Social Emergence

Can we understand important social issues by studying individual personalities, decisions, and behaviors? Or are societies somehow more than the people in them? Sociologists have long believed that the study of individual decisions and behaviors cannot fully explain the complex social phenomena that emerge when people interact in organizations, institutions, and societies. In contrast, most psychologists and economists tend to treat social phenomena as if they were reducible to the actions of individuals, whose independent choices can simply be added together to explain complex social processes.

Social Emergence takes a new approach to these long-standing questions. Sawyer argues that societies are complex dynamical systems and that the best way to resolve these debates is by developing the concept of emergence, focusing on multiple levels of analysis – individuals, interactions, and groups – and on how social group phenomena emerge from communication processes among individual members. This book makes a unique contribution not only to complex systems research but also to social theory.

R. KEITH SAWYER is Associate Professor of Education at Washington University. He is the author or editor of six previous books, including *Group Creativity* and *Improvised Dialogues*. He has also published a wide range of scholarly journal articles on contemporary issues in sociological theory and on computational modeling of societies.

Social Emergence

Societies as Complex Systems

R. Keith Sawyer

Washington University

CAMBRIDGE UNIVERSITY PRESS
Cambridge, New York, Melbourne, Madrid, Cape Town, Singapore, São Paulo

Cambridge University Press
40 West 20th Street, New York, NY 10011-4211, USA

www.cambridge.org
Information on this title: www.cambridge.org/9780521606370

First published 2005
Reprinted 2007

Printed in the United Kingdom at the Cambridge University Press, Cambridge

A catalog record for this publication is available from the British Library.

Library of Congress Cataloging in Publication Data

Sawyer, R. Keith (Robert Keith)
Social emergence : societies as complex systems / R. Keith Sawyer.
  p. cm.
Includes bibliographical references and index.
ISBN 0-521-84464-9 (hardback)
ISBN 0-521-60637-3 (pbk.)
1. Social evolution. 2. Social systems. 3. Sociology.
4. Communication – Social aspects. I. Title.
HM626.S39 2005
303.4 – dc22   2005011488

ISBN 978-0-521-84464-2 hardback
ISBN 978-0-521-60637-0 paperback

Contents

Figures and tables

Figures

Tables

Acknowledgments

This book was written during 2003 and 2004 while I was an Associate Professor of Education at Washington University in St. Louis. It is based on ideas, discussions, and research extending back at least ten years. The project began in earnest in 1999 when I discovered an intriguing footnote in a 1951 reader edited by Melvin Marx called *Psychological Theory*; the article, by Edward C. Tolman and originally published in 1932, mentioned that emergence was "now becoming so popular among philosophers" (p. 414). Although I was originally inspired to study emergence by my background in psychological theory, that chance encounter with a footnote led me to pursue the concept through the philosophy of science, computational modeling, and sociological theory. I would like to thank my editor at Cambridge, Sarah Caro, for her enthusiasm for the project and her professionalism throughout the editiorial process.

Some of the chapters in this book draw heavily from articles that have appeared elsewhere, and this material appears with permission. However, all material has been substantially rewritten, in some cases to such a degree that its origin is unrecognizable. Consequently, this book should be considered to supersede the following five articles:

Sawyer, R. Keith. 2001. "Emergence in sociology: Contemporary philosophy of mind and some implications for sociological theory." *American Journal of Sociology* 107:551–85.

Sawyer, R. Keith. 2002. "Durkheim's dilemma: Toward a sociology of emergence." *Sociological Theory* 20:227–47.

Sawyer, R. Keith. 2002. "Emergence in psychology: Lessons from the history of non-reductionist science." *Human Development* 45:2–28.

Sawyer, R. Keith. 2002. "Unresolved tensions in sociocultural theory: Analogies with contemporary sociological debates." *Culture and Psychology* 8:283–305.

Sawyer, R. Keith. 2003. "Artificial societies: Multi agent systems and the micro-macro link in sociological theory." *Sociological Methods and Research* 31:37–75.

1 Emergence, complexity, and social science

> How it is possible that institutions ... can arise without a common will aiming at their creation [is] the significant, perhaps the most significant, problem of the social sciences.
>
> Carl Menger

Societies have often been compared to other complex systems. Inspired by the rise of science and technology, writers in the eighteenth century compared societies to complex artificial mechanisms like clocks; such metaphors are now broadly known as _mechanistic_ (La Mettrie [1748] 1912). Inspired by Darwin's influential theory of evolution, nineteenth-century _organicists_ compared the various institutions of society to the organs of the human body (Paul von Lilienfeld, Albert Schäffle, and Herbert Spencer). Just after World War II, Talcott Parsons' influential structural-functional theory was inspired by cybernetics, the study of "control and communication in the animal and the machine," the subtitle of a seminal book published by mathematician Norbert Wiener in 1948. Cybernetics was centrally concerned with developing models of the computational and communication technologies emerging in the post-war period, but many cyberneticians applied these models to biology, anthropology, and sociology. In the 1960s and 1970s, general systems theory continued in this interdisciplinary fashion; it was grounded in the premise that complex systems at all levels of analysis – from the smallest unicellular organisms up to modern industrial societies – could be understood using the same set of theories and methodologies (Bertalanffy 1968; J. Miller 1978).

Common to all of these approaches is the basic insight that societies are complex configurations of many people engaged in overlapping and interlocking patterns of relationship with one another. Some key questions raised by these society-as-system metaphors are, How do complex social systems originate, when they are not consciously designed by anyone? What do social relations and configurations look like? Which societies are the most effective, and which are stable and long-lasting? How could

1

a stable complex system ever change and evolve, as societies often do? What is the role of the individual in the system? These questions have long been central in sociology.

Beginning in the mid-1990s, several scientific developments converged to create a qualitatively more advanced approach to complex systems, and these developments have significant implications for social scientists. The general systems theories of previous decades were always more successful at explaining natural systems than social systems; in spite of the universalist ambitions of such theorists, social scientists generally ignored them. In contrast, the latest work in complex dynamical systems theory – which I refer to as a *third wave* of systems theory (Chapter 2) – is particularly well suited to sociological explanation. In this book, I argue that sociologists should bring these developments into the heart of their discipline; the third wave has the potential to contribute to resolutions of long-standing unresolved issues in sociology and provides methodologies that are of immediate practical use for sociologists (Chapters 8, 9, and 10).

Third-wave systems theory grew out of developments in computer technology. From the 1970s through the early 1990s, computer use in sociology was focused on systems dynamics simulations, in which changes in macrovariables of society – population, poverty rates, urban densities – were mathematically modeled (e.g., Forrester 1971). In the 1990s, however, computer power advanced to the point where societies could be simulated using a distinct computational agent for every individual in the society through a computational technique known as *multi-agent systems* (Chapters 8 and 9). A multi-agent system contains hundreds or thousands of agents, each engaged in communication with the others. The researcher can use these simulations to create *artificial societies* and to run "virtual experiments" – in which properties of agents and of the communication language are varied and the subsequent changes in the overall macrobehavior of the system are observed. Multi-agent systems have been used by complexity researchers to simulate a wide range of natural systems, including sand piles, industrial processes, and neuronal connections in the human brain; in the late 1990s, this methodology was increasingly used to simulate social systems.

This new methodology has led complexity theorists to become increasingly concerned with *emergence* – the processes whereby the global behavior of a system results from the actions and interactions of agents. Philosophers of science, who have been concerned with emergence for almost a century (Chapter 3), refer to properties of system components as being "lower-level properties" and to emergent properties of the entire system as "higher-level properties." In both psychology (Chapter 4) and sociology (Chapter 5), the relation between lower-level and higher-level properties has often been theorized in terms of emergence. But these various treatments of emergence in the social sciences have been scattered and are often contradictory. In Chapters 3, 4, and 5, I critically review these various treatments and develop a foundational account of social emergence.

Like "emergence," the term "complexity" has also been used somewhat loosely in the last decade. In the most general sense, complex phenomena are those that reside between simplicity and randomness, at "the edge of chaos," in Kauffman's (1993a) terms. When the laws governing a system are relatively simple, the system's behavior is easy to understand, explain, and predict. At the other extreme, some systems seem to behave randomly. There may be laws governing the behavior of a system of this type, but the system is highly nonlinear – small variations in the state of the system at one time could result in very large changes to later states of the system. Such systems are often said to be *chaotic*. Complex systems are somewhere in between these two extremes. A complex system is not easy to explain, but it is not so chaotic that understanding is completely impossible (as argued by researchers associated with the Santa Fe Institute, including Murray Gell-Mann and Stuart Kauffman).

In complex systems so conceived, relatively simple higher-level order "emerges" from relatively complex lower-level processes. Canonical examples of emergence include traffic jams, the colonies of social insects, and bird flocks. For example, the V shape of the bird flock does not result from one bird being selected as the leader, and the other birds lining up behind the leader. Instead, each bird's behavior is based on its position relative to nearby birds. The V shape is not planned or centrally determined; it emerges out of simple pair-interaction rules. The bird flock demonstrates one of the most striking features of emergent phenomena: Higher-level regularities are often the result of simple rules and local interactions at the lower level.[1]

In the social sciences, a comparable example of an emergent phenomenon is language shift. Historians of language have documented that languages have changed frequently throughout history, with vocabulary and even grammar changing radically over the centuries. Yet until the rise of the modern nation state, such changes were not consciously selected by any official body, nor were they imposed by force on a population. Rather, language shift is an emergent phenomenon, arising out of uncountable everyday conversations in small groups scattered throughout the society

---

[1] A computer simulation of bird flock emergence has been developed by Reynolds (1987).

(Sawyer 2001a). In this social system, the "lower level" consists of the individual speakers, their interactions are the individual conversations, and the "higher level" is the collective social fact of language as a group property.

Common to both of these examples is that emerging at the global system level are patterns, structures, or properties that are difficult to explain in terms of the system's components and their interactions. Whether or not a global system property is emergent, and what this means both theoretically and methodologically, has been defined in many different ways, and one of the primary purposes of this book is to identify and clarify these many senses of the term in the social sciences. For example, in some accounts system properties are said to be emergent when they are *unpredictable* even given a complete knowledge of the lower-level description of the system – a complete knowledge of the state of each component and of the interactions of all the components. In other accounts, system properties are said to be emergent when they are *irreducible*, in any lawful and regular fashion, to properties of the system components. In yet other accounts, system properties are said to be emergent when they are *novel*, when they are not held by any of the components of the system (see Cilliers 1998 for an extensive list of the characteristics of complex systems). Philosophers of science have debated such properties since the burst of emergentist theory in the 1920s (Chapter 3); some philosophers emphasize one or another of these features, and others argue that there are no such properties in nature. Social scientists have applied widely different definitions of emergence, resulting in conceptual confusion (Chapter 5).

Nonetheless, there is a consensus that complex systems may have autonomous laws and properties at the global level that cannot be easily reduced to lower-level, more basic sciences. Thus the paradigm of complexity is often opposed to the paradigm of reductionism (Cederman 1997, Chap. 3; Gallagher and Appenzeller 1999). For example, philosophers of mind generally agree that mental properties may not be easily reduced to neurobiological properties, due to the complex dynamical nature of the brain. In an analogous fashion, I use complex dynamical systems theory to argue against methodological individualism, the attempt to explain groups in terms of individuals. In Chapters 5, 8, 9, and 10, I show why methodological individualism will have limited success as a potential explanation for many group phenomena.

Complexity theorists have discovered that emergence is more likely to be found in systems in which (1) many components interact in densely connected networks, (2) global system functions cannot be localized to any one subset of components but rather are distributed throughout the entire system, (3) the overall system cannot be decomposed into subsystems and these into smaller sub-subsystems in any meaningful fashion, (4) and the components interact using a complex and sophisticated language (Chapter 5). Not all complex systems have all of these features; for example, interaction between birds in a flock involves very simple rules, but it manifests emergence because of the large number of birds. Conversely, the complex musical communication among the four musicians in a jazz group leads to emergent properties, even though there are only four participants (Sawyer 2003c). These properties of emergence were originally proposed to explain complexity in biological and physical systems; in this book, I argue that all four of these properties are found in social systems, perhaps to an even greater extent than in natural systems.

These properties are interrelated in most complex systems. For example, social systems with a densely connected network are less likely to be decomposable or localizable. In modern societies, network density has become progressively greater as communication and transportation technology has increased the number and frequency of network connections among people; some complexity theorists suggest that this results in *swarm intelligence* (Kennedy and Eberhart 2001). Swarm intelligence and network density were first explored by French sociologist Émile Durkheim, who referred to the phenomenon as *dynamic density* (cf. Durkheim [1895] 1964, 114–5), and in Chapter 6, I argue that Durkheim was the first social emergence theorist and that contemporary complexity theory sheds new light on several poorly understood aspects of Durkheim's writings.

The individual and the group

The social science disciplines that emerged in the nineteenth century were centrally concerned with the uniquely complex nature of human societies, and the relationship between the individual and the collective has always been one of the most fundamental issues in the social sciences. This relationship was a central element in the theorizing of the founders of sociology and economics, including Comte, Weber, Smith, Menger, Durkheim, Simmel, and Marx. The processes whereby aggregated individual actions lead to macroeconomic phenomena have been a central focus of neoclassical microeconomics. Contemporary organizational theory is deeply concerned with how organizational structure influences individual action and how individual behavior results in the emergence of global organizational properties (Carley and Gasser 1999; Cyert and March 1963; Marion 1999). In sociology, this relationship is known as the *micro-macro link* (J. C. Alexander et al. 1987; Huber 1991; Knorr-Cetina and Cicourel 1981; Ritzer 2000). Theories of the micro-macro link are central, if implicit, to many twentieth-century sociological paradigms, including structural functionalism (Parsons [1937] 1949, 1951), exchange theory (Blau 1964; Homans 1958, 1961), and rational choice theory (Coleman 1990).

Drawing on both philosophical discourse and on systems theory, many sociological accounts of the micro-macro link use the term "emergence" to refer to collective phenomena that are collaboratively created by individuals, yet are not reducible to individual action (Archer 1995; Bhaskar 1979, 1982; Blau 1981; Edel 1959; Kontopoulos 1993; Mihata 1997; Parsons [1937] 1949; Porpora 1993; T. S. Smith 1997; Sztompka 1991; Whitmeyer 1994; Wisdom 1970). Emergence theories attempt to explain the nature of society as a complex system by accounting for how individuals and their relations give rise to global, macro social phenomena, such as markets, the educational system, cultural beliefs, and shared social practices (e.g., politeness and power dynamics). However, despite the broad appeal of the term "emergence," it has never been adequately theorized by social scientists, and as I show in Chapter 5, there is much confusion surrounding the term.

For example, microeconomists and some sociologists attempt to explain macro social properties by identifying the micro-to-macro process of emergence – how individual actions and dyadic interactions aggregate to result in macro social phenomena, such as institutions, social movements, norms, and role structures. Sociologists use the phrase "methodological individualism" to describe this bottom-up approach to modeling social phenomena. Sociologists who attack this approach argue that there are macro social phenomena so complex that they could never be successfully modeled in this way. Instead, they argue that sociology will always have irreducibly social terms and laws. In Chapters 5 through 7, I explore theories of emergence in sociology, show that these treatments have been inadequate and remain confused, and propose a clarifying framework that draws on philosophy of science and complexity theory.

In the latter decades of the twentieth century, a renegade group of psychologists known as *socioculturalists* have used "methodological individualism" to invoke a different enemy – the individualist focus of mainstream psychology. Sociocultural psychologists argue that traditional psychology must be redefined to incorporate social and cultural context. In their writings, "methodological individualism" refers to the experimental methods of research psychology, where the unit of analysis is a single randomly sampled individual and where the variables are all measured properties of individuals. Socioculturalists emphasize the collective creativity of human collaborative action in small groups, such as in family settings, classrooms, and the workplace (e.g., Sawyer 2003c). In Chapters 4 and 7, I explore emergence in sociocultural studies of small groups because this work has recently begun to address long-standing sociological issues.

Although both sociologists and socioculturalists share a rejection of individualist reductionism, the forms of reductionism they explicitly oppose are somewhat different. The Austrian economists who first elaborated methodological individualism in the middle of the twentieth century – Hayek, Popper, and Mises – took pains to distinguish it from methodological psychologism, the true foil of the socioculturalists. These economists never thought that economics would reduce to psychology. My discussion speaks to both sociologists and socioculturalists and uses emergence theory to fruitfully explore these different anti-individualist approaches.

To date, complex systems conceptions of emergence have had almost no impact on these debates. In Chapters 8, 9, and 10, I draw on the study of complex dynamical systems to provide new perspectives on these important unresolved issues – the relations between individuals and groups, the emergence of unintended effects from collective action, and the relation between the disciplines of economics and sociology. In short, my conclusion is that whether or not a social system can be understood solely in terms of its component individuals and their interactions is an empirical question, to be resolved anew with respect to each social system. Theories of emergence from complexity science show why some social properties cannot be explained in terms of individuals. Thus, economics and psychology cannot assume that methodological individualism can exhaustively explain human behavior in social groups. However, not all social systems are irreducibly complex, and some social properties can be explained by identifying their processes of emergence from individuals in interaction. Complex systems theory can help to determine which approach will be most appropriate for which social property.

Studies of social groups must be fundamentally interdisciplinary because a focus on emergence requires a simultaneous consideration of multiple levels of analysis: individuals, their communication language, and the group. The explanation of any given social system cannot be provided by psychology, sociology, or economics alone; it will require interdisciplinary teams (and perhaps even a new type of graduate student training) of the sort that are currently being attempted in the computational modeling of social systems (Chapter 8).

Sociology and symbolic communication

A second goal of this book is to suggest a potential rapprochement between microsociology and macrosociology. Within both sociology and economics, theorists interested in emergence – in the relations between agent action and interaction at the lower level and the global properties of the society at the higher level – have not considered the role of symbolic communication. However, artificial societies show that when the agent communication language changes, the processes of emergence change, and the global properties that emerge often change as well. In Chapter 9, I combine two strands of current research to show that sociologists and economists must foundationally incorporate sophisticated theories of symbolic communication in their models of emergence. First, I discuss several artificial societies and show how changes in agent communication result in changes in emergence. Second, I discuss recent empirical studies of emergence in small social groups (Sawyer 2003c, 2003d); these empirical studies show that group properties emerge from rather complex and subtle differences in symbolic communication. To date, the role of communication in social emergence has been neglected.

The third-wave view of social systems as agents in interaction reveals the importance of complex communications among individuals. The complexity of human language distinguishes complex social systems from the complex systems studied in the natural sciences. As a result, social systems have unique properties that are not held by other complex systems in nature, and social systems require elaborations of the notions of emergence and complexity that were originally developed to explain complex systems in nature. The study of the unique properties of social systems can contribute to complex dynamical systems theory more generally, and this book will be of interest not only to social scientists but also to researchers in the interdisciplinary field of complexity science.

The complexity of social systems does not entail that methodological individualism will always fail. After all, emergence and complexity have been more fully embraced by economists than sociologists – for example, economists participate actively in interdisciplinary complexity groups such as the Santa Fe Institute and the University of Michigan Center for the Study of Complex Systems – and neoclassical microeconomics is foundationally based in methodological individualism. In Chapter 5, I show how social properties may be emergent from individual action and interaction, yet not reducible to explanation in terms of them, and I provide an account that clarifies which properties of social systems can be explained with methodological individualism and which cannot. The theory of social emergence allows the distinctive perspectives of economists, sociologists, and psychologists to be considered and integrated.

The primary audience for this book will be sociologists, who will learn how these new developments in complexity science have the potential to transform sociological research. Psychologists and economists will learn how these transformations in sociology might affect their disciplines (particularly in Chapter 10). A secondary audience will be complexity researchers more broadly, who may gain insights into how they might extend their formalisms and models to adequately capture a broader range of complex dynamical systems – not only natural systems but also social systems.

The first wave of social systems theory is Parsons's structural function-alism, the second wave is derived from the general systems theory of the 1960s through the 1980s, and the third wave is based on the complex dynamical systems theory developed in the 1990s. This book focuses on the third wave of systems thinking in sociology. Third-wave systems the-ory has more potential relevance to sociology than the first two waves, and it offers theoretical concepts and methodological tools that have the potential to speak to unresolved core sociological issues. Because the third wave has not yet had much impact on the social sciences, a primary goal of this book is to demonstrate that third-wave theory addresses weaknesses of the first and second waves and to show the practical and theoretical implications for the social sciences.

First- and second-wave systems theories often discussed social emer-gence, but these prior treatments were overly brief and insufficiently developed; foundational questions related to emergence were not addressed. For example, both individualists and collectivists often refer to themselves as emergentists, yet their positions are theoretically incom-patible (Chapter 5). Collectivists argue that although only individuals exist, collectives possess emergent properties that are irreducibly com-plex and thus cannot be reduced to individual properties and relations. Yet emergence has also been invoked by methodological individualists in sociology and economics. Methodological individualists accept the exis-tence of emergent social properties but claim that such properties can be explained in terms of individuals and their relationships.

Thus, contemporary uses of emergence in sociology and economics are contradictory and unstable; two opposed paradigms both invoke the concept of emergence and draw opposed conclusions, one consistent with methodological individualism and one inconsistent with it (also see Kontopoulos 1993). The problem arises in part because neither sociolo-gists nor economists have developed an adequate account of emergence. Contemporary sociologists are not the first to be confused about emergence; ever since the term was first used well over 100 years ago (Chapter 3) comments have been made on the confusion surrounding it. The conceptual clarification of emergence in Chapter 5 can help achieve a rapprochement between sociology and economics by demonstrating that both are concerned with the emergence of macrosocial behavior from a complex system of individuals engaged in microinteraction. In Chapter 8, I show how a late 1990s complexity methodology – multi-agent systems simulation – can help to resolve and integrate economic and sociological perspectives. And in Chapter 10, I propose a new relationship between economics and sociology.

Methodological individualists often conceive of their work as contributing to a theoretical foundation underlying all of the social sciences. Books by sociologists bear names like *Foundations of Social Theory* (Coleman 1990), *Nuts and Bolts for the Social Sciences* (Elster 1989), and *Social Behavior: Its Elementary Forms* (Homans 1961). Economists go even further, claiming that economics is "the universal grammar of social science" (Hirshleifer 1985, 53; see Chapter 10). Complexity theorists have likewise emphasized the foundational nature of their generative approach, as evidenced by Epstein and Axtell's subtitle *Social Science from the Bottom Up* (1996; see Chapter 8). Microeconomics and its individualist approach have co-opted the position that Comte and Durkheim claimed for sociology: to be the pure science discipline at the root of all of the social sciences, the abstract study of humans interacting in groups. Although Durkheim's sociological realism is opposed to methodological individualism, both Durkheim and contemporary individualists emphasize emergence and complexity in social systems. Durkheim's vision for a foundational sociology was grounded in social emergence and is surprisingly compatible with contemporary complexity approaches (Chapter 6). My account of social emergence suggests that individualism as currently conceived may be significantly limited in its ability to explain complex social systems; the science of social emergence may ultimately be grounded in sociology rather than in microeconomics. Sociology refigured as the study of emergence in complex social systems would be foundational to anthropology, history, economics, and political science, thus reclaiming the central position that Durkheim claimed for sociology (I elaborate this position in Chapter 10).

In addition to sociology, I draw on other disciplines concerned with emergence: economics, psychology, philosophy of science, and multi-agent simulation. Consistent with the long tradition of systems theory, my approach is deeply interdisciplinary. But unlike most complexity theorists, I conclude that social systems have additional complex features that make them unlike any other systems found in nature, and I attribute these features to the complexity of human symbolic communication (Chapter 9).

The first wave: Talcott Parsons and structural functionalism

Many sociologists associate systems theory with Talcott Parsons's mid-century theoretical writings. Parsons's influential *structural-functional* theory of society was famously based on systems concepts derived from cybernetics. Cybernetics was a postwar interdisciplinary effort to understand "control and communication in the animal and the machine," the subtitle of a seminal book published by mathematician Norbert Wiener in 1948. Postwar cybernetics attempted to explain and to engineer systems that were self-regulating through the use of negative feedback loops. Between the 1937 publication of Parsons' first book, *The Structure of Social Action*, and the 1951 publication of *The Social System*, cybernetics and information theory began to influence Parsons, and he began to think that "control in action systems was of the cybernetic type" and not coercive (Parsons 1970, 850). Cybernetics became the model for all contemporary systems theory; like later systems theories, it was an interdisciplinary endeavor that was based primarily on mathematics but that engaged figures as diverse as anthropologist Gregory Bateson and neurophysiologist Warren McCulloch. Parsons was the first to apply cybernetic systems theory to sociology, and I refer to his theory as the first wave of sociological systems thinking.

Parsons' conception of systems as structures assumed they were hierarchical and decomposable. Decomposable systems are modular, with each component acting primarily according to its own intrinsic principles. Each component is influenced by the others only at well-defined input points; its function (its internal processing of those inputs) is not itself influenced by other components (Simon 1969). In such a system, the behavior of any part is *intrinsically determined:* it is possible to determine the component's properties in isolation from the other components, despite the fact that they interact. The organization of the entire system is critical for the function of the system as a whole, but that organization does not provide constraints on the internal functioning of components. This was the concept of system that Parsons borrowed from cybernetics; his structural functionalism assumed decomposability in its elaborate identification of systems and subsystems and in its focus on status-role sets as decomposable components of systems (Parsons 1951).

Complexity scientists have recently discovered that decomposable systems are less likely to manifest emergence than nondecomposable systems. In nondecomposable systems, the overall system organization has a significant influence on the function of any component; thus, component function is no longer intrinsically determined. Dependence of components on each other is often mutual and may even make it difficult to draw firm boundaries between components (Bechtel and Richardson 1993, 26–27). Parsons acknowledged this possibility with his concept of "interpenetration" (e.g., Parsons and Shils 1951, 109) but this phenomenon remained a challenge to the essentially decomposable emphasis of his systems model. Systems that are not *nearly decomposable* (Simon 1969) are more likely to have emergent system properties that are difficult to explain in reductionist fashion, by working up from analyses of the components and their relations.

Parsonsian theory also assumed *functional localizability* in social systems. In Parsons's AGIL (*a*daptation, *g*oal attainment, *i*ntegration, and *l*atency) scheme, each of the four major systems is defined in terms of its function. Likewise, the lowest-level components – roles – are defined in terms of the function they serve for the system: "There is the same order of relationship between roles and functions relative to the system in social systems, as there is between organs and functions in the organism" (Parsons 1951, 115). Collectivities are likewise conceptualized in role terms and are also defined in terms of their functions (Parsons and Shils 1951, 190–7). The allocation process – which together with the integration process allows systems to maintain equilibrium – serves the function of allocating functions to roles and to subsystems (Parsons and Shils 1951, 108, 198).

Contemporary complexity theory has argued that in functionally localizable systems, emergence is less likely to occur. A system is localizable if the functional decomposition of the system corresponds to its physical decomposition and if each property of the system can be identified with a single component or subsystem. If system functions or properties cannot be identified with components but are instead distributed spatially within the system, the system is not functionally localized (Bechtel and Richardson 1993, 24). Many social functions and properties are not localizable. For example, "being a church" cannot be localized to any of the individuals belonging to the church, nor to any subnetwork of those individuals. In an improvising collaborative group, the topic, tone, style, and genre cannot be localized to any one individual nor to any specific moment in the dialogue (Sawyer 2003d).

Parsons's concept of system was perhaps appropriate for the classically Weberian bureaucracy typically found in midcentury American hierarchical organizations such as large corporations and government agencies. However, in the latter part of the century, due to a range of changes in the economy, new forms of organization emerged to challenge hierarchical organization (Bell 1973). Many writers in organization theory and management science have noted the flattening of the modern corporation; hierarchy is out, and heterarchy – structures with multiple lines of reporting and with flexibly reconfiguring task groups – is increasingly embraced (Weick 2001). The structures of many contemporary organizations have become more similar to informal social groups such as social movements, improvised ensembles, and ephemeral organizations, and the shifts that have taken place require an updating of systems theory in social science. A sociologist of science or a historian of ideas could profitably explore how these economic developments influenced 1990s systems theory, although this has not yet been done (but see Thrift 1999).

The second wave: General systems theory and chaos theory

In the 1960s and 1970s, a *second wave* of systems thinking emerged. The second wave had no single influential sociological advocate comparable to Parsons. Sociological applications have appeared periodically since Buckley's 1967 book *Sociology and Modern Systems Theory*, but none has had much influence on mainstream sociology. Like cybernetics, the second wave – within which I include both general systems theory (GST) and the chaos theory of the 1980s and 1990s – was an interdisciplinary project. Stuart Kauffman (1993b) of the Santa Fe Institute made explicit the connection between complexity and 1960s-era cybernetics: "The history of this emerging paradigm conveniently begins with the 'cybernetic' revolution" (p. 76). Second-wave advocates attempted to develop universal principles and laws of systems that would apply to systems at any level of analysis, from the microorganism to the world system. A seminal work was Ludwig von Bertalanffy's book *General Systems Theory* (1968); another important work was James Miller's book *Living Systems* (1978). Many systems theorists drew on the concept of "autopoiesis" developed in biology by Humberto Maturana and Francisco Varela (1980). Grounded in these traditions, Niklas Luhmann ([1984] 1995) developed one of the best-known second-wave social systems theories. Second-wave models of societies, like the first wave, were inspired by cybernetics-related models. Cybernetics and related systems theories continued to evolve through the 1960s, after Parsons's theoretical framework rose and fell, and these later developments distinguish the second wave.

I group chaos theory with GST because, despite their differences, they share many important features.[1] For example, they both attempted to develop universal and generalizable models that could apply to any level of analysis; in the writings of 1990s second-wave theorists, examples of seemingly similar phenomena from physics, biology, and the social sciences are frequently juxtaposed as evidence for the potential of a unified science of complexity (e.g., Johnson 2001; Kauffman 1993a). In this approach, complexity is defined as the search for algorithms and principles found in nature that display common features across many levels of organization. Kauffman's (1993b) examples of these universal features include the "edge of chaos" principle, in which all complex systems in nature fall between chaos and order (p. 78), and the power laws of many-body physics. The applicability of these features to biological systems (e.g., Kauffman 1993a; 1993b, 87) led Kauffman to speak of "a physics of biology" (1993b, 79).

Second-wave complexity theory is not a unified body of work but rather "a scientific amalgam . . . an accretion of ideas, a rhetorical hybrid" (Thrift 1999, 33). Many of those using chaos theoretic algorithms have used the terms "chaos" and "complexity" interchangeably, but chaos theory and complexity theory are distinct areas of research and methodology. "Chaos" refers to turbulent behavior in a low-dimensional system (i.e., with low degrees of freedom) where the behavior is completely determined by nonlinear laws that may exaggerate minor changes in the initial conditions and thus make the system's behavior unpredictable in practice beyond a certain time period. "Complexity" refers to ordered phenomena in a high-dimensional system (i.e., with high degrees of freedom) that emerge from a large number of interactions among system components. Whereas second-wave social systems theory drew on chaos theory, the third wave draws on complexity theory.

Perhaps the most distinctive feature of second-wave systems theory is its focus on dynamics and change; in contrast, the first wave was primarily concerned with structure and stability. A shift from a static focus to a process orientation is common in complexity studies, from physics to economics (Arthur 1999). British social theorist Walter Buckley's 1967 book *Sociology and Modern Systems Theory* is canonically referenced by second-wave systems sociologists; Buckley agreed with critics of Parsonian theory who argued that it was overly focused on equilibrium and stasis, and he presented a dynamical version of systems theory that accommodated

---

[1] Although some readers may question my grouping of GST with chaos theory, others have noted the same parallels, including Bertalanffy himself (Bailey 1994; Bertalanffy 1968, 151; Loye and Eisler 1987, 55; Reed and Harvey 1992, 376n8).

both the maintenance of equilibrium and the potential for radical change. Dynamical systems are in constant change over time, yet in spite of this constant change, they remain *self-organizing* or *self-maintaining*; Maturana and Varela's (1980) biological theories of autopoeisis are often cited by these theorists.

Finding additional inspiration in the chaos theory of the 1980s and 1990s, second-wave authors increasingly emphasized the *nonlinearity* of dynamical systems (e.g., Kiel and Elliott 1996). In nonlinear systems, the effect may not be proportional to the cause; a small change in initial conditions can lead to a radical change in a later state of the system – the so-called "butterfly effect" – or, inversely, a large change in initial conditions might not lead to any significant change in later states of the system. Chaotic equations are a specific type of nonlinear equation. Systems described by chaotic equations are often observed to possess *attractors*, relatively steady states that the system tends to gravitate toward, and these attractors are sometimes said to "emerge" from the equations governing the system (although note that such a conception of emergence is quite different from those discussed in the Preface, which involve two levels of analysis, a higher level and a lower, componential level from which it emerges). Second-wave systems theorists argued that the reductive methods of traditional science were difficult to apply to such systems because many of the mathematical tools used in traditional science were developed for linear systems and are not applicable to nonlinear systems (Casti 1994).

Murray Gell-Mann (1994) argued that in chaotic systems, reduction to explanation in terms of components is practically impossible: "Scientists are accustomed to developing theories that describe observational results in a particular field without deriving them from the theories of a more fundamental field. Such a derivation, though possible in principle when the additional special information is supplied, is at any given time difficult or impossible in practice for most cases" (p. 111). Kauffman (1993a) took an even stronger position: that the derivation is not possible even in principle. This unpredictability is in large part due to extreme sensitivity to initial conditions, so extreme that scientists could never identify and characterize the initial conditions with the requisite degree of detail to allow prediction of the dynamic path of the system.

Thus for both practical and theoretical reasons, second-wave theorists emphasized nonlinearity and opposed the reductionist scientific program. This emphasis on nonreductionism was not found in the first wave. Although first-wave theory considered social systems as well as individuals, neither Parsons nor any other first-wave theorist provided explicit arguments that these systems could not be reduced to individual-level explanation, and their failure to do this was the focus of methodologically individualist critiques such as that of George Homans (1958).

Many sociologists, particularly of a realist bent, are attracted to this line of nonreductionist thinking because it argues for a collective level of analysis and against reduction of social system behavior to explanations in terms of individuals (e.g., Byrne 1998). For example, the laws of thermodynamics work quite well without any knowledge of their reduction to statistical mechanics; for example, when heat is applied to a volume of gas, the pressure rises in a completely lawful way, and this requires no knowledge whatsoever of the component molecules and their interactions. In most cases, the reduction is prohibitively difficult and is only valid for a single state of the system, whereas the higher-level laws work just as well and are more general, in that they apply to the heat-pressure relation regardless of the position and motion of the component molecules.

During the 1970s and 1980s, several nonreductionist sociologists drew inspiration from general systems theory. Bruce Mayhew published an early paper in a collection edited by von Bertalanffy (Mayhew, Gray, and Mayhew 1971), and his well-known 1980 article cited systems theorists such as Krippendorff (1971). The social realist Margaret Archer (1982, 1995) often cited second-wave systems theorist Walter Buckley (1967), who held that institutional structures were "emergent phenomena" that were generated through "morphogenetic processes" (p. 125). However, Buckley's "complex adaptive system model" did not elaborate a theory of emergence.

And more generally, the second wave does not resolve the issue of social emergence, nor the issue of the reality of the social (contrary to what some second-wave authors argue, such as Byrne 1998, 48). Microeconomists – guided by methodologically individualist assumptions – have been equally attracted to second-wave methods, and many have begun to apply nonlinear equations to develop more sophisticated ways of reducing properties of collectives to individual action. (I explore these conflicting positions further in Chapter 5.)

A third distinguishing feature of second-wave systems theory is the emphasis on *open systems* – systems in which energy, information, or matter flows between the system and its environment. Many theorists argue that first-wave cybernetics-derived theory is only appropriate for *closed systems*. A common citation in this context is the work of Nobel prize–winning physicist Ilya Prigogine on dissipative structures, systems far from thermodynamic equilibrium (Nicolis and Prigogine 1977; Prigogine and Stengers 1984). The best-known dissipative structure is the Bénard convection cell. Bénard convection cells form when a layer of liquid is heated from below; at a given temperature, the heated molecules at the bottom of the layer start to rise, and the cooler ones on top start to sink. If the temperature is too high, the liquid reaches a turbulent state without any regular, stable structure, but at just the right temperature, the flow between the top and bottom of the liquid results in the emergence of regular, stable patterns known as *Bénard cells*, typically hexagonal in shape, with the hotter fluid rising up the center of the cell and the cooler fluid sinking at the edges. Although a system in this state is quite chaotic and individual particles are moving rapidly, the cells remain remarkably stable. This is an open system because it requires the application of an external heat source to occur. In fact, it is generally thought that the structures of open, nonequilibrium many-particle systems are more complex than the structures found in systems at equilibrium.

Beginning in the late 1980s, second-wave authors in sociology began to draw metaphors from chaos theory: notions like bifurcation, strange attractors, and state space have frequently been applied to social phenomena (Byrne 1998; Loye and Eisler 1987; Marion 1999; Reed and Harvey 1992). In particular, these sociologists were attracted to the concept of nonlinearity – the notion that outputs are not proportional to inputs – and to the idea that there may be an unpredictable "bifurcation sequence" between many distinct states of the system. Second-wave sociologists often associated these processes with emergence because the final state of the system could not be predicted from the initial state but rather was said to emerge from the dynamical properties of the system (although such discussions tend to strike nonlinear mathematicians as nonrigorous and purely metaphorical). For example, Byrne (1998) associated emergence with interaction effects among variables in a nonlinear equation (p. 65). Prigogine and coauthors have not hesitated to draw sociological implications from their work: "nonlinearities clearly abound in social phenomena, where a yawn, a desire for an automobile with fins, or a lifestyle can spread contagiously throughout a population" (Prigogine and Allen 1982, 7). Of course, sociologists have long known that such collective behaviors are nonlinear (Evans 1969). Second-wave theorists have elaborated these metaphors: "dissipative social systems display far-from-equilibrium behavior. That is, their evolution is chaotically driven. . . . [D]issipative social systems can be studied in a manner similar to the study of natural dissipative systems" (Harvey and Reed 1996, 306).

Within GST and chaos theory alike, it is a foundational assumption that all systems will follow similar laws of complexity, but this "unification of the natural and social sciences" (Kiel 1991, 440) is not a proven fact but rather a hope; many social scientists are critical and can readily point to distinctive features of social systems. To take one set of common metaphors from chaos theory that have been applied to social science, it is hard to see how societies are far-from-equilibrium systems or dissipative structures in any interesting sociological sense. In Prigogine's dissipative systems, emergent structure requires a continuous influx of energy from outside of the system to be maintained. But the examples of collective behavior cited by Prigogine and Allen (1982) – fads, lifestyles – do not seem to be even metaphorically dissipative in this sense. In a limited biological and materialistic sense, societies require energy from the environment in the form of food and raw materials; thus, the greatest success in applying chaos models to the social sciences has been in urban geography – the study of the spatial evolution of urban areas (Allen et al. 1985). However, the role of *sociological* inflows – of information, power, or monetary goods – through mass communication or external network links is generally much less significant than internal interactions within the system, contra the claims of second-wave systems theorists (e.g., Baker 1993; Byrne 1998; Harvey and Reed 1996; Kiel 1991). Although there are exceptions – client states that are unpopular with their people can be maintained with massive and continuing economic and military support from a superpower – most states are internally self-organizing and self-maintaining and are at equilibrium rather than far-from-equilibrium. Like second-wave theory more generally, Prigogine's work has provided many helpful metaphors, but it has never been fruitfully used in a more substantive way by sociologists. Although providing a useful set of metaphors for thinking about social systems – nonlinearity, self-organization, nonreducibility – the substance of chaos theory itself, its mathematics and its underlying physical theory, has limited applicability to the social sciences (cf. Paolucci 2002).

Neo-organicism? Problems with the second wave

Complex dynamical systems theorists have studied a range of complex systems – including the human mind and social insect colonies – in which higher-level regularities emerge from complex actions and interactions of components. To date, complexity theory has not incorporated the unique properties of human social systems; rather, models are developed for systems composed of much simpler entities (neurons in the brain, ants in colonies) and are then applied by analogy to social systems, with the explicit assumption that social systems are not qualitatively different from these simpler complex systems.

The development of this approach has been heavily nurtured by the Santa Fe Institute, and the maturation of the second wave is evidenced by the founding of the journal *Complexity* by the Santa Fe Institute in 1995. The methodologies and perspectives reflect the dominant home disciplines of those at the institute (biology, physics, and mathematics); most of the work in this journal models organisms, genetic evolution, social insects, and ecology. Biological systems are an appropriate topic for complexity research because biological organisms are the most complex entities found in nature, and they are self-reproducing and adaptive.

Like sociological functionalism since the nineteenth century, much of this second wave has been based on biological models; James Miller (1978) and Maturana and Varela (1980) explicitly invoked biological life-forms as metaphors for systems more generally. For example, biologists have used nonlinear equations to model evolutionary "fitness landscapes," in which organisms that are selected for high fitness are represented by a point attractor (Kauffman 1995). Although the terminology is new, such ideas remain rooted in 1950s cybernetics; the General Problem Solver (Newell, Simon, and Shaw 1963) also displayed multipeaked landscapes and first raised the problem of intelligent agents that get stuck at locally optimal solutions.

When examining how biologically inspired models of complexity have been applied to social systems in the second wave, sociologists with a long view will recognize these applications as modern variants of nineteenth-century *organicism*, the school of thought that proposed that society was analogous to a biological organism (proponents of this view included Paul von Lilienfeld, Albert Schäffle, and Herbert Spencer). Most sociologists consider organicism to be a form of functionalism, and both have generally been rejected by contemporary sociologists. Viewing second-wave GST within this historical context provides a helpful perspective on the debate concerning whether social systems have unique properties distinct from those of natural complex systems. Second-wave theorists generally argue that social systems are not qualitatively different from natural systems; the third wave, which I describe in the next section, breaks with this assumption.

Although the second wave introduced several important metaphors and concepts into social science, it has several core features that make it inappropriate as a complete theory of social system complexity. First, the quantitative formalisms used in chaos theory were originally developed to model physical systems and are difficult to apply to sociological phenomena. The various concepts and components of chaos models have no clear correspondence to the entities of the social world – individuals, communications among individuals, and emergent social properties. Social processes rarely seem well characterized by chaos metaphors such as "bifurcations" and "strange attractors." Second, the "general systems"

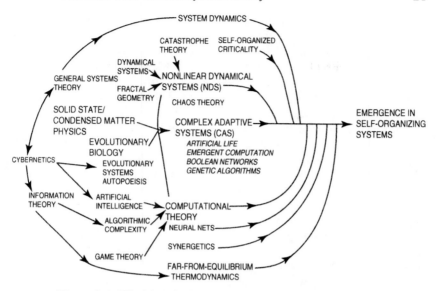

Figure 2.1. The historical development of third-wave emergence theory (from Goldstein 1999, 55).

focus of much of this research has the effect of eliding those elements of social systems that have no easy analog in the physical or biological world, such as the self-referential capabilities of human language (see Chapter 9).

Apart from a few economists and political scientists – many of them affiliated with the Santa Fe Institute – social scientists have not participated in the development of second-wave systems theory. And all of the social science contributions to second-wave systems theory have been from methodologically individualist social scientists. This history has left second-wave systems theory with severe weaknesses that make it inappropriate for application to sociology. For example, sociological research suggests that social systems have properties not held by other complex systems in nature and that universalist second-wave approaches may not be applicable to social systems.

The third wave: Emergence and complexity

This book describes a third wave of systems theory that is more appropriate for explaining complex social phenomena. This third wave emerged from recent developments in computer science and sociological theory (see Figure 2.1). What social scientists want to better understand is how successive symbolic interactions among autonomous individuals result in the emergence of collective phenomena. Although second-wave theory has provided many useful metaphors – of nonlinearity, of dynamical process – it has not helped social scientists to understand these microsocial interactions and how they contribute to social emergence.

First- and second-wave theorists were not focused on emergence. First-wave systems theorists like Parsons assumed the analytic independence of distinct levels of social reality, but they never developed arguments for the nonreducibility of higher levels of analysis (cf. J. Goldstein 1999). Parsons' 1951 book *The Social System* assumes but does not argue that the social system is an autonomous level of analysis, emergent from and not reducible to the individual participants. Second-wave general systems theorists likewise assumed the independence of the higher level. James Miller's massive 1,100-page book (1978) on general systems theory reads like an encyclopedia of all systems in nature – proposing 8 autonomous levels of systems, with each level containing the same 20 subsystems and processes (drawn primarily from first-wave cybernetics). But despite occasional uses of the term "emergence," Miller does not argue that the levels are independent and autonomous, and Miller does not explain how one of his proposed levels might be later proven to be nonautonomous and thus mergable with a nearby level. In the second-wave paradigm of chaos theory, emergence is conceived of as the unpredictable movement of a system into one of many attractors at points of bifurcation or is associated with interaction effects in multivariate equations (Byrne 1998). Although this notion of emergence captures the key insights of nonlinearity and unpredictability from initial conditions, it isn't very helpful in understanding the actual social processes whereby macrosocial properties emerge from communicative interactions among thousands of independent agents. Certainly a chaotic equation can be observed to fall unpredictably into one or another of many attractors as the initial conditions are modified, but this dynamic process has no clear connection to how richly complex phenomena like societies and institutions emerge from collective action.

Third-wave systems theorists are fundamentally concerned with emergence, component interactions, and relations between levels of analysis (see Table 2.1). A third-wave journal founded in 1999 by the New England Complex Systems Institute is titled *Emergence,* and the editors consider emergence to be the natural integrated development of diverse areas, including chaos theory, nonlinear dynamical systems, and complex adaptive systems (see www.emergence.org, accessed 24 March 2005).

Unlike second-wave theorists, many in the third wave have explored the unique features of human social systems. Drawing on recent developments in complexity research, I argue that the most important missing

Table 2.1. *The Three Waves of Social Systems Theory*

	First Wave	Second Wave	Third Wave
Dynamical	No	Yes	Yes
Nonlinear	No	Yes	Yes
Microlevel agents	No	No	Yes
Agent communication	No	No	Yes
Social emergence	No	No	Yes
Society is unique	No	No	Yes

element is the sophistication of human symbolic communication. In Chapters 9 and 10, I outline the role played by symbolic communication in emergence processes, showing that societies are uniquely complex systems because of complex properties of human language.

Like the first two waves, the third wave conceives of societies as systems and draws on a range of interdisciplinary work from outside sociology. This third wave is generally called "complex dynamical systems theory" or "complex adaptive systems theory." In some circles of late, particularly the popular press, the field is sometimes referred to simply as "complexity theory," although this term conflates the second and third waves and elides important distinctions between modeling technologies such as nonlinear dynamical equations and multi-agent systems. As my paradigm case of complexity modeling, I focus on *multi-agent system technologies* that emerged only in the late 1990s but have already begun to be applied to social simulation (see Chapters 8 and 9).

It is widely acknowledged in sociology today that social theory must be centrally concerned with process and mechanism (Abbott 1995; Archer 1995; Giddens 1984; Hedström and Swedberg 1998). Nonetheless, sociologists have found it difficult to develop an adequate theory for capturing social processes, and even more difficult has been the empirical study of social processes. As a result, much of modern sociology neglects process (cf. Cederman 2002; N. Gilbert 1997, para. 3.3). Complex dynamical systems can provide tools to explore these processes; they are "dynamical" because processes of change over time are of central interest. The occasional alternate name, "complex *adaptive* systems," suggests that the changes are toward ever increasing improvements in functionality of the system in response to feedback from the environment. Second-wave theorists were distinguished from the first wave by their emphasis on dynamics; however, they were less successful at representing adaptation and at providing useful explanations of the detailed evolution of the process.

Although some systems theorists maintain that reduction to a lower level of explanation is impossible, there is not yet a principled and foundational argument for why systems could not, in theory, be reduced to analyses at lower levels. For example, most social-scientific applications of complexity concepts have been undertaken by neoclassical microeconomists, and they have considered complexity science to provide a new methodology with which to accomplish their reductionist, methodologically individualist program. Using complexity methods – nonlinear dynamical modeling and multi-agent systems – microeconomists have attempted to reproduce empirically observed macrophenomena by modeling microevents and microinteractions – individuals' calculations of optimal outcomes and their rational decisions to pursue those outcomes. In economics, "emergence" is considered to be consistent with the program of methodological individualism.

The reductionist, individualist challenge posed by economics has not been successfully answered by sociology, and the relation between the disciplines remains unstable. Economists have been the social scientists most enamoured with complex systems thinking; for example, economists associated with the Santa Fe Institute have been applying complex dynamical systems theory to social systems since the late 1980s (Waldrop 1992). Methodological individualism has increased in influence in the second half of the twentieth century, with the growth and success of microeconomics, rational choice theory, and game theory. Some sociologists have responded by embracing the reductionist system approaches of economics; Coleman's 1990 *Foundations of Social Theory* outlined how sociologists could proceed using rational choice methods, and such methods have become increasingly widespread in sociology since that time.

Although economists and sociologists both are concerned with emergence, they maintain distinct versions of emergence (Chapter 5). Economists tend to believe that because social phenomena emerge from collective individual action, the best way to study those phenomena is to study the lower level of individual action from whence they emerge. This is the reading of complex dynamical systems theory that one often finds in the writings of economists: a reductionist, atomistic version, perhaps most explicitly demonstrated in multi-agent system computer models of societies (Chapter 8). Yet this version of systems thinking is not acceptable to many sociologists because it seems to deny the reality of social phenomena like networks, symbolic interactions, and institutions. In contrast, many sociological theories of emergence argue that emergent social properties cannot be analyzed in terms of the individuals constituting society because once emergent they take on autonomous properties and seem to exert causal force over the participating individuals.

The problem is that neither economists nor sociologists have prepared a sustained analysis of the concept of emergence. In this book, I explore these issues by drawing on systems theory, philosophy of science, and sociological theory. I address foundational issues in both sociology and economics and outline the various ways that the two disciplines may be related and perhaps even find an eventual congruence. The third-wave focus on social emergence provides an opportunity for sociologists and economists to find common ground. In Chapter 10, I propose a new relationship between sociology and economics.

Complex dynamical systems theory is sometimes said to have emerged from chaos theory as the study of systems that manifest nonlinear relations (see Figure 2.1). However, chaos theory as such is not very useful for social scientists other than as a source of provocative metaphors. The main problem is that its mathematical formalisms are exceedingly difficult to apply to social systems because they do not provide an opportunity to explore the emergence processes of the micro-macro link (Chapters 3 and 4 of Byrne 1998 are an attempt to accomplish this difficult task). In contrast, this book draws on a more recent method of modeling complex systems known as *multi-agent systems*. In multi-agent systems, each individual is represented by its own autonomous computational entity, and the simulator provides the individuals with a "language" in which to communicate. The simulation consists of choosing the number of agents, programming them with various goals and internal states, and then letting an "artificial society" emerge on its own. In Chapters 8 and 9, I provide several examples that demonstrate how this methodology can help social scientists study social emergence.

Third-wave theories allow for the incorporation of theories of symbolic communication, and the third-wave methodology of multi-agent system modeling provides a way to experiment with different conceptions of symbolic communication and explore how these conceptions change the micro-macro relation. Thus multi-agent methodologies help to address a third problem with the second wave: the tendency to consider all complex systems as theoretically equivalent and to consider issues of relations between contiguous levels of analysis as identical issues. For example, the relation between an organism's genes (which exist at a lower level) and the fitness of the species (which exists at a higher level) is considered to be theoretically identical to the relation between an individual's goals and the emergent properties of the society. In contrast, I argue that owing to the uniquely complex character of human symbolic communication, emergence processes in social systems are qualitatively different from emergence processes in natural and biological systems (Chapter 9). First- and second-wave system theories do not model agent communication and its role in emergence and thus cannot make this principled distinction.

The chapters to follow outline an approach to complexity in social systems that is designed to address these unique properties of social systems. For the third wave of systems theory to be genuinely applicable to sociological theory, it will require complex systems theorists to elaborate and extend their formalisms along these lines:

1. In the natural world, complex systems are bounded physical systems, highly integrated and with visibly (objectively, physically) interconnected parts. In the social world, it is difficult to identify a physical boundary for a social system. Thus, these systems are radically more open than other complex systems. It is a commonplace in systems theory that open systems are resistant to reductionist analysis.

2. In social systems, the interconnections between components are not physically visible; in natural systems they are. For example, neurons are visibly connected via synapses. The nature of the information passed between individuals is not well understood; linguists, conversation analysts, and semioticians are still developing a basic theory of situated communicative action. Interaction among individuals is much more complex than synaptic transfer; semiosis, meaning, and intersubjectivity become important. Unlike synaptic transfer between neurons, the content of these communications is not physically observable and describable because it is semiotic and intentional.

3. In social systems, the components (individuals) contain representations of the emergent macropatterns, unlike in any other complex system. Weber (1968) emphasized the importance of this difference in his critique of functionalism, claiming that, in the case of social collectivities, "We can accomplish something which is never attainable in the natural sciences, namely the subjective understanding of the action of the component individuals" (p. 15). Neurons do not have interpretations, meanings, and intentional action; individuals do.

In sum, the first two waves of systems theory were inadequate to the study of societies because their models and formalisms were originally developed for natural systems. The third wave – with its focus on emergence from agent communication – provides an opportunity to develop a truly *social* system theory.

3 The history of emergence

Emergence is a central concept in third-wave systems theory. The term "emergence" often appears in writings by first- and second-wave theorists, but these theorists did not present a foundational argument concerning emergence. This lack of foundational clarity has led to the problems that I noted in Chapters 1 and 2: that "emergence" has been used in widely varying and often contradictory ways by theorists in different paradigms and different disciplines. My goal in this book is to provide a foundational account of social emergence, one that will allow social scientists to evaluate and reconcile these varying conceptions of the individual-social relation.

In this chapter, I begin the exploration of social emergence by going back to the source: the very first writings on emergence. Discussions of emergence began among philosophers in the mid-nineteenth century. The nineteenth-century founders of both psychology and sociology were heavily influenced by these discussions, and they each engaged with emergentist theory in their works. An awareness of this history can offer an important perspective on contemporary discussions of emergence. My goal therefore is to present an account that is not simply of historical interest but that will be a valuable background when I move on to clarify competing contemporary conceptions of emergence in psychology (Chapter 4) and in sociology (Chapter 5).

Atomism, holism, and emergentism

Since the nineteenth century, most physical and biological scientists have been reductionist atomists, believing that the only scientific way to understand a complex system is to first analyze it into its component parts, then discover the rules and laws that describe these components, and finally analyze interactions among the parts. In the twentieth century, reductionist methods were increasingly successful in the physical sciences, identifying *bridging laws* between levels of analysis that were formerly thought to be incommensurable; canonical examples include the reduction of thermodynamics to statistical mechanics and the reduction of the regularities of the periodic table to the laws of quantum mechanics (Nagel 1961). These successes led to a form of reductionism known as *physicalism* – the belief that all science ultimately reduces to the laws of physics – that was closely associated with logical empiricism. One of the most distinctive features of contemporary complexity science is that it breaks with this tradition of physicalist reductionism.

In philosophy, the traditional opposite of atomism has been *holism*: the position that there are some complex systemic phenomena that must be studied in their own terms; that mechanistic, reductionist methods are not applicable to such systems; and that no part can be understood except in its relation to the entire system (Gellner [1956] 1968; Phillips 1976). The term "holism" is sometimes used in an even broader sense, to indicate a belief that components must be studied not only in isolation but also to see how their behavior changes when they come into relation with other parts in complex systems. But even reductionists accept that component behaviors can change in different contexts: "If this is emergence, then this is a sort of emergence that the most reductionist and mechanist physicalist will never have dreamed of denying" (Smart 1981, 111; also see Phillips 1976, 35). Holists can be more or less receptive to incorporating some analyses of parts, but they all assign analytic primacy to the arrangement of the parts in a complex system.

Since the origins of the social sciences in the nineteenth century, they have included both reductionist atomists and antireductionist holists. For example, the nineteenth-century structuralist psychology associated with Wundt and Titchener was reductionist; by asking subjects to report in detail on the nature of their subjective experience, they attempted to identify the component sensations of various mental states. Behaviorism rejected this methodology of introspection, but it was equally reductionist. In his seminal 1913 paper, Watson wrote that after psychology accepts behaviorism, psychology can then be unified with the physical sciences: "The findings of psychology...lend themselves to explanation in physico-chemical terms" (p. 177). Gestaltism, in contrast, was a form of psychological holism; it was foundationally based on the claim that humans perceived irreducible wholes, or *gestalts*. Consequently, its attacks on behaviorism and introspectionism targeted their reductionist assumptions: "The processes of learning, of reproduction, of striving, of emotional attitude, of thinking, acting, and so forth...do not consist of independent elements, but are determined in a situation as a whole" (Köhler 1929, 193).

Holists have always faced the difficult task of ontologically grounding their antireductionism. For example, Durkheim dedicated a great deal of theoretical effort attempting to ground his sociological holism, opposing it to the nonholist theories of Tarde, Simmel, and others (Chapter 6). If the holist accepts the ontological position of materialism – only physical matter exists – then on what grounds can an antireductionist argument be made? After all, a higher-level phenomenon is nothing but its component matter. From the late nineteenth century through the 1920s, many holists rejected materialism and held to dualist ontologies such as *vitalism* and *organicism*. Vitalism holds that living organisms contain a "vital" force or substance in addition to physical matter. If this were true, reduction to physical matter would be impossible and science would have to remain dualistic. In social philosophy, many vitalists were also *organicists*, drawing analogies between society and complex biological organisms. As science became more firmly detached from metaphysics, nonmaterialist holisms – including vitalism, dualism, spiritualism, and idealism – became increasingly difficult for serious scientists to maintain, although metaphysical philosophers continued to make such arguments through the 1920s. Today, dualist ontologies such as vitalism are rejected as unscientific by the mainstream of all scientific disciplines; all science is now materialist and is based on the metaphysical position that all existence is material in character and there are no entities that exist independently of matter.

Emergentism is a form of nonreductionism that accepts the ontological position of materialism. With regard to the complex natural phenomena under study, emergentism accepts that nothing exists except the component parts and their interactions, and thus it avoids the ontological problems of holism. However, the emergentist also rejects atomism and argues that reductionism, physicalism, mechanism, and epiphenomenalism are not necessary consequences of materialism. Some complex natural phenomena cannot be studied with reductionist methods; these phenomena are complex systems in which more complex and differentiated "higher-level" structures emerge from the organization and interaction of simpler, "lower-level" component parts. Emergentists make a wide range of philosophical arguments for this latter claim; the arguments are quite complex and are found not only in complexity theory but also in philosophy, psychology, and sociology. The consensus among these scholars – discussed here and in Chapters 4 and 5 – is that reductionism is not the only valid scientific method and that for many natural phenomena it will not be successful.

Because emergentists are materialists, they hold that higher-level properties *supervene* on the system of lower-level components (Davidson 1970; Fodor 1974; Kim 1993b; Sawyer 2002b). Supervenience is a relation between two levels of analysis such that if two events are identical with respect to their descriptions at the lower level, then they cannot differ at the higher level. If a collection of lower-level components with a given set of relations causes higher-level property E to emerge at time t, then on every other occasion when that same collection of components in that same set of relations occurs, E will again emerge. Note that this implies that an entity cannot change at a higher level without also changing at the lower levels. Although emergentists accept supervenience, many of them also hold that higher-level structures can have causal powers over the lower-level components (Davidson 1993; Fodor 1989; Horgan 1989; Sawyer 2003e).

The observation that some complex systems manifest emergent higher-level properties that are not attributable to the components is not in itself incompatible with reductionism. The pressure of a volume of gas is an emergent property – no component molecule can be assigned the property "pressure" – yet the pressure can be reduced to statements about molecular movement and interaction using the laws of statistical mechanics. Such examples have led some scientists to argue that "emergence" only reflects the incomplete state of science and is not a fact about the natural world. For example, reductionists in sociology – known as *methodological individualists* – hold that although we may identify laws about social groups that we cannot at present reduce to laws about individuals, these are only incomplete and interim explanations; as our scientific knowledge advances, we will ultimately be able to effect the reduction to laws about individuals (see Chapter 5). These issues have been central in over a century of sociological debate, including disputes between Durkheim and Tarde (Chapter 6) and between Homans and Blau (Chapter 5); these issues remain unresolved, and I discuss the implications for contemporary sociology in Chapters 5 through 10.

In contrast to the almost total dominance of reductionism in the physical sciences – at least until the burst of interest in complexity theory in the 1980s and 1990s – psychology and sociology have been influenced by emergentism from their late nineteenth century origins through the present. Early versions of emergentism first arose in the mid to late nineteenth century and include the theories of French sociologists Auguste Comte ([1842] 1854) and Émile Durkheim ([1895] 1964), American psychologist William James (1890), English philosopher George Henry Lewes (1875), and several German social organicists. For psychologists such as Wundt and the later Gestaltists, emergentism provided grounds for a nonreductionist science of psychology. For sociologists like Durkheim and Parsons, emergentism was a way of creating a science of social phenomena that is not derivative from psychology.

Both complexity scientists and social scientists could benefit from a greater familiarity with this tradition of nonreductionist, emergentist science. Most complexity scientists have homes in natural science disciplines that have been predominantly reductionist, and consequently the nonreductionist features of complexity theory seem particularly radical to them. However, the social sciences have a sustained history of scientific inquiry in a nonreductionist approach, and familiarity with this history could provide a valuable perspective on the contemporary tensions between reductionism, emergentism, and holism.

Psychological emergence

The history of emergence in psychology is important for understanding emergentism in the social sciences more broadly. Throughout the nineteenth and twentieth centuries, emergentist thinking in psychology and emergentist thinking in sociology have mutually influenced each other. A focus on social emergence requires an interdisciplinary analysis of both individuals and collectives; social emergence implies that sociologists will need to draw on psychology and that psychologists will need to draw on sociology (see Chapters 4, 5, and 10).

I group emergentist arguments in psychology into four schools: British emergentism of the 1920s, Gestalt psychology of the 1920s and 1930s, American pragmatism from the 1890s through the 1930s, and contemporary philosophy of mind and cognitive science from the 1970s through the 1990s.

British emergentism

The British emergentists were a group of philosophers who elaborated a theory of emergence in the 1920s, focusing primarily on biological evolution (see Ablowitz 1939; Blitz 1992; McLaughlin 1992; Teller 1992). Most 1920s emergentists rejected vitalism and dualism, accepting a materialist ontology (i.e., the view that only physical matter exists). Higher-level entities and properties were grounded in and determined by the more basic properties of physical matter; this was referred to as "supervenience." By the late 1920s, emergence was a full-fledged intellectual fad, expanding beyond evolutionary thought to be applied to a wide range of topics, including creativity and sociality. British emergentists cited Mill as the source of the concept of emergence. In his *Logic* (1843), in Book III, Chapter 6, "Of the Composition of Causes," Mill elaborated the implications of the science of chemistry and proposed two types of causation: mechanical causation, which was additive, and *heteropathic* causation, or emergent causation, which was not additive and not mechanical (vol. 2, 427).

However, Mill did not use the term "emergent"; this term was coined by a friend and colleague of his, George Henry Lewes (1875). Like Mill, Lewes distinguished between mechanical and chemical effects, referring to them as "resultants" and "emergents," respectively. The classic example of emergence invoked by both Mill and Lewes was the combination of hydrogen and oxygen, which results in water. Water does not have any of the properties of either hydrogen or oxygen; its properties are emergent effects of the combination:

Although each effect is the resultant of its components, the product of its factors, we cannot always trace the steps of the process, so as to see in the product the mode of operation of each factor. In this latter case, I propose to call the effect an emergent. It arises out of the combined agencies, but in a form which does not display the agents in action. (Lewes 1875, vol. 2, 412)

If all effects were resultants, Lewes noted, the power of scientific rationality would be absolute, and mathematics could explain all phenomena. But Lewes claimed that "effects are mostly emergents" (p. 414). Thus, science must proceed by experiment and observation rather than rational reasoning, since emergent effects are unpredictable before the event.

Mill's distinction between mechanical and heteropathic causation and Lewes's concept of the emergent were elaborated by several English language philosophers during and after World War I, including C. Lloyd Morgan (1923), Samuel Alexander (1920), and Edward Spaulding (1918). Morgan (1923), who was responsible for reintroducing Lewes's term "emergence," claimed that in *emergent evolution* "one cannot predict... the emergent expression of some new kind of relatedness among pre-existent events" (p. 6). Although emergent phenomena follow the laws of nature, they will not always submit to scientific study; "such novelty is for us unpredictable owing to our partial knowledge of the plan of emergence up to date, and our necessary ignorance of what the further development of that plan will be" (p. 282).

During this period, several emergentists were also vitalists, proposing that complex systems contained some nonmaterial substance, such as Driesch's *entelechies* and Bergson's *élan vital*. In particular, Bergson's book *Creative Evolution* ([1907] 1911) was widely studied by British philosophers, particularly by those who most strongly advocated emergentism in the 1920s. This book was a critique of what Bergson called "radical mechanism" and "radical finalism"; he argued that both positions exaggerated the predictability of natural phenomena and that both evolution and mental processes were unpredictable for similar reasons: because they "endure" in time. He appealed to a vitalist, nonmaterial force, the *élan vital*, to account for novelty in evolution. For some British emergentists (such as S. Alexander 1920), such lingering vitalist influences contributed to a tendency to be dissatisfied with a strict materialist ontology, and this vestigial vitalism led many scientists of the day to dismiss emergentism entirely. Bergson was the first to elaborate the process metaphysics that became an element of many later antireductionist theories: "Everything is obscure in the idea of creation if we think of *things* which are created and a *thing* which creates. . . . There are no things, there are only actions" (p. 248). Bergson referred to the human tendency to fixate on stable forms as the "cinematographical illusion," a metaphor for the false belief that reality is a succession of fixed structures (pp. 305–7). As I showed in Chapter 2, third-wave complexity science also focuses on the processes of dynamical change over time. Interestingly, a process ontology is central to the influential sociological theory of Anthony Giddens, which rejects emergentist theories. The exact relationship between process and emergence remains unresolved in contemporary sociology, and the tension between them is the topic of Chapter 7.

Morgan's work was influential because it explicitly rejected vitalism and yet seemed to provide a nonreductionist version of materialism. It resulted in a dramatic burst of activity, including conference symposia and special issues of journals (see Lovejoy 1927; Pepper 1926; Russell, Morris, and MacKenzie 1926). These British emergentists argued that life and mind – what philosophers today call "consciousness" and "intentional states" – were emergent and were supervenient on material reality. Through the 1930s, the nonreductive materialism of the British emergentists had a wide-ranging impact in psychology and the social sciences, and they were explicitly acknowledged as influences by theorists as diverse as Wolfgang Köhler, George Herbert Mead, and Talcott Parsons. These same theorists acknowledged their debt to Alfred North Whitehead (1926), whose theories were also heavily emergentist. Philosophers of science continued to elaborate on the writings of the British emergentists through the 1950s and 1960s (e.g., Hempel 1965, 258–64; Mandelbaum 1951; Meehl and Sellars 1957). Although emergentism continued to influence psychologists and sociologists, in the 1930s it was rejected by physical scientists owing to developments in quantum mechanics and other sciences that reinforced the physicalist belief that all science would ultimately reduce to physics (McLaughlin 1992, 89).

Gestalt psychology

Emergentism in psychology has its roots in nineteenth-century *organicism*: the theory that the organism is different from the sum of its parts and that it depends on the structural arrangement of the parts. Social organicism – the notion that society formed an integrated unity similar in some sense to that of living organisms – can be traced to classical social philosophy, but the publication of Darwin's account of evolution gave new energy to social organismic theories (see Giddens 1970, 172). In the nineteenth century, organicism was prominent in German social philosophy; influential advocates included Albert Schäffle and Paul von Lilienfeld. Like the views held by Bergson and other vitalist biologists and philosophers of the nineteenth century, organicist social theories retained elements of vitalism; they were not strictly materialist in ontology and therefore did not meet the contemporary definition of emergentism. However, these theories were widely read and influenced German psychologists, including Wundt and the early Gestaltists. Both Wundt and the Gestaltists drew on the emergentist insights of social organicism to develop nonvitalist, materialist forms of nonreductionist psychology.

Wundt (1912) included emergence as one of his fundamental principles, the "principle of creative resultants," writing that it "attempts to state the fact that in all psychical combinations the product is not a mere sum of the separate elements that compose such combinations, but that it represents a new creation. But at the same time ... this product is formed by the elements, so that further components are not necessary for its creation" (p. 164). Wundt had formulated the principle of creative resultants in his 1902 edition of *Grundzüge der physiologischen Psychologie* (*Principles of Physiological Psychology*, [1902] 1904), although these passages appeared in the final chapter of the final volume, which has never been translated into English (for a translated passage, see Wheeler 1928, 60–1). Wundt is often considered to be a structuralist psychologist, and his method was essentially reductionist; however, his writings were contradictory – at times he wrote as if he held to associationism (which is additive and thus mechanical), yet at other times he emphasized creative synthesis (see Boring 1929, 336, 607–9).

Drawing on organicist precedents, the Gestalt psychologists opposed the reductionist claim of physiological psychology that the brain took simple sensations and by a process of association identified and evaluated them. Gestalt antireductionism was opposed to structuralist psychology – represented by E. B. Titchener – which claimed that mental experiences could be analyzed into elementary units such as sensations, feelings, and thoughts. The Gestaltists drew on emergentism to philosophically ground their antireductionism. Köhler (1929) explicitly noted that his Gestalt psychology was emergentist (p. ix) and frequently appealed to emergence in terms strikingly familiar to contemporary complexity theory – arguing, for example, that higher-level structures emerge from "dynamical self-distribution" (p. 140) and presenting Gestalt theory as an analysis of how "a process dynamically distributes and regulates itself" (p. 193). However, the Gestaltists were more holist than emergentist; their emphasis was on the study of irreducible wholes, and they did not explore how those wholes emerged from lower-level components and their interactions (Jean Piaget attacked Gestaltism on exactly this point; see "The Cognitive Revolution" below).

Kurt Lewin's research on *group dynamics* was a particularly interesting elaboration of Gestalt psychology; it shifted emergence arguments from the individual to the group level of analysis. Lewin, working alongside Köhler and Wertheimer in Berlin, applied Gestalt holism to group phenomena, using Köhler's term "dynamical whole" to refer to groups. Lewin argued that, by analogy with a perceptual Gestalt, a change in any component of a group changed the state of the other components. The research in Lewin's school focused on the internal characteristics of groups – cohesiveness, internal communication processes, and group structure and position (Deutsch 1954). When Lewin first began to develop and publish his theories on group dynamics, most psychologists denied the existence or reality of groups. Rather, they held a reductionist, atomist view of social phenomena: Only individuals were real, and to talk about properties of groups was considered to be nonscientific or mystical. Thus, one of Lewin's major contributions was to help make the concept of "group" acceptable to psychologists, and this contribution was thus foundational for late twentieth century social psychology. Of course, a belief in the emergent existence of groups was common among French sociologists of Durkheim's school (see Chapter 6); yet apparently Lewin developed his conceptual framework without influence from sociology (Deutsch 1954), again demonstrating the pervasive influence of emergentist thought in both psychology and sociology throughout the twentieth century.

Pragmatism and symbolic interactionism

American pragmatism was formed at the same time as the theoretical discussions described in the preceding section were most prominent, and consequently emergentist elements had significant influence on the development of pragmatist thought. William James was often cited by both British emergentists and process metaphysicians and was also widely read by French sociologists, including Durkheim. In rejecting associationism, materialist monism, and epiphenomenalism, James (1890) argued that "thoughts and feelings exist" (vol. 1, vi) and that "we ought to continue to talk in psychology as if consciousness had causal efficacy" (vol. 1, 138). Chapter 6 of *The Principles of Psychology* is a critique of psychological atomism – of the "mind-stuff theory" that "our mental states are composite in structure, made up of smaller states conjoined" (James 1890, vol. 1, 145).

George Herbert Mead and John Dewey developed their theories under the influence of James, Whitehead, and the British emergentists, and each developed a distinct variant of emergentism. Dewey's concept of "experience" was a theory of agent-environment interaction; experience emerges from the active process of an intelligent agent engaging with an environment: "Experience is the result, the sign, and the reward of that interaction of organism and environment which ... is a transformation of interaction into participation and communication" (1934, 22). In focusing on interaction between a complex organism and its environment, Dewey's emergentism is subtly different from the version I emphasize here, in which higher-level properties *within* a complex system are emergent from and yet irreducible to lower-level components. In his focus on process and change and his critique of static, structuralist theories, Dewey was influenced by the process metaphysics of Bergson and Whitehead.

Arthur Murphy, in his introduction to Mead's 1932 *The Philosophy of the Present*, noted that "'process,' 'development' and 'emergence' are catchwords of recent thought" (p. xi) and described Mead's work as an elaboration of both Alexander's theory of emergence and Whitehead's process metaphysics. Dewey, in his prefatory remarks in the same book, stated, "Long before the words 'emergent evolution' were heard, [Mead's problem was] that of the emergence of the new ... one can appreciate how much more fundamentally he took the doctrine of emergence than have most of those who have played with the idea" (p. xxxviii). Like James, Mead opposed an epiphenomenalist materialism that attributed causal force only to the lowest level physical particles (e.g., 1932, 38). In Mead's conception of emergence, both the lower-level *and* the higher-level entities have causal power; the emergent, higher levels of reality have causal influence on the lower, component levels (e.g., p. 69). Mead's term for this principle was "sociality." Sociality is a property of emergence processes because such processes are emerging simultaneously within different systems at different levels of analysis. Mead's choice of the term "sociality" reveals that emergentism is at the core of his social psychology; it indicates that Mead equated emergence with the existence of the social and with the causal autonomy of the social.

In addition to their theoretical work, Mead and Dewey were concerned with the empirical mechanics of emergent processes. The philosophical theory of process, emergence, and sociality led Mead (1934) to propose an empirical focus on symbolic social process, and this was the foundational inspiration for symbolic interactionism, an empirical branch of microsociology that focuses on joint action (Blumer 1969) and that is one of the roots of sociocultural psychology, a contemporary psychological paradigm that increasingly draws on sociological theory (see Chapter 4). Symbolic interactionists reject explanations that reduce joint activity to individual psychology and argue that joint activity is the only appropriate level for social scientific study.

The cognitive revolution

Several authors have noted connections between the early stages of the cognitive revolution and Gestalt psychology (Murray 1995; Simon 1999). From the emergentist perspective, the most important connection is that they share antireductionist, antiphysicalist impulses. The behaviorism and associationism that dominated psychology in the first half of the twentieth century were consistent with reductionist atomism in holding that the physical processes of the brain are causally complete and that reference to consciousness or mental states is not necessary for understanding behavior. If higher-level mental phenomena are merely epiphenomenal, with no causal powers, then why should scientific psychology attempt to study them? The cognitive revolution represented a new approach to psychology – one that rejected the reductionist atomism of behaviorism and proposed that mental phenomena could be scientifically studied without first reducing them. The first cognitive psychologists were heavily influenced by cybernetics and systems theory, which had identified feedback and homeostasis processes at the level of complex systems (the same influence was foundational for Talcott Parsons; see below). Philosophers responded with proposals for new forms of materialism that were mentalist and thus nonreductionist. Perhaps the first was the neuroscientist R. W. Sperry, who drew on the British emergentists and as early as 1965 proposed theories of emergentism and *nonreductive mentalism* to ground the new cognitive science (see Sperry 1980). In the philosophy of mind, the cognitive revolution reactivated a dormant mind-brain debate, with *identity theorists* holding to the epiphenomenalist position (mental states cannot have any causal force) and *nonreductive materialists* holding that mental properties and events are not reducible to physical ones (Davidson 1970; Fodor 1974; Lowe 1993) and may indeed have causal power over the physical brain (Andersen et al. 2000; Campbell 1974; Lowe 1993). At various points in this recent debate, the 1920s-era concepts of emergence and supervenience have been influential (Beckermann, Flohr, and Kim 1992; Horgan 1993; Humphreys et al. 1997; Kim 1993b).

Jean Piaget's developmental psychology, another major influence on cognitivism, was also opposed to the reductionist atomism of behaviorism (see Taylor 1985, 140). Piaget was influenced by a strong line of holist thinking in French philosophy, having studied Durkheim and Lévy-Bruhl early in his career.[1] Piaget noted that the nonreductionist task of his "genetic epistemology" was analogous to Durkheim's emergentist project (Piaget [1950] 1995, 39–40; see Chapter 6). In spite of this general influence, on several occasions throughout the writings collected in his *Sociological Studies* Piaget explicitly rejected Durkheim's sociological emergentism, arguing in contrast a position more similar to that of Durkheim's nemesis Gabriel de Tarde: that any social totality must be conceived of as the set of all social interactions and that "one can reduce all 'social facts' to interactions between individuals" (1995, 97; also see pp. 45, 134–9).

Piaget's constructivism was quite similar to emergentism, in that schemas at one stage emerge from the interaction between activity and schemas at the prior stage (Sawyer 2003b). His empirical research focused on the detailed incremental mechanisms of this emergence. By providing bottom-up explanations of the emergence of mental schemas through time, Piaget was rejecting the claim of the Gestaltists that higher-level phenomena can be analyzed and explained without reference to their components. The form of emergentism found in Piaget's constructivism was formative for cognitive psychology and its rejection of behaviorism because it provided an account whereby cognitive schemas could be emergent from a past process of ontogenesis and thus not reducible to present behavior.

Sociological emergence

Emergentism has been even more influential in sociology than in psychology. The emergence arguments of sociologists and psychologists have mutually influenced each other since the late nineteenth century, reflecting both the generality of the underlying philosophical arguments and the interlevel nature of emergence theories.

The founding of French sociology

A society therefore can no more be decomposed into individuals, than a geometric surface can be resolved into lines, or a line into points. (Comte [1854] 1966, vol. 2, 153)

Emergence was not a British invention; rather, it originated with Auguste Comte, who was a major influence on both Mill and Lewes.

---

[1] Piaget's comments on his early holism and on the formative influence of the Durkheim-Tarde debate can be found in Piaget 1952, 240–2.

Mill was strongly influenced by Comte before and during the writing of his 1843 *Logic*; he asserted that Comte's *Cours* was "the greatest yet produced on the Philosophy of the Sciences" (Mill 1843, vol. 1, 421), and he initiated an extensive correspondence with Comte in 1841 (Mill and Comte 1994). Lewes was also heavily influenced by Comte's positivism, and he wrote an English summary of Comte's *Cours de philosophie positive* in 1853, claiming that Comte was "the greatest thinker of modern times" (Lewes 1853, iii).

Comte rarely appears in accounts of emergentism. That Comte was the source of British concepts of emergence has not been noted, perhaps because Comte's own emergence theory has not been recognized by English-speaking scholars. Comte argued for both the irreducibility of higher levels and the causal power of higher levels in the first two volumes of his six-volume *System of Positive Philosophy*; these volumes were published in 1830 and 1835. Although Comte is sometimes read as a reductionist, he explicitly argued that reductionist study would not work for sociology: "The methodical division of studies which takes place in the simple inorganic sciences is thoroughly irrational in the recent and complex science of society, and can produce no results" ([1842] 1854, vol. 2, 81).

Comte's writings were a major influence on late nineteenth century French sociologists, including Le Bon, Tarde, and Durkheim. In *The Crowd* ([1895] 1896), Le Bon proposed a psychology of crowd behavior, beginning a long sociological tradition of associating emergence with collective behavior. The crowd's psychology was qualitatively different from individual psychology: "When, however, a certain number of these individuals are gathered together in a crowd ... there result certain new psychological characteristics" (p. 5). He explored how crowds form and how this collectivity then influences the participants' mental states. Thus, like Comte, Le Bon was interested in the dialectic between emergence and downward causation. Like Mill and Comte, Le Bon ([1895] 1896) drew metaphors with chemistry and cell biology to make his emergence argument:

The psychological crowd is a provisional being formed of heterogeneous elements, which for a moment are combined, exactly as the cells which constitute a living body form by their reunion a new being which displays characteristics very different from those possessed by each of the cells singly. ... In the aggregate which constitutes a crowd there is in no sort a summing-up or an average struck between its elements. (p. 30)

Although Le Bon was influenced by organicist and emergentist thinking, he did not elaborate a theory of emergence, and he applied his ideas only to crowd behavior, not to normal social behavior.

In the nineteenth century, the theory of social emergence was most fully developed by Durkheim. Durkheim's foundational argument for sociology was heavily emergentist, and it has many parallels with third-wave social systems theory. I elaborate these parallels at some length in Chapter 6 ; the following is a preview. Emergence was the central concept of *Rules of the Sociological Method*, of the essay "Individual and Collective Representations," and of *Suicide*. In the Preface to the second edition of *Rules*, Durkheim ([1901] 1964) responded to reductionists' criticisms of the first edition by giving examples of emergence from other sciences:

Whenever certain elements combine and thereby produce, by the fact of their combination, new phenomena, it is plain that these new phenomena reside not in the original elements but in the totality formed by their union. The living cell contains nothing but mineral particles, as society contains nothing but individuals. Yet it is patently impossible for the phenomena characteristic of life to reside in the atoms of hydrogen, oxygen, carbon, and nitrogen. . . . Let us apply this principle to sociology. If, as we may say, this synthesis constituting every society yields new phenomena, differing from those which take place in individual consciousness, we must, indeed, admit that these facts reside exclusively in the very society itself which produces them, and not in its parts, i.e., its members. . . . These new phenomena cannot be reduced to their elements. (pp. xlvii–xlviii)

In "Individual and Collective Representations," Durkheim ([1898] 1953) explicitly noted the analogy between emergence arguments as applied to collective phenomena and emergence arguments as applied to psychological phenomena. Durkheim observed, "Not without reason has it been said that the self is itself a society" (p. 111), probably in reference to William James, who was widely read in France owing to his relationship with Durkheim's professor, Charles Renouvier. Durkheim noted that mental emergents are caused by neuronal activity but are not merely epiphenomenal; they exert causal force on those neurons: "They are caused, but they are in their turn causes" (p. 4). Otherwise "ideas have no power" (p. 10). In situations of higher-level causation, reductionist analysis is inappropriate because the component elements are changed by their association (p. 11). Durkheim argued that analogous threats of reductionism faced both sociology and psychology and that if psychological phenomena exist, then so must social phenomena. Psychologists who attack sociologists for studying something that doesn't really exist apart from its components – the members of the social group – are themselves subject to a similar reduction to biology, unless they make the same emergentist arguments (see Chapter 6).

The first English language writer to include society in an emergence theory was the Harvard entomologist William Morton Wheeler, in his 1928 book *Emergent Evolution and the Development of Societies*. In this text, he criticized the British emergentists for leaving the social level of analysis out of their schemes; for Morgan and Alexander, the next level above the mind was the Deity. Wheeler's perspectives on complex emergent systems were developed over decades of studying social insect colonies, including ants, termites, bees, and wasps. By 1911, Wheeler had formulated an organicist and nonvitalist perspective on social insect colonies and had an insight similar to Durkheim's, that all complex systems – including living organisms – were "sociogenic" in a similar way: "If the cell is a colony of lower physiological units . . . we must face the fact that all organisms are colonical or social and that one of the fundamental tendencies of life is sociogenic" (Wheeler 1911, 324).

As the emergence fad crossed the Atlantic from England to Harvard in the 1920s, Wheeler rather quickly perceived that this new concept represented the same phenomenon he had spent his career studying. In his 1928 book, Wheeler connected his organicist theories of social insects to the British emergentists, the French sociologists, and the German organicists, writing that "social emergence bears an interesting analogy to that of mind" (p. 26). Wheeler provided several examples of social emergence from the insect world. Referring to the nests of social insects, he wrote, "These structures, though the result of the cooperative labor of most of the personnel of the colony, are nevertheless true *Gestalten*, being no more mere sums of the individual activities than is the diverse architecture of cities built by human hands" (p. 33). Both human and animal societies manifest emergence: "[Nonhuman societies], no less than human society, are as superorganisms obviously true emergents" (p. 25).

It is no coincidence that an expert on social insects would be one of the first scholars to perceive the sociological importance of emergence theory. In fact, in the 1990s, some of the first third-wave complexity projects simulated emergence in groups of social insects; the multi-agent simulation language developed by the Santa Fe Institute was dubbed "Swarm" to reflect this inspiration, and the contemporary phrase "swarm intelligence" (Kennedy and Eberhart 2001) harkens back one hundred years to the original insights of Durkheim and Wheeler: social group emergence has parallels to psychological emergence.

Talcott Parsons

The influential sociological theorist Talcott Parsons drew heavily on emergence concepts in his first major work, *The Structure of Social Action* ([1937] 1949). Parsons defined the discipline of sociology as the study of the emergent properties of "social action systems" (p. 768) and drew on emergence to argue for the irreducibility of his chosen levels of analysis:

the *unit act* and *action systems*. He argued that reductionism was an inappropriate methodology for the scientific study of social action because it "consists in the progressive elimination, as the breaking down into parts is carried farther, of the emergent properties of the more complex systems." In contrast, Parsons argued that the science of social action must focus on a level of analysis that is not reducible to physical science: "Action systems have properties that are emergent only on a certain level of complexity in the relations of unit acts to each other" (p. 739). He defined three emergent levels of analysis, which are the objects of study of economics, politics, and sociology, respectively (p. 768). In a later major work, *The Social System* (1951), Parsons drew on systems theory and cybernetics and presented what became known as *structural-functional* sociology. Although Parsons rejected the reduction of sociology to psychology, as an emergentist he also rejected a sociological holism that denies the relevance of psychology. Scientists who study the "higher levels of emergence" have to be familiar with the sciences of the lower levels as well: "The 'mechanisms' of the processes that a sociologist is interested in will always prove to involve crucially important elements on these 'lower' levels" ([1937] 1949, 772). Like today's third wave of complexity science, Parsons realized that explanations of social emergence require a generative and processual focus on social mechanisms.

Methodological individualism in economics

The opposition between sociological holism and reductionism has been central not only in sociology but also in economics. Reductionism in both disciplines is known as *methodological individualism*: the position that all social phenomena can and should be explained in terms of individuals and relations among individuals and that there are no irreducible social properties.[2] Like sociologists, economists accept that society often manifests emergent properties. However, rather than using this observation to ground a nonreductionist science of society, as Durkheim and Parsons attempted, economists consider emergence to be compatible with methodological individualism. Like those physical scientists who observe that the properties of water only seemed to be emergent until the quantum mechanical bridge laws had been identified, methodological individualists argue that emergent social properties only seem to be irreducible owing to the limitations of our current state of scientific

---

[2] The term "methodological individualism" was coined in German by the economist Schumpeter in 1908 in a work never translated into English (see Machlup 1951, 150) and was first used in English by Popper ([1944–1945] 1957).

knowledge. Thus, economists generally hold that the existence of emergent social properties is compatible with methodological individualism, just as the existence of water, which has emergent properties not held by hydrogen and oxygen, does not demonstrate the falsity of physicalism.

Carl Menger, founder of the influential Austrian school of economics, insisted – in opposition to German social organicism and other forms of sociological holism – that even emergent social phenomena, including law, language, money, and markets, could be analyzed by reducing them to the analysis of individuals pursuing individual interests, using a reductionist, atomist method that he called the *exact orientation* ([1883] 1963, 151–9). Menger was influenced by Mill, who was quite explicit in denying that his chemical method of heteropathic causation was necessary for the social sciences: "The Laws of the phenomena of society are, and can be, nothing but the actions and passions of human beings. . . . Men are not, when brought together, converted into another kind of substance, with different properties; as hydrogen and oxygen are different from water" (Mill 1843, vol. 2, 469).

F. A. von Hayek, in his three-part essay *Scientism and the Study of Society* (1942, 1943, 1944), elaborated Menger's theories to develop an influential statement of methodological individualism. In this essay, Hayek argued that social phenomena must be explained in terms of individuals. Like Menger, Hayek (1942) rejected sociological holism, and described higher-level social phenomena as emergent from, although reducible to, individual action:

The conscious action of many men produce undesigned results . . . regularities which are not the result of anybody's design. If social phenomena showed no order except in so far as they were consciously designed, there would indeed be no room for theoretical sciences of society and there would be, as is often argued, only problems of psychology. . . . The reason of the difficulty which the natural scientist experiences in admitting the existence of such an order in social phenomena is that these orders cannot be stated in physical terms. (p. 288)

His examples included the forest trails that form gradually as hundreds of people each seek the best path; the task of social science is to discover explanations for how such patterns emerge. The "compositive theory of social phenomena" (Hayek 1944, 27) has as its goal the resolution of what Menger ([1883] 1963) called "the most noteworthy problem of the social sciences" (p. 146): how the independent actions of many people can produce higher-level social structures that are not intentionally designed. Although an emergentist of sorts, Hayek was critical of sociological realism, instead proposing a science of bottom-up emergence processes: "It is only by the individualist or compositive method that we can give a definite meaning to the much abused phrases about the social processes and formations being in any sense 'more' than 'merely the sum' of their parts" (1944, 30). Although such passages may seem reductionist, Hayek and other individualist economists maintained that their discipline could not be reduced to psychology; unlike psychology, economics was concerned with emergent phenomena in complex systems with large numbers of individuals – the canonical example being how the price of a good emerges from many exchanges among individuals in a free market.

In the 1950s, there was a wide-ranging debate among theorists about the merits of Hayek's methodologically individualist stance (O'Neill 1973). J. W. N. Watkins (1955, 1957) formulated an even stronger version of methodological individualism. Whereas Hayek (1944, 30–1) held that an understanding of social phenomena using the compositive method could never be complete due to the extreme complexity of the task and the limitations of the human mind, Watkins (1957) was more optimistic: "We shall not have arrived at rock-bottom explanations of such large-scale [social] phenomena until we have deduced an account of them from statements about the dispositions, beliefs, resources and inter-relations of individuals" (p. 106).

Methodological individualism continues to be debated within economics theory. Economist Kenneth Arrow (1994) recently argued that economics – although its paradigm follows a rhetoric and belief system of explaining everything in terms of individual behavior – in fact must use social categories because they are "irreducible," not just "figures of speech" (p. 1). He concluded that "social variables, not attached to particular individuals, are essential in studying the economy or any other social system and that, in particular, knowledge and technical information have an irremovable social component, of increasing importance over time" (p. 8). Coming from a Nobel prize winner in economics – one of the most firmly reductionist of all social sciences – and from one of the people responsible for introducing rational choice analysis into economics (Arrow 1951), such a claim is indicative of the continued viability and relevance of emergentism in the social sciences and of the continuing and unresolved tensions between different versions of social emergence. The remaining chapters are an attempt to resolve these tensions.

Conclusion

Emergentist theories have had an influence on social science theory since the founding of these sciences in the nineteenth century. Originally, emergentist theories in psychology and sociology were based on nineteenth-century philosophical thinkers such as Comte, Mill, and Lewes; the founders of the modern social sciences were all influenced by these ideas. Wundt, the founder of modern psychology, advocated a form of emergentism, and many contemporary psychologists draw on emergentism in their theories (Chapter 4). In sociology, Émile Durkheim's work was foundationally emergentist and continued to impact sociological thought throughout the twentieth century. I analyze contemporary sociological theories of emergence in Chapter 5, and I elaborate on Durkheim's emergentism in Chapter 6. Chapter 6 explores the relation between process ontologies and social emergence in contemporary sociological theory. In economics, Menger's seminal writings – as well as the writings of the later Austrian economists – were equally emergentist, although emergentist theory was used to advocate a methodologically individualist position, in contrast to Durkheim's sociological realism. I discuss these tensions between sociology and economics in Chapter 5 and again in Chapter 10.

4 Emergence in psychology

First, sociology is a type of knowledge worthy of study in its own right, especially with regard to its relations (of difference as well as similarity) with psychological knowledge. Second, the very object of sociological knowledge is of vital interest to epistemology, since human knowledge is essentially collective.

Jean Piaget

In Chapter 3, I traced the long history of emergentist thought in the social sciences, from its nineteenth-century origins to the mid-twentieth century. This history demonstrates that emergentism has always been an influential element in the foundational theories of both psychology and sociology. In this chapter, I bring the story up to the present by reviewing emergentist elements in contemporary psychology. In the bulk of the chapter, I identify five unresolved issues that emergentism has encountered throughout its history, and I suggest several implications for contemporary schools of psychology. Most of these issues are essentially sociological, and this discussion leads into the more sociological material of Chapters 5 through 7.

Emergence is a central concept in two contemporary psychological paradigms – socioculturalism and connectionist cognitive science – and both of them have important implications for sociology. The *connectionist* and *distributed* models of contemporary cognitive science hypothesize a "society of mind" (Minsky 1985; Rumelhart and McClelland 1986); that is, they consider the mind to be a society of independent, autonomous entities, with mental states emerging from their interaction. These parallels between society and mind were first observed by Durkheim, as I noted in Chapter 3; I further explore their implications for sociology in Chapter 5. *Socioculturalism* focuses on human behavior in social and cultural contexts, and many socioculturalists study processes of social emergence in small groups. Although this research is not widely known by sociologists, it has begun to encounter the long-standing issues discussed in Chapters 2 and 3: emergence, communication, and complexity.

Socioculturalism will return to center stage in Chapter 7, where I show that it has much to contribute to the debate between emergence theorists and structuration theorists.

Sociocultural psychology

Socioculturalism is a revival of a range of nineteenth and early twentieth century intellectual trends that each contributed to emergentism in the 1920s and 1930s: German social organicism, Bergson and Whitehead's process metaphysics, and the psychological holism of the Gestaltists, particularly the social version of Lewin's school. The school of sociocultural psychology emerged in the 1980s and 1990s to study socially and culturally situated action. Within socioculturalism, I include cultural psychologists, Vygotskian-influenced educational theorists, and those studying situated action and cognition (Bruner 1990; Cole 1996; Forman, Minick, and Stone 1993; Lave and Wenger 1991; Rogoff 1990, 1998; Stigler, Shweder, and Herdt 1990; Suchman 1987; Valsiner 1998b; Wertsch 1998). Socioculturalists have attempted to extend psychology by taking into account how meaningful activity is generated in social contexts. In doing so, they reject reduction of these phenomena to individual-level explanations by appealing to an *event* or *situated action* level of analysis.

Following American pragmatists like John Dewey and George Herbert Mead, socioculturalists consider intelligent behavior to emerge from the socially situated interactions of individuals rather than to be a product that resides in the head. Barbara Rogoff, for example, argued that knowledge itself is collective and nonreducible to individual cognitive representations: "[T]he assumption of abilities or skills as stable possessions of individuals . . . we argue should be dropped in the sociocultural approach." Instead, the focus is on "the process and individuals' participation in and contributions to the ongoing activity" (Rogoff, Radziszewska, and Masiello 1995, 144). Several theorists have used organicist language to describe situated social action: "By analogy, the organs in an organism work together with an inherent interdependence. . . . [Any component] would lose all meaning if it were actually separated from the whole" (Rogoff 1992, 317).

Socioculturalism has been heavily influenced by the American discovery and elaboration of Vygotsky's writings in the 1960s and 1970s. Since Vygotsky's works were composed primarily between 1924 and his death in 1934, it is not surprising that he was directly and indirectly influenced by the multiple strands of emergence theory that were prominent during that time, including British emergentism, German Gestaltism, Durkheimian sociology, and the process metaphysics of Bergson and

d. Like the Gestaltists, Vygotsky rejected the reductionist atom-
⏟ith behaviorism and introspectionism (Vygotsky 1971, 18; also
⏟e Cole and Scribner 1978, 5, and Wertsch 1985, 4). Although he was
heavily influenced by the Gestaltists, Vygotsky argued that they did not
explain the origins of complex mental phenomena. Vygotsky drew on several strands of nineteenth-century sociological holism in proposing that
irreducible psychological wholes originated in collective life; his belief in
the social origins of higher psychological processes was influenced by the
Durkheimian school of French sociology (see Cole and Scribner 1978, 6);
he closely read Lévy-Bruhl (Vygotsky 1971, 9), who made extensive use of
the research and theory of Durkheim's school, particularly the concept of
"collective representation" (e.g., Lévy-Bruhl [1910] 1925).[1] Vygotsky's
sociological holism led him to focus on social units of analysis that were
irreducible, functionally integrated wholes. Since "all higher mental
functions are internalized social relationships," Vygotsky expanded on
Gestaltist theory by examining both psychological and social wholes
and how they were related in development: "how individual response
emerges from the forms of collective life" (Vygotsky 1981, 164).

I refer to Vygotsky as a sociological holist because he did not attempt to
explain social phenomena in terms of how they emerged from individuals
and interactions. Like holism more generally, sociological holism holds
that macrosocial phenomena have primacy over individuals in explaining
behavior and cannot be redefined in terms of individual behavior. In sociological holism, minimal attention is given to the individual's influence
on society; the structures of society are primary and are responsible for
shaping the individual. Sociological holists are not emergentists because
they are not concerned with the micro-to-macro processes through which
individuals collectively create macrosocial structures (cf. Archer 1995);
rather, their concern is with the macro-to-micro influences of society on
individuals (also see Kontopoulos 1993).

Although they are influenced by Vygotsky's sociological holism, American socioculturalists are rarely sociological holists because they seek
to explain sociological phenomena as emergent from individual mental
states and behaviors. In developing an emergence theory, socioculturalists have drawn heavily on the emergentism of the American pragmatist
philosophers, and their focus on situated action continues the symbolic
interactionist tradition of focusing on joint actions as the basic units of
analysis. The sociocultural approach focuses on processes rather than
products and consequently is implicitly concerned with the durational

---

[1] Lawrence and Valsiner (1993) also noted the influences of Janet (who was in the same
university class with Durkheim at the *École Normale Supérieure*) and Baldwin.

mechanisms of the emergence of social-level phenomena from individual actions and interactions. (Note the parallels with the process metaphysics of Bergson and Whitehead.)

In turning to sociological emergentism, socioculturalism finds itself in the midst of long-standing issues in sociological theory; in Chapter 3, we saw the historical roots of sociological emergentism in both Durkheim and Parsons, and these issues remain central to the debate in contemporary sociology between individualism and collectivism (the following positions are elaborated further in Chapters 5 through 7). *Ontological individualists* are analogous to materialists in physical science; they hold that only individuals exist. An ontological individualist holds that the group is not a real entity but that "group" is merely a term used to refer to a collection of individuals. Social structure does not really exist; the term "social structure" is merely convenient shorthand for summarizing individual behavior in the aggregate.

Sociological realists, in contrast, hold that the group is just as real as the individual and that both the group and the individual are abstract, analytic units rather than concrete entities. Thus they reject both ontological and methodological individualism. Realists also note that sociological properties seem to have some causal influence over individuals; yet an ontologically individualist position entails that these higher-level properties are epiphenomenal. Contemporary realists include Keat and Urry (1975), Bhaskar (1979), and Archer (1995); several realists have explicitly invoked emergence arguments (Archer 1995; Bhaskar 1979).

Antirealist sociological theories include Giddens's structuration theory (1984), the methodological individualism of rational choice theory (Coleman 1990), and the interactional reductionism of Collins (1981). These critics claim that sociological realists propose a dualist ontology, one that "hypostatizes" or "reifies" sociological concepts. Antirealists reject holism and argue that because groups are not real, explanations in terms of groups will be incorrect, misleading, or at best approximations of individual-level explanations.

Several social scientists hold to the intermediary position of accepting ontological individualism and nonetheless rejecting methodological individualism. Ontological individualism is the position that only individuals exist; but even if only individuals exist, there may be grounds for rejecting a methodology that explains all social phenomena in terms of individuals (Brodbeck [1958] 1968; L. J. Goldstein [1958] 1973). Even many theorists who are individualists in principle accept that, owing to the extreme complexity of many social systems, it may be impossible in practice to fully identify how macrophenomena emerge from the millions of individuals engaged in trillions of daily interactions.

By taking an implicitly emergentist stance, socioculturalism is at the center of this active, and unresolved, theoretical debate. Historical debates concerning social emergence are directly relevant to foundational issues in contemporary social science. Familiarity with this debate could be beneficial for the development of sociocultural theory by providing additional clarity to the ontological and methodological foundations of socioculturalism.

Contemporary cognitive science

In Chapter 3, I noted the emergentist influences on the cognitive revolution. Several contemporary schools of cognitive science have drawn even more explicitly on emergentist foundations. These include situated robotics, connectionism, and distributed cognition.

The socioculturalist focus on situated cognition is paralleled by a contemporary paradigm in cognitive science, *situated robotics*, which expanded in popularity roughly contemporaneously with socioculturalism, in the late 1980s and early 1990s. Situated robotics researchers argue that intelligent behavior emerges from the interaction of an agent with a rich, complex environment (Agre and Rosenschein 1995; A. Clark 1997; Suchman 1987). By focusing on agent-environment interaction, situated robotics was a shift from "classic AI," which attempted to model the intelligence of the agent by developing internal mental representations of higher-level cognitive processes, including semantic networks, short-term memory, attention processes, and language perception and comprehension.

Situated robotics emphasized that intelligent agents are situated in an environment. Agents typically have incomplete knowledge of the environment; thus, they must be able to respond to unexpected events and interactions, modifying their plans opportunistically. Situated robotics resulted in a shift in designers' approaches to planning and representation because rather than maintaining explicit representations of the world and preparing detailed plans of action, situated agents are viewed as exhibiting behavior that emerges from agent-environment interaction and is not simply the result of internal representations. Opportunistic planning requires on-the-fly improvisation because no prepared plan could anticipate all possible environmental contingencies. These ideas have occasionally influenced socioculturalism, for example, through the work of Suchman (1987) and Hayes-Roth (1992); also note the distant parallels with Dewey's concept of experience.

In its rejection of the representational approach of classic AI, situated robotics was preceded and enabled by another emergentist paradigm in computational modeling, *connectionism*. Connectionist systems do not explicitly represent or model higher-level mental processes. Instead, in connectionist simulations, intelligent behavior emerges from the interactions of many rather simple units. Connectionist concepts can be traced back to the neural nets of the 1940s (McCulloch and Pitts 1943), yet the birth of contemporary connectionism is typically dated to the 1986 publication of *Parallel Distributed Processing* (Rumelhart and McClelland 1986). Connectionists are loosely inspired by the neuronal structure of the brain; they note that individual neurons are not themselves intelligent, yet intelligent behavior emerges from the interactions of many neurons. Connectionists argue that the human brain is a complex system and as such displays emergent behavior that cannot be predicted from a full and complete description of the component units of the system (Bechtel and Richardson 1993). Rumelhart and McClelland (1986) proclaimed that "we certainly believe in emergent phenomena in the sense of phenomena which could never be understood or predicted by a study of the lower level elements in isolation" (p. 128).[2] Because this complexity prevents prediction in advance (as the British emergentists first argued; see Chapter 3), simulations must be run to determine how the system will behave at the macrolevel. Connectionists attempt to directly simulate the microprocesses whereby intelligent macrobehavior emerges from the complex interactions of many neurons. In addition to connectionism, work on distributed cognition has influenced sociocultural theory (e.g., Hutchins 1995).

Connectionist and situated robotics concepts of emergence developed in parallel with *developmental systems theory*, a synthesis of developmental biology and developmental psychology (Griffiths and Gray 1994; Oyama 1985). Developmental systems theory argues that genes do not have primacy in explanations of ontogenetic development; rather, gene-environment interaction should be the focus, and researchers should focus on the process of construction of phenotypes rather than the transmission of genotypes. Developmental systems theory holds that "development is a process of emergence" and that the goal of developmental study is to identify "the conditions under which emergent form arises and the ways in which emergence can be constrained" (Elman et al. 1996, 359). Several themes deriving from developmental systems theory – including self-organization, complexity, and emergence – have begun to filter into developmental psychology, and the result is sometimes

---

[2] Ultimately, however, theirs is a weak form of emergence because they believe that a global system property can be explained and reduced if one takes into account all of the interactions between the components (also see Stephan 1998, 654).

referred to as the *dynamic systems approach* (e.g., Lewis 2000; Thelen and Smith 1994).

Connectionism studies what A. Clark (1997) called *direct emergence*: The macroproperties of a system emerge from interactions among its components. Sociological emergence is a form of direct emergence because the macroproperties of a group emerge from the group's component individuals and their interactions. Situated robotics studies *indirect emergence*, where the action of the system emerges from interaction with an external environment. A robotic agent executing a plan within a complex environment represents indirect emergence. Indirect emergence is analogous to the socioculturalist's focus on situated cognition and echoes Dewey's conception of *experience* as an individual-environment system. Direct emergence is also used implicitly by socioculturalists to ground their claim that properties of the group are emergent from, and irreducible to, participants' actions and interactions.

The preceding overview reveals broad theoretical parallels. Contemporary descriptions of complex dynamical systems have earlier echoes in the texts of the nineteenth-century organicists, the Gestaltists, and the British emergentists. To argue for the nonreducibility of human cognition and consciousness, many contemporary scholars defend cognitivism by drawing explicitly on emergence.

Unresolved issues

In Chapter 3, I demonstrated that the concept of emergence has had a long-standing influence on psychological thought, and in the earlier sections of the present chapter, I showed that its influence continues to the present day, in connectionism, the philosophy of mind, and sociocultural psychology. Both connectionism and socioculturalism are grounded on emergence principles. Both emphasize (1) the simultaneous consideration of two levels of analysis, a higher-level emergent one and a lower-level componential one; (2) the examination of how the higher-level entities emerge from the complex interactions among the component parts; and (3) the examination of how the higher-level emergent entities influence the future behaviors of the components. In socioculturalism, the components are individuals, and group properties are the higher-level emergent properties; in connectionism, the components are neurons, and mental properties are the higher-level emergent properties. Both connectionism and socioculturalism argue that analytic reduction to the science of the lower level may not be sufficient for a full and complete explanation of the higher-level phenomena and that the higher-level phenomena may not be predictable from a full and complete knowledge of the components and their interactions.

Throughout the long history of emergence theory, these antireductionist views have been hotly debated. In the following sections, I discuss five unresolved issues in an attempt to indicate a path to a more robust emergence theory.

The ontological issue: Does the higher level really exist?

A materialist must accept that the universe consists of nothing but physical matter and interactions among elementary particles. A metaphysics that holds that something exists other than matter is known as *vitalism* or *dualism*. Vitalism is a nineteenth-century position that rejected materialism, holding that life involved a nonmaterial "vital force" that existed independently of physical matter. British emergentists like Morgan explicitly rejected vitalism. Nonetheless, reductionist atomists often confused the British emergentists with vitalists. After all, the reductionists reasoned, living beings contained nothing but physical matter; therefore, all science should be reducible to physics.

In a similar way, individualists argue that the methodology of sociocultural psychology is based on an invalid ontology because, after all, a social group contains nothing but individuals. Most socioculturalists implicitly accept that the social is just as real as the individual and thus seem to hold to a dualist ontology. In a parallel fashion, contemporary sociological realists are criticized for proposing a dualist ontology, a world in which individuals and social entities compose autonomous realms of reality. (I return to these issues in Chapter 7.)

Socioculturalists can respond to such criticisms by being more explicit about their ontological commitments, for example, being careful to distinguish ontological claims (the social is real) from methodological claims (the social cannot be meaningfully explained in terms of individuals). To hold to the ontological claim – sociological realism – the socioculturalist must present a more sophisticated ontology. And if a socioculturalist accepts ontological individualism yet intends to argue for methodological collectivism, he or she must develop an argument showing that reductionism is impossible, even though groups consist of nothing more than individuals. Emergentism can potentially provide such an argument.

One possibility for socioculturalists is to turn to sociological theory, where these same issues have been central to theoretical discussion for an entire century (see Chapter 5). The 1980s and 1990s have seen a great deal of theoretical work in sociology on what is known as the *micro-macro link*, the relation between individual situated action and macro-social structure (J. C. Alexander and Giesen 1987). Sociological realists from Durkheim onward have been accused of proposing a dualist ontology, a world in which individuals and groups compose distinct realms of reality, each autonomous and each exerting causal influence on the other. Their responses, particularly those of contemporary realists and emergentists, can be instructive for socioculturalists. For example, the debate between Giddens's structuration theory (1984) and the analytic dualism of Archer's (1995) emergentism is directly relevant to the ontological and methodological stance being developed by sociocultural theorists. As Archer noted, both structuration and emergentism reject the exclusive focus on either individual or society typical of traditional sociological theories and attempt to develop theories that can incorporate both in close and constant interaction. Structuration theory holds that it is not possible to analytically separate individual action and macro-social structure; the two cannot be meaningfully distinguished because both individual and society are constituted through the same situated practice. Some socioculturalists hold to quite similar positions, rejecting a stratified conception of reality and holding that individual and group "mutually constitute" each other (Matusov 1998). In this context, it is interesting to note that structuration theorists have explicitly rejected emergence as a theory of the individual-collective relation (e.g., Giddens 1984, 169–74). In contrast, Archer (1995) proposed an emergentist theory that retains an *analytic dualism* (in which individual action and social structure are both recognized) and is heavily critical of structuration theory. In Chapter 7, I draw on both sociocultural theory and sociological theory to clarify and elaborate these theoretical issues.

Nonreductionist scientists can also draw on the contemporary philosophy of mind. In rejecting the extreme reductionism of physicalism and logical positivism, philosophers of science accept that one can hold to materialism – nothing exists except for physical matter – and nonetheless reject two implications of physicalism: theoretical reductionism (higher-level theories can be translated into lower-level theories) and methodological reductionism (the best way for science to proceed is to focus on analysis of the lower levels; see Ayala 1974). Psychologists who hope to reject reductionism must make explicit their arguments on this point. Philosophers of mind have made significant progress in this area; in fact, the current dominant view is not the reductionist identity theory but is rather nonreductive materialism.

Connectionist work, although drawing on emergence concepts, is at present a fundamentally reductionist theory because it models only the lower-level units and their interactions; the higher-level patterns that emerge are fully explained by the lower-level representation of the system, and they do not have any causal power. Any apparent causation of the emergent pattern can be fully explained in terms of local interactions between pairs of units. The preceding discussion suggests that connectionist theory could fruitfully proceed by relaxing its firmly reductionist assumptions (as argued by Elman et al. 1996, e.g., 359). Connectionists could, for example, explicitly represent emergent macropatterns as computational objects. This would involve a partial return to the earlier paradigm of symbolic AI, which was a form of nonreductionist cognitive science that argued that psychology could be a science of the mental not necessarily reducible to neurons and their interactions. At present, connectionists are quite averse to any form of symbolic AI, which they pejoratively refer to as "GOFAI" (an acronym for "good old-fashioned AI"); it may take some time before connectionism is ready to move toward an emergentist synthesis with symbolic AI. I predict that such a synthesis will eventually occur and will retain the emergentist insights of connectionism while extending them to incorporate elements of nonreductionism.

The holism issue: Is the higher level independent of the lower level?

Holism is the position that the science of the lower level is largely irrelevant to the higher-level science, that the higher level has explanatory primacy, and that the behavior of the components can only be explained in terms of their relations within the entire system. For example, sociological holism holds that social phenomena can be analyzed and studied without consideration of the science of individuals and that many aspects of individual behavior are best explained by reference to macro-social phenomena. Hayek attacked sociological holism and argued that it could not be connected to individual action except in a deterministic, top-down fashion (see Chapter 3). In fact, as I noted in the previous section, holism has largely been rejected in contemporary sociological theory in favor of accounts that incorporate both a theory of the individual and a theory of the dialectic relations between individuals and social phenomena (cf. Kontopoulos 1993).

Sociocultural psychology can draw on such theoretical work and its criticisms of methodological individualism. The methodological individualist criticizes sociocultural psychology, arguing that individuals have explanatory primacy and that social phenomena do not exist and thus cannot have any causal power over individuals. By drawing on arguments of sociological emergentists, sociocultural psychologists can better ground their methodological stance. To develop a robust response to methodological individualism, these sociological theories have had to develop sophisticated positions vis-à-vis individualism (cf. J. C. Alexander and Giesen 1987; Archer 1995; see Chapter 5). Contemporary rejections of reductionism in sociology – including Archer's emergentist theory and micro-macro theory in general – have not been holist because they have accepted the necessity of a theory of the individual and the necessity of a theory of the relations between individuals and higher-level social phenomena.

Emergentism is a form of nonreductionism that is not holist; in emergentism, higher-level properties are supervenient on lower-level components and could potentially be systematically analyzed in terms of their connections to the lower levels. However, due to complexity, some global system properties are resistant to reductionist analysis even though they are supervenient on their parts. Because emergentism accepts supervenience, the science of the higher level has to be compatible with that of the lower level; thus to some extent emergentist theory is compatible with a limited form of reductionism – reductionist explanation can contribute a piece of the overall solution, even if not the complete scientific explanation.

Within an emergentist framework, the question with regard to any complex systemic phenomenon is the relative degree to which lower-level and higher-level explanation should be combined to develop a complete scientific explanation of the phenomenon. Certain aspects of system behavior can be explained by undertaking traditional reductionist analysis; some properties of the component elements will play a role in the types of macrophenomena that emerge. For example, contemporary economists accept a form of emergence and yet pursue a methodology that explains emergent social phenomena by reduction to individuals; using this individualist methodology, they have developed reductionist explanations of some collective phenomena, such as the price of a good. Of course, there are well-known and significant concerns about the scope of social and human phenomena that such a methodology can explain (see Chapter 10). In response, nonreductionist emergentists hold that not all emergent phenomena will be explainable or predictable in terms of the lower levels, although they generally accept that there is some role for the study of micro-to-macro processes of emergence.

Thus, nonreductive psychology needs to elaborate, in more explicit detail, how its theories connect to sciences of the lower levels and yet are not reducible to them. Connectionism has avoided the holism issue because it is a variant of emergentism that is quite close to reductionism: all explanations are framed in terms of the lower level of analysis, the units and their interactions. Yet as a price for this, the status of higher-level emergents, and of mental causation, remains problematic. Socioculturalism does not yet have a unified theory that systematically relates social phenomena to individual mental states, largely because the relation between the micro- and macrolevels remains hotly debated. Socioculturalists are divided on how to resolve this theoretical point, with each researcher proposing a different micro-macro theory; I contrast the positions of several prominent socioculturalists in Chapter 7. Sociocultural theory could benefit by drawing on the recent decades of theoretical work on sociological emergence and on the micro-macro link.

The issue of higher-level causation

Scientists of the higher levels typically wish to attribute causal force to the phenomena that they study. Psychologists propose causal laws relating mental states, and they assume that mental events have downward causal power over neurons. We explain the fact that an individual moved his hand away from the fire by saying that his feeling of pain caused his hand to move. Likewise, sociologists propose causal laws relating social states, and they assume that social structures have causal power over individual behavior. Socioculturalists, by maintaining that the social and the individual mutually constitute each other, imply that the social can causally influence the individual. Such scientists can appeal to emergence theory as a way of accounting for this higher-level causation that is nonetheless compatible with materialism or individualism.

Some emergentists take a position on downward causation that is compatible with reductionism: they deny that it exists and focus only on "upward" emergence. This is the conventional position in economics, which accepts the existence of emergent social properties yet claims to have fully explained them using methodological individualism. On this view, social properties do not have an autonomous existence and cannot have causal power over individuals. Likewise, connectionists focus on bottom-up emergence but without providing any account of the apparent downward causation of the mind over the brain.

An opposing extreme is for the emergentist to hold that the emergent higher level is real (Archer 1995; Bhaskar 1979). If what emerges is ontologically autonomous, then its causation is not problematic, but this leads to the problems associated with realism – how to explain the emergence of something from a lower level that is ontologically autonomous from its emergence base? To maintain the realist stance requires a rather sophisticated philosophical argument, and realism remains hotly debated in both sociological theory and the philosophy of mind.

An emergentist path between these two extremes could attempt to account for downward causation within a monistic ontology. This is the path that mental realists have taken in the philosophy of mind; they hold that mental properties are real and not reducible to physical properties, even though they are ontological materialists. The unresolved issue then becomes this: If the higher level is not ontologically autonomous, how can it have causal power? The status of mental causation is controversial in contemporary philosophy of mind (e.g., Andersen et al. 2000; Heil and Mele 1993), and the status of social causation is foundational for sociology: It was the downfall of Durkheimian sociological realism and led to Parsons's critique ([1937] 1949) as well as later American critiques. If emergentists reject a dualist ontology and at the same time argue that higher-level phenomena have causal force, the argument must root that causal force in their emergence from lower-level components.

Thus, an emergence theory that is both nonrealist and nonreductionist requires simultaneous consideration of two directions of causation: emergence of the higher-level phenomena from the lower level and downward causation from the higher level to the lower level. The caveat for psychology is that neuroscience must be considered; the caveat for both sociology and sociocultural psychology is that individual psychology must be considered. These are the central issues of Chapter 5.

The methodological issue: How to study multiple levels of analysis?

Drawing on emergence arguments, both connectionism and socioculturalism emphasize that it is not possible to analytically reduce the higher level to the lower level; however, both draw different methodological conclusions. Their different methodologies reflect their different stances on the above issues.

Connectionists assume that higher-level mental phenomena are not real, and they deny that the higher level is independent of the lower level. They also deny the possibility of mental causation; the higher-level emergent patterns are epiphenomenal. However, unlike reductionist atomists, connectionists generally believe that prediction of the system's behavior from a complete knowledge of its lower-level components is impossible. Connectionists thus reject the conventional approach of analytic reduction – the belief that one has fully described a system once one fully understands the components and their interactions. Instead, due to the extreme complexity of cognitive systems, connectionists emphasize the need for simulation. This is sometimes called a *compositive* method, in contrast to the analytic method of reductionism. In fact, the compositive method used by connectionists has been applied to sociological emergence in social simulations using multi-agent systems techniques; designers of these simulations explicitly claim that they have modeled sociological emergence (see Chapter 8). Few socioculturalists would be satisfied with this compositive approach to sociological emergence, because it denies that the social level is real and that the social level has any causal power.

Like connectionists, socioculturalists note the difficulty of analytic reduction of complex social phenomena. But compared to connectionists, socioculturalists maintain a wider range of positions on the above issues. The majority of socioculturalists reject holism in their focus on the interrelations among the social and individual levels of analysis. Many socioculturalists believe that the social level is just as real as the individual level, and most socioculturalists accept the possibility of social causation. Although socioculturalists often fail to make their ontological stance explicit, their method – in assuming that group-level properties can be studied, can influence individuals, and yet cannot be reduced to individuals – implies an acceptance of sociological realism.

The definitional task: Which systems manifest emergence?

The history of science suggests that no scientist can assume a priori that a given higher-level phenomenon is emergent and thus nonreducible. For example, the favorite example of the British emergentists – that chemical combinations had emergent properties that could not be reduced to the laws of physics – had to be abandoned with the advance of quantum mechanics. Reductionism has a long history of success in the physical sciences; this success has contributed to the widespread acceptance of methodologically individualistic methods in the social sciences, including economics, most of psychology, and even prominent trends in sociological theory, including rational choice theory and exchange theory. Nonreductionist scientists of the higher level require a foundational theoretical argument for why their systems must be treated as emergent and an empirical account that demonstrates the methodological value of the emergence approach. This is the *definitional task*: to identify characteristics that distinguish those systems that require emergentist explanation from those systems that will submit to reductionist atomist analysis and explanation. These characteristics are likely to be subtle; sociological realists and methodological individualists in economics have noted the same general phenomena, yet have drawn opposing conclusions about the potential for reducibility.

Because emergentism is a form of materialism and holds that higher-level phenomena are supervenient on lower-level component systems, reductionist methods always have the potential to offer a part of the complete scientific solution. To deny that the science of the lower level can contribute to the understanding of the higher level is holism; yet, we have seen that most emergentists, including socioculturalists and connectionists, reject holism. Once holism is rejected, the emergentist must define the scope of the science of the higher level and identify which higher-level phenomena cannot be usefully reduced to lower-level explanation. In the philosophy of mind, theories that attempt this include multiple realizability (Fodor 1974) and complexity (Bechtel and Richardson 1993). Philosophers who hold these views argue that the issue of whether a reductionist or holist approach is appropriate for any given higher-level property or phenomenon is an empirical issue that can only be resolved via scientific inquiry. In sociological theory, no equivalent consensus has emerged; I work through these issues in Chapter 5.

Both connectionists and socioculturalists have failed to confront the definitional task; thus, the bounds of these paradigms are not yet clear. Connectionists, for example, have never argued convincingly that the phenomena they simulate will not submit to higher-level description (in the languages of symbolic AI). Such a theoretical argument is not considered to be necessary, since their focus is on the pragmatic concerns of engineering: What is the most efficient way to simulate the desired behavior? If a connectionist simulation is more efficient than a direct representation of the higher-level emergents, the behavior is said to be "emergent," even if a higher-level explanation exists. This is a pragmatic definition of emergence: Emergent behavior is higher-level systemic behavior that cannot be predicted from knowledge of properties of the lower-level components, except via simulation. Yet under this definition, the meaning of "emergent" will continue changing as better analytic methods are developed to derive global properties from local ones.

Although connectionist systems are commonly said to manifest emergence, only a few researchers have attempted to define the properties of emergent systems or to define different classes of emergence (Baas 1994; Bedau 2002; Cariani 1991; Crutchfield 1994; Darley 1994; Sawyer 1999). Although such definitional concerns have not been primary for connectionists, a few theorists have proposed contributing variables such as the number of units in the simulation and the complexity of the communication among the units (see Chapter 5).

Socioculturalists likewise have not presented an argument for the emergence and consequent irreducibility of social systems, nor have they distinguished social systems that will submit to methodological individualism from those that might require an emergentist approach, along the lines of micro-macro sociological theory. Instead, socioculturalists often assume that *all* social action is irreducible. Emergentist theories in sociology and philosophy suggest that this assumption cannot be made a priori but requires a foundational and empirical argument. Promising theoretical paths are suggested by contemporary sociological theory, which typically proposes a hybrid between extreme micro and extreme macro approaches (Chapter 5). For example, the relative influences of individual and structural factors have been explored by *network exchange theorists*, sociologists who attempt to reconcile the methodological individualism of *exchange theory* (which holds that macro-social phenomena are best explained in terms of individual's responses in pairwise exchange relations) and the holism of *network theory* (which holds that individuals' actions derive from their position in a complex social network; Cook and Whitmeyer 1992). Several such studies have reached a high level of theoretical sophistication, for example, showing both that network structure has causal effects on individuals and also that when different individuals occupy the same network positions, those downward causal effects can qualitatively change. An effect that seems to inhere in structure alone is actually part of a complex dialectic of emergence and downward causation.

In part, socioculturalists have not addressed the definitional task because they are split between an objectivist branch and a subjectivist, interpretivist branch. For those psychologists and philosophers who hold to Dilthey-derived subjectivist dualisms – for example, Charles Taylor and Kenneth Gergen – the definitional task is a nonissue: Subjectivity, meaning, and consciousness are fundamentally unique natural phenomena that are irreducible to material phenomena (see Chapter 10). Subjectivism has also been an influential sociological response to micro-macro issues, playing a prominent role in the hybrid theories of both Giddens and Bourdieu. For subjectivists, there will always be two sciences, a natural science and a human science; such claims are metaphysical variants of dualism.

Objectivist socioculturalists share with the subjectivists the claim that whereas reductionism works fine for many types of natural phenomena, psychological or sociocultural phenomena are somehow different. But those socioculturalists who are materialist and objectivist – thus holding that sociocultural analysis is a part of the natural sciences – have to explain why reductionism is not an appropriate methodology for the phenomenon in question. Socioculturalists often do not explicitly state where they stand on these issues, and these theoretical tensions remain unresolved.

Conclusion

In this chapter, I have focused on two contemporary psychological paradigms that have embraced emergentist thinking. However, these paradigms are somewhat marginalized in psychology proper; for the most part, the mainstream of contemporary psychology holds to a view of science that is atomist and reductionist. In fact, many psychologists believe that psychology will ultimately be unified with biology, and some of the most rapid growth in psychology today has been in the most extremely reductionist paradigms: cognitive neuroscience, behavioral genetics, and evolutionary psychology.

Because most of psychology is implicitly reductionist, emergence has remained largely unexplored by mainstream psychologists. The task of theorizing emergence – engaging with and working toward the resolution of the issues discussed in this chapter – remains uncompleted within psychology. Those who wish to establish a nonreductionist science of psychology must make explicit the relations between their science, the science of the lower level (biology), and the science of the higher level (sociology). For example, socioculturalists must make explicit the relations between their (collective) objects of study and individual psychology. The sociological theories of emergence discussed in Chapter 5 can provide the necessary theoretical foundations.

Emergentism is compatible with materialism and yet holds that reductionist methodology does not necessarily work for psychological (or social) phenomena. We don't yet know whether reductionism will ultimately be successful at explaining all complex natural systems, including the human mind and complex societies. Yet emergentism provides a materialist, scientifically plausible account of why reductionist explanation may not be possible for certain classes of complex systems. The lesson for psychology, for its lower-level science (neurobiology), and for its higher-level science (sociology) is that empirical studies of the relations between levels of analysis should be an active area of research. Such studies are central to both Rogoff's "three planes of analysis" framework (1995) and Wertsch's "irreconcilable tension" between mediational means and situated action (1998). Given the current state of empirical knowledge, neither sociology, psychology, or neurobiology can safely assume a priori that its level of analysis will explain the others or that it will not ultimately be explained by the others. A scientific attitude of skepticism requires one to admit that reductionism may or may not be applicable to the mental or the sociocultural levels of analysis, pending further empirical study.

5   Emergence in sociology

From its nineteenth-century origins, sociology has been faced with a foundational question: In what sense do social phenomena exist? Sociologists study social groups, collective behavior, institutions, social structures, social networks, and social dynamics, and after all, such social phenomena are only composed of the people that are in them. Thus, social phenomena seem to have no ontological status; and if not, sociology can ultimately be reduced to facts about individuals.

For this reason, the relationship between the individual and the collective is one of the most fundamental issues in sociological theory. This relationship was a central element in the theorizing of the nineteenth-century founders of sociology, including Weber, Durkheim, Simmel, and Marx, and was a central element, if implicit, in many twentieth-century sociological paradigms, including structural functionalism (Parsons [1937] 1949, 1951), exchange theory (Blau 1964; Homans 1958, 1961), and rational choice theory (Coleman 1990). In recent years, this relationship has become known as the "micro-macro link" (J. C. Alexander et al. 1987; Huber 1991; Knorr-Cetina and Cicourel 1981; Ritzer 2000).

Many accounts of the micro-macro link have explicitly used emergence to argue that collective phenomena are collaboratively created by individuals, yet are not reducible to individual action (Archer 1995; Bhaskar 1979, 1982; Blau 1981; Edel 1959; Kontopoulos 1993; Mihata 1997; Parsons [1937] 1949; Porpora 1993; T. S. Smith 1997; Sztompka 1991; Whitmeyer 1994; Wisdom 1970). Most of these accounts argue that although only individuals exist, collectives possess emergent properties that are irreducibly complex and thus cannot be reduced to individual properties. Some of these accounts reject sociological realism and instead take the weaker position of methodological collectivism (cf. Brodbeck [1958] 1968). Others defend the stronger claim that emergence can be used to ground sociological realism (Archer 1995; Bhaskar 1979).

However, emergence has also been invoked by methodological individualists in sociology and economics. Methodological individualists accept the existence of emergent social properties yet claim that such properties can be reduced to explanations in terms of individuals and their relationships. Methodological individualism's focus on micro-to-macro processes is explicitly considered to be a study of how social properties emerge from individual action (Axelrod 1997, e.g., 4; Coleman 1987, 171; 1990; Epstein and Axtell 1996, e.g., 6–20; Homans 1964a). For example, Homans argued that "emergence, and the nature of the properties that emerge, are to be explained by psychological propositions," and he claimed that he had demonstrated this reducibility in his 1961 book *Social Behavior* (1964a, 229). Many of these sociologists draw inspiration from economics, where emergence is conceived of as the process whereby unintended macro-social phenomena arise from the actions of many participating individuals (Hayek 1942, 1943, 1944; Menger [1883] 1963). In contrast to sociologists who believe that emergence is incompatible with reductionist individualism – I will call them *collectivist emergentists* – individualist emergentists believe that macro-social properties and laws can be explained in terms of properties and laws about individuals and their relations.[1]

Thus, contemporary sociological uses of emergence are contradictory and unstable; two opposed sociological paradigms both invoke the concept of emergence yet draw opposed conclusions. As I first suggested in Chapters 2 and 3, this problem arises in part because neither social scientists nor complexity theorists have developed an adequate account of emergence. Contemporary sociologists are not the first to be confused about emergentism; throughout the long history of philosophical usage of the term (Chapter 3), one finds comments on the confusion surrounding it (Broad 1925, 59; Edel 1959, 192; Kim 1992, 122). In this chapter, I clarify the different sociological theories of emergence by drawing on recent arguments in the philosophy of science. In Chapter 3, we saw that philosophical interest in emergence has gone through several cycles since the term was first coined in 1875 by the philosopher G. H. Lewes; in this chapter, I focus on emergentist theories from the 1970s through the 1990s that have been inspired by developments in

---

[1] Some sociologists define the micro and macro levels in terms of the size of social units (e.g., Münch and Smelser 1987, 356–7; Ritzer 2000, 499–505). However, both individualist and collectivist emergentists agree that the micro-macro debate must be couched in terms of relations between properties at multiple levels of analysis, not in terms of group size. Any given social system may have some properties that are merely aggregative and others that are emergent (Archer 1995, 8–9; Stephan 1997; Wimsatt 1986, 260).

cognitive science (Chapter 4). Although philosophical arguments about emergence and reducibility have focused on the mind-brain relation, they can be generalized to apply to any hierarchically ordered sets of properties, as noted by many philosophers (Fodor 1989; Humphreys 1997, 3; Jackson and Pettit 1992, 107; Kincaid 1997, 76; Yablo 1992, 247n5).

In this chapter, I demonstrate the relevance of these philosophical debates to sociological theory. I necessarily brush over many subtle differences in presenting what most philosophers of mind agree is the current consensus. I begin by summarizing this consensus; I then summarize the two competing uses of the term "emergence" in sociology, beginning with individualist emergentism and then turning to collectivist emergentism. In both cases, I use arguments from the philosophy of science to evaluate these competing theories of emergence, and I conclude that none of these theories has adequately addressed all of the implications of the philosophical account. I conclude by identifying several unresolved issues facing sociological theories of emergence, issues that are further addressed in Chapters 7 through 10.

Nonreductive individualism

To help clarify and compare these various stances toward emergence, I briefly summarize a philosophical account of emergence that is based in a nonreductive form of individualism.[2] This argument for *nonreductive individualism* is grounded in the tradition of more general arguments for *nonreductive materialism*.[3] The nonreductive materialist rejects the claim that all science can ultimately be reduced to physics, even though there is nothing in the universe other than physical matter. The canonical arguments for nonreductive materialism, formed in the 1970s and 1980s, did not use the language of emergence; instead, they used the concepts of supervenience, multiple realizability, and wild disjunction. However, as the concept of emergence reappeared in the 1990s, philosophers

---

[2] The following philosophical account is a condensed version of philosophical arguments that I have presented elsewhere (Sawyer 2002b, 2003e, 2004a, 2004b). There has been significant philosophical activity surrounding emergence, including journal special issues ("Emergence and Downward Causation," *Principia* 6, no. 1 (2002); "Emergence and Supervenience: Alternatives to Unity by Reduction," *Philosophy of Science*, 64, no. 4, suppl (1997); "Reduction and Emergence," *Philosophical Studies*, 95, nos. 1–2 (1999)). There is no clear consensus as of yet, and significant differences are apparent within this debate. Regardless of the exact nature of its relation to emergentism, most philosophers agree that the current consensus in the philosophy of mind is nonreductive materialism.

[3] In philosophy of biology as well, the dominant view is *emergent mechanism* (Bechtel and Richardson 1993) or *physicalist antireductionism* (Rosenberg 1997). Here I restrict my arguments to the philosophy of mind, but the issues are similar in both cases.

began to note that the issues debated were fundamentally the same (e.g., Cunningham 2001; Kim 1999; Pihlström 2002; Stephan 1997).

Supervenience

Most sociologists, both individualists and collectivists, try to avoid hypostatizing or reifying social groups; they accept that the only real entities are individuals. This position is known as *ontological individualism*: the ontological position that only individuals exist. In the philosophy of mind, the emergentist argument of nonreductive materialism starts with a parallel ontological assumption: all that exists is physical matter. Because there is only physical matter, there are only physical events; thus, mental events are the same events as neurophysiological events. This is known as the *token identity thesis*: any token mental event is identical to a physical event. Token event identity entails that emergent higher-level properties *supervene* on the system of lower-level components (Davidson 1970; Fodor 1974; Kim 1993b). Supervenience is a relation between two levels of analysis, and this relation is such that if two events are identical with respect to their descriptions at the lower level, then they cannot differ at the higher level. If a collection of lower-level components with a given set of relations causes higher-level property E to emerge at time t, then on every other occasion when that same collection of components in that same set of relations occurs, E will again emerge. The supervenience relation is asymmetric; an entity cannot change at a higher level without also changing at the lower levels, but an entity could change at the lower levels and retain the same description at the higher level.

Several philosophers of social science have suggested that the individual-collective relation is one of supervenience (Bhargava 1992, 62–8; Currie 1984, 357; Kincaid 1997; MacDonald and Pettit 1981, 119–20, 144–5; Mellor 1982, 16; Pettit 1993, 148–54). Although a few sociologists have argued that supervenience can provide an argument for social realism (Healy 1998; also see Le Boutillier's 2001 critical response), these philosophers have shown that supervenience is compatible with methodological individualism and that it does not entail the irreducibility of the social. Likewise, philosophers of mind generally agree that supervenience alone is not sufficient to establish the irreducibility of the mental (Bunge 1977; Heil 1998, 1999; Humphreys 1997; Margolis 1986; Wimsatt 1997, S373) because supervenience is compatible with the *type identity thesis*: the claim that all higher-level types or properties are identical to some type or property in the physical language. To develop an argument for irreducibility, philosophers of mind have extended supervenience by using the notions of multiple realizability and wild disjunction.

Multiple realizability and wild disjunction

Fodor's (1974) influential argument against reductionist physicalism is based on the concept of types as *natural kind terms* and on a certain notion of what counts as a scientific law. A law is a statement within which the basic terms are natural kind terms of that science. To reduce a law to the science of the lower level, a *bridge law* must be identified that translates the law. To accomplish this, each of the natural kind terms of the higher-level science must be translatable into natural kind terms of the lower-level science.

Fodor argued that a simple translation – in his case, from a psychological term to some combination of neurobiological terms – may not be possible. His argument is based on the notion of *multiple realizability*: the observation that although each mental state must be supervenient on some physical state, each token instance of that mental state might be implemented, grounded, or realized by a different physical state. For example, the psychological term "pain" could be realized by a wide range of different neurobiological terms and concepts, and each token instance of "pain" might be realized by a different supervenience base. Multiple realizability is thus an account of how one could accept token identity and yet reject type identity (also see Batterman 2000; Heil 1999; Sober 1999).

Multiple realizability alone does not necessarily imply irreducibility; if there are only a few realizing states, or if those states display some common features, the reduction may not be problematic. However, reduction would be difficult if the neurobiological equivalent of a psychological term was an otherwise unrelated combination of many neurobiological concepts and terms (see Figure 5.1). Fodor termed such a realization "wildly disjunctive." If a higher-level property is realized by a wildly disjunctive set of lower-level properties, then the physical equivalent of a

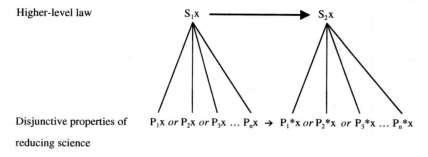

Higher-level law $\qquad$ $S_1x \longrightarrow S_2x$

Disjunctive properties of $\qquad$ P_1x *or* P_2x *or* P_3x ... P_nx → $P_1{}^*x$ *or* $P_2{}^*x$ *or* $P_3{}^*x$ ... $P_n{}^*x$

reducing science

Figure 5.1. Wild disjunction and the reduction of higher-level laws.

psychological law must contain wildly disjunctive terms. Fodor argued that a true scientific law cannot have wildly disjunctive components and that wild disjunction thus implied that there could be lawful relations among events, described in psychological language, that would not be lawful relations in the language of physics. Whether or not one holds to this definition of a law, it is clearly of limited scientific usefulness to have laws with wildly disjunctive terms because they provide only limited understanding of the phenomena; they are of limited explanatory value because they apply to collections of specific token instances, whereas the higher-level law is likely to be more generally applicable. Such reductions can nonetheless be useful for explaining exceptions to the higher-level laws; Fodor's argument explains why laws in sciences other than physics will always have exceptions.

When supervenience is supplemented with wildly disjunctive multiple realizability – the observation that a single higher-level property might be realized by many different lower-level supervenience bases and that these different supervenience bases may have no lawful relations with one another – we have an account of emergence that shows why certain social properties and social laws may be irreducible. There may be a social property that in each token instance is supervenient on a combination of individual properties, but each token instance of that property may be realized by a different combination of individual properties. Many social properties seem to work this way. A token instance of a collective entity that has the social property "being a church" also has a collection of individual properties associated with each of its component members; for example, each individual I_n may hold properties "believing in X_n" or "intending Y_n" where the sum total of such beliefs and intentions are (in some sense) constitutive of the social property "being a church." Yet the property of "being a church" can be realized by a wide range of individual beliefs and dispositions. The same is true of properties such as "being a family" and "being a collective movement." Microsocial properties are no less multiply realizable: examples include "being an argument," "being a conversation," and "being an act of discrimination." In fact, most social properties of interest to sociologists seem to have wildly disjunctive individual-level descriptions (just as most of the properties of interest to other sciences have wildly disjunctive lower-level realizations, including biology, psychology, and geology; see Fodor 1997).

Emergentism does not claim that all higher-level properties are irreducible; some of them are predictable and derivable from the system of lower-level components (see Bedau 2002). Only in cases where the relation between higher- and lower-level properties is wildly disjunctive beyond some threshold of complexity will the higher-level property not be lawfully reducible (see Sawyer 2004a). Whether or not this is indeed the relation between any given set of higher- and lower-level properties is an empirical question to be determined by empirical study (see Chapters 8, 9, and 10).

Downward causation

In sociology, arguments for irreducible emergence have always been linked with arguments for social causation. Durkheim's emergentist account of the autonomy of sociology was foundationally based on emergent (or "sui generis") social properties having causal force on the individual. His defining criterion of the social fact was its external constraint on individuals (Chapter 6). Durkheim's theory of social causation was famously criticized for seeming to hypostatize the social. For similar reasons, higher-level causation is problematic in the preceding account of emergence. Several philosophers of mind have argued that this account does not constitute an argument for mental causation; they argue that in nonreductive materialism the mental is epiphenomenal (e.g., Kim 1992, 1993a; Lowe 1993). In response, other philosophers of mind have attempted to extend nonreductive materialism to allow the mental to be more than epiphenomenal. Although nonreductive materialists accept supervenience, many of them also hold that higher-level properties can have causal powers over lower-level properties (Davidson 1993; Fodor 1989; Horgan 1989). For example, several philosophers have argued that some complex systems exhibit *downward causation* in which an emergent higher-level property or pattern causes effects in the lower level, either in the component entities or in their patterns of interaction (Andersen et al. 2000). Others reject this "downward causal" claim (see especially Kim 1993a). Kim noted that emergentism and nonreductive materialism entail a commitment to downward causation, and he argued that the attempt to account for downward causation was the primary motivation for emergentist accounts (1993a, 121). According to Kim's critique, such emergent causation can only derive from the causal powers of the supervenience base, and a higher-level property can only cause another higher-level property by causing its supervenience base (Kim 1992, 136; Sawyer 2003e). This is usually referred to as the argument for *causal fundamentalism* or *causal exclusion*: the claim that the lower level is causally complete (Papineau 1993, 16; Pettit 1993, 151; Yablo 1992, 246). With respect to the mental, physics is causally complete; with respect to the social, individualism is causally complete. The probability at time t that an event will occur at time $t + dt$ is fixed by the lower-level properties that the system has at time t; this probability is unaffected by taking into

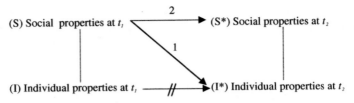

Figure 5.2. Social and individual causal relations.

account the system's higher-level properties at time t as well. Because Kim held to such arguments, he referred to downward causation as either "epiphenomenal causation" or "supervenient causation" (1984; also see Loar 1992; Sober 1999).

In response, arguments for mental causation have taken a specific philosophical form: that there can be a lawful causal relation between a mental property and a physical property even though there is no lawful causal relation between the realizing physical properties of that mental property and the caused physical property. In what follows, I apply the structure of this argument from the philosophy of mind to defend social causation.

Arguments for social causation require a rejection of the causal exclusion principle and the causal completeness of the lower level postulate. For example, Horgan argued that higher-order causal properties are not necessarily nomically coextensive with lower-level causal properties. In Horgan's (1994) view, a single event can be subject to a variety of different explanations involving properties from a variety of different counterfactual relation patterns.[4] Horgan called this "robust causal compatibilism": the view that properties at multiple levels may each be causal.[5]

Nonreductive individualism makes an analogous argument for autonomous social causation (Sawyer 2003e). Nonreductive individualism accepts that the causal consequences of social properties obtain in virtue of their realizing individual supervenience base. However, (owing to multiple realizability) it could be the case that a social property S, with supervenience base I at time t_1, could lawfully be identified as the cause of social property S^* and individual property I^* at time t_2, even though I cannot be lawfully identified as the cause of I^*, due to wild disjunction (see Figure 5.2). If the individual-level equivalent of a social property is wildly disjunctive, then explanations in terms of I and I^* are not

---

[4] This also seems to be Pettit's (1993) position.
[5] Also see Horgan's (1993) account of *preservative irrealism*: Preservative irrealism treats the higher-order discourse as legitimate and indispensable while repudiating its apparent ontological commitments (p. 581).

necessarily lawful, even when the relation between S and S^* is lawful. Supervenience entails that social causes have their effects via intervening mechanisms at the individual level (Sawyer 2004a). But in spite of the necessary existence of such mechanisms, multiple realizability and wild disjunction suggest that we may never be able to describe that base causal relation in a lawlike way. In complex systems in which wild disjunction obtains, methodologically individualist explanation may be in principle impossible.

A full and complete description of observed sociological regularities may require social causal laws that cannot be reduced to individual causal laws. A methodological individualist might counter: Why can't the causal law $S \rightarrow S^*$ simply be reduced to an individual causal law by substituting the equivalent individual supervenience bases, deriving the law $I \rightarrow I^*$? A large body of argument in the philosophy of mind has been directed at exactly this question. Epiphenomenalists like Kim would argue that if $S \rightarrow S^*$ is a lawful relation, then $I \rightarrow I^*$ must also be a lawful relation. My defense of social realism is analogous to the defense of mental realism: That $S \rightarrow S^*$ is lawful does not necessarily entail that $I \rightarrow I^*$ is a lawful relation. Disjunctive lower-level properties are not causal properties; on any occasion when a disjunctive lower-level property is instantiated, the causal work is done not by the whole disjunction but only by whatever specific disjunct is instantiated on the given occasion (e.g., Horgan 1997, 167).

In arguing that socially emergent properties have autonomous causal powers, I draw on philosophers of mind such as Davidson, Fodor, Horgan, Kim, and McLaughlin (see Sawyer 2003e) to argue that nonreductive individualism is compatible with the existence of irreducible causal laws of two forms (numbered arrows in Figure 5.2):

1. *Social constraint.* Social property S at time t_1 lawfully causes individual property I^* at time t_2 even though the supervenience base I at time t_1 does not lawfully cause I^*.
2. *Macrosocial laws.* Social property S at time t_1 lawfully causes social property S^* at time t_2 even though the supervenience base I at time t_1 does not lawfully cause the supervenience base I^* at time t_2 nor social property S^* at time t_2.

A social realist holds that the question whether a social property S is causally responsible is equivalent to the question whether there are causal laws about S that are not reducible. If there are, then even if the properties in the higher-level science are supervenient on the properties that the lower-level science talks about, the properties that the higher level talks about are not epiphenomenal. Social properties can be causally responsible if there are irreducible social causal laws. Whether there are social laws has been a long-standing topic of debate in the philosophy of social science (Blau, 1977; Kincaid 1990, 1997; Mandelbaum 1957; Mellor 1982; Pettit 1993; Porpora 1983).[6] Methodological individualism is committed to the claim that there are no social laws that are irreducible to laws concerning the behavior of individuals. Many methodological individualists accept that there can be *reducible* social laws, although they rarely address the causal complexities of the philosophical debate here described. For example, several theorists (Macdonald and Pettit 1981; Porpora 1983, 1987) have argued that social laws must depend on intervening individual-level laws, otherwise they could not be lawlike; this argument is analogous to Kim's critiques of mental realism. But these theorists have not addressed the implications of wild disjunction.

In the preceding, I have proposed an account of social emergence that is based on the philosophical account of nonreductive individualism. A social property may be said to be emergent when it is multiply realized in wildly disjunctive complex systems of individuals. Such emergent social properties participate irreducibly in causal relations. Consequently, social emergence is a form of sociological realism. In the terms used by philosophers of science, this is an argument for *strong emergence* (e.g., Bedau 2002; Pihlström 2002). Many philosophers instead choose to argue for various versions of weak emergentism that do not allow for downward causal powers. But these philosophers have not addressed the nonreductive argument for higher-level property realism outlined here. My argument against the causal exclusion principle supports the emergence of higher-level properties that cannot be reduced and that have downward causal powers even though social groups are composed of individuals. To argue that physics is causally complete, one must argue that the special sciences do not, in fact, carve nature at its joints; one must reject natural kinds, types, and higher-level properties; one must be a nominalist and reject universals. However, to date there has not been much overlap between philosophers of emergence and philosophers of universals (Pihlström 2002, 156–7).

In the following two sections, I discuss theories of emergence that are reductive and methodologically individualist and then theories that are nonreductive, collectivist, or realist. Throughout these discussions, I

---

[6] Beginning in the 1980s and 1990s, social mechanists have advocated a turn away from covering law explanations, arguing that sociology should concern itself with describing the basic causal mechanisms of social systems – mechanistic explanations rather than laws (see Hedström and Swedberg 1998) As Chapter 8 makes clear, I find much of value in social mechanism, yet I believe that mechanistic explanations are compatible with the existence of social laws (Sawyer 2004a).

evaluate these theories by reference to the preceding account of nonreductive individualism. Following these discussions, I discuss a few critical responses, I identify a set of unresolved issues, and I provide a list of empirical features of social systems that are likely to manifest irreducible emergent properties.

Individualist theories of emergence

Individualist emergentists claim that the existence of emergent system properties that are not possessed by the parts does not entail irreducibility of those properties. Most scientists call a system property emergent relative to properties of the system's parts if it depends on their mode of organization, and this is generally considered to be consistent with reduction (Cottrell 1978, 130; Phillips 1976, 13; Wimsatt 1997, S372). The physical sciences can provide many examples of successful explanation of higher-level emergent properties from the lower-level components' properties and their relations. The classic example that the 1920s British emergentists borrowed from Mill and Lewes, chemical combination, demonstrates this point. Lewes (1875), in coining the term "emergent," observed that water has properties that are not held by hydrogen nor oxygen: it is transparent, it is a liquid, it is colorless, it observes certain pressure and fluid laws. However, in the twentieth century, quantum mechanics provided the reduction. The transparency of water can now be explained in terms of – reduced to – the properties of hydrogen and oxygen and their relation of combination even though neither hydrogen nor oxygen have the property "transparency." A second example is the reduction of the laws of thermodynamics to statistical mechanics. Although the pressure of a volume of a gas is a property of that whole, and none of the component molecules can be said to possess the property of "pressure," the laws of statistical mechanics allow the reduction of the pressure of the whole to the aggregated individual motions of the component particles. Such developments in the physical sciences contributed to the rejection of emergentism that accompanied logical positivism and the unity of science movement (McLaughlin 1992); Hempel (1965, 258–64) and others argued that emergence is not a property of reality but is rather an artifact of our incomplete knowledge of the world.

In sociology, the observation that social groups have properties that cannot in principle be held by any single individual is likewise compatible with *methodological individualism*, the stance that sociological explanation should always be in terms of processes of individual-to-social emergence. Methodological individualists argue that the task of sociology is to explain social properties by reduction to properties of individuals and their interactions; this perspective is foundational in neoclassical micro-economics and in several influential sociological theories, including behavioral sociology (Homans 1958, 1961), exchange theory (Emerson 1972), and rational choice theory (Coleman 1990). Methodological individualists draw on concepts of emergence to account for the micro-to-macro link, yet they are reductionist nonetheless: They hold that social properties can be fully explained in terms of properties of individuals and their interactions.

Since the origin of sociology in the nineteenth century, the field has included reductionist individualists. Mill claimed that sociological phenomena could be understood by analysis of the component individuals and their interactions (e.g., Mill 1843, vol. 2, 469), and many early sociologists emphasized the study of individuals and interaction, including Simmel, Tarde, and Weber. In part influenced by Mill's writings, Carl Menger, founder of the Austrian school of economics, insisted – in opposition to German social organicism and other forms of sociological holism – that even unintended organic social forms, including law, language, money, and markets, could be analyzed by reducing them to the analysis of individuals pursuing individual interests using a reductionist atomist method that he called the "exact orientation" ([1883] 1963, 151–9). During and after World War II, several scholars elaborated Menger's theories to develop a position that became known as "methodological individualism," and in the 1950s, there was a wide-ranging debate among philosophers about its merits (Chapter 3).

During this same period, Homans shifted from an earlier holism to methodological individualism. In his first books, Homans held to a nonreductionist emergentist view (1941, 1950; see Blain 1971, 5; Buckley 1967, 35, 140; Wallace 1969, 52). For example, Homans (1950) referred to groups as "complex organic wholes" (p. 91), acknowledged that groups experience "emergent evolution" (p. 94), and wrote that the sociologist studies "the very act of emergence" (p. 272). Yet by 1958 he had discarded talk of complex wholes and had become an "ultimate psychological reductionist" (Homans 1958, 597). This approach led to the foundational emphasis of exchange theory: to derive all of the laws of sociology from "elementary" social behavior (i.e., the behavior of individuals in interaction). For example, a group's equilibrium must be explained by appeal to the behaviors of each individual in exchange with other members of the group, in contrast to Parsons's (1951) explanation of equilibrium as a functionally necessary feature of groups (p. 601).

Consistent with methodological individualism, Homans (1964a) argued that propositions about groups or societies should be explained by reduction to propositions about the behavior of people (p. 227) and that "new properties are always emerging.... [T]he question is how the emergence is to be explained. I say that the emergence, and the nature of the properties that emerge, are to be explained by psychological propositions" (p. 229). In his 1961 book *Social behavior*, Homans's goal was to show how emergent properties could be explained using psychological propositions (p. 229).

Homans believed that emergent properties were the same as the "composition effects" noted in the physical sciences and were not qualitatively different from aggregate or additive properties (1964b, 970). Yet, on several occasions he admitted that with very complex composition effects we may never have a complete reductionist explanation; many large groups cannot be explained in this way, and some institutions, like money and markets, cannot be explained because we do not have sufficient historical data (1964a, 227). Homans suggested that later developments in computers might help in this task, a prescient statement considering the recent growth of multi-agent system models (1964a, 225–6; see Chapter 8). Homans's claim that a social causal law is not an explanation is questionable; under such a conception, psychological laws are not explanations either, because their true explanation can only be found in terms of neurobiology (as Blau argued; 1970a, 337–8). Homans claimed that a social explanation must always be in terms of its implementing mechanism at the individual supervenience base. Yet as Fodor (1974) noted in connection with his wild disjunction argument, the claim that there are higher-level types that are irreducible to the lower level does not entail that there are no implementing mechanisms. In fact, token identity and supervenience require there to always be such an implementing mechanism. However, if wild disjunction holds, then the existence of an implementing mechanism does not mean that there will be a lawful reduction, and it does not mean that higher-level causal laws can be translated into lawful lower-level causal laws. A description of the implementing mechanism of a given token instance may be of some limited interest but will not constitute an explanation of the higher-level type or law.

Rational choice theory is also individualist emergentist; it holds that social institutions and social change must be explained in terms of their emergence from the action and interaction of individuals (Coleman 1990; Elster 1989). Like most individualist emergentists, Elster viewed social terms and laws as "shorthand" for what ultimately must be explained in terms of individuals (1989, 158). Elster (1985) famously read Marx as a methodological individualist because Marx focused on the unintended consequences of human action (p. 1) and attempted to provide "causal explanation of aggregate phenomena in terms of the individual actions that go into them" (p. 2). Coleman's (1990) influential focus on "the internal analysis of system behavior" (p. 2) is methodologically individualist because it examines component parts of the system, explains the behavior of the system in terms of the behavior of its parts, and shows how one can compose and synthesize systemic behavior from the actions of the parts. Coleman explicitly accepted emergence: "Interaction among individuals is seen to result in emergent phenomena at the system level, that is, phenomena that were neither intended nor predicted by the individuals" (p. 5). System behavior is "an emergent consequence of the interdependent actions of the actors who make up the system" (Coleman 1986, 1312); it is emergent because it results from social organization, not "merely aggregated individual behavior" (Coleman 1987, 157; also 1990, 22). Coleman accepted that there may be emergent social properties and that lawlike generalizations between them could be identified (1990, 28). But like all methodological individualists, Coleman maintained that these propositions are temporary shorthand for, and are less general than, the individual-level explanation (1990, 20).

As we saw in Chapter 2, emergence has been an important concept in complex dynamical systems theory. Complex social systems have been modeled using multi-agent system technologies (Chapter 8), and these "artificial society" models are grounded in individualist concepts of emergence (Conte et al. 2001). In an artificial society, macro-structural phenomena emerge, attain equilibrium, and remain stable over time. In Chapter 8, I describe several artificial societies that begin with no social structure and in which differentiated and hierarchically structured groups emerge during the simulation. One well-known example is Axelrod's (1995) simulation of the emergence of new political actors: supranational entities that can regulate resource use at the global level. In his model, each agent represents a national state, and in repeat runs of the model, clusters of commitment emerge surrounding strong states. Thus, higher-level actors emerge from the interactions among lower-level actors. This is a simpler version of Coleman's (1990) theory of how corporate actors emerge from the rational action of component members. Yet despite its simplicity, the simulation allowed an examination of the unexpected effects of micro-theoretical assumptions. For example, Axelrod's simulation reproduced historically observed patterns, such as *imperial overstretch*, when powerful empires are weakened by being dragged into fights involving weaker actors to whom they have developed commitments. Based on such simulations, Axelrod (1997) defined emergence in artificial society simulations in reductionist terms: "The large-scale effects of locally interacting agents are called 'emergent properties' of the system" (p. 4).

How do these variations of individualist emergentism compare with the philosophical account of emergence presented earlier? Individualist emergentists claim that the existence of emergent system properties that are not possessed by the parts does not entail irreducibility of those properties. This is consistent with the philosophical account of token identity and supervenience; those accounts show that emergence, conceived of as supervenience alone, is compatible with reductionism. However, the philosophical account leads to potential irreducibility for those emergent properties that are multiply realizable and wildly disjunctive; this possibility poses several problems for individualist emergentists.

First, they fail to address the implications of multiple realizability; there are two serious implications. First, a plausible account of an instance of the micro-to-macro emergence of a social property may be provided, but that account might not describe what actually led to the emergence of that property in that token instance; due to multiple realizability, the instance of the social property being modeled might have emerged from a different supervenience base. But suppose that all agree that the micro-to-macro emergence of a social property has been successfully modeled for one token instance of that social property. This still leaves us with the second, more foundational problem: that account may not be applicable to any other token instances of the same social property, owing to multiple realizability, and it may not provide any explanatory power beyond that token instance, owing to wild disjunction. The philosophical account shows that individualist emergentism can only work if a form of type identity between social and individual properties holds.

A second failing is that individualist emergentists do not address the causal implications of wild disjunction. If social properties are implemented in wildly disjunctive sets of individual properties, then social terms and laws may not be lawfully reducible to individual terms and laws. If a social property has a wildly disjunctive individual base, then the social property can participate in causal laws even though there is no equivalent lawful description in the language used to describe individuals. In such cases, an old-fashioned covering law provides a better explanation than a description of the mechanism associated with any given token instance (Sawyer 2004a).

These two failings are related to a common error among methodological individualists: making the assumption that ontological individualism entails methodological individualism. The logical error of making ontological arguments in support of methodological claims is quite common in the philosophy of social science and is found in Popper's (1962) confusion of materialist metaphysics with epistemology (e.g., p. 341), in Elster's (1985) methodologically individualist reading of Marx, and in Giddens's

(1984) attacks on structural sociology (e.g., chap. 4). The fact that social properties are nothing more than their individual supervenience bases does not entail that an explanation can necessarily be provided in the language used to describe individuals.

Collectivist theories of emergence

In the the preceding section, I showed that methodological individualists conceive of their approach as a way of explaining the micro-to-macro emergence of social phenomena from individual action. Methodological individualists hold that emergence is compatible with reduction to individual-level explanation of social phenomena. How can one reconcile these claims with those of contemporary sociological theorists who have explicitly drawn on emergence to ground nonreductionist, nonindividualist sociological theories? In this section, I review these collectivist versions of emergence, and I evaluate them against nonreductive individualism. With regard to the complex social phenomena under study, this form of emergentism accepts that nothing exists except the component individuals and their interactions but nonetheless maintains that some complex social phenomena cannot be studied with reductionist methods. I discuss five theorists: Peter Blau, Roy Bhaskar, Margaret Archer, Douglas Porpora, and Kyriakos Kontopoulos.

Peter Blau

The simpler social processes that can be observed in interpersonal associations and that rest directly on psychological dispositions give rise to the more complex social processes that govern structures of interconnected social associations, such as the social organization of a factory.... Although complex social systems have their foundation in simpler ones, they have their own dynamics with emergent properties. (Blau 1964, 19–20)

Blau's concept of emergence evolved over his career, but both his earlier more reductionist writings and his later structuralist work represent variants of emergentism. His 1955 account of status exchange was reductionist because it showed how a stable and differentiated social structure emerges from a process of exchange between members (Homans 1958, 604). In his 1964 book, Blau elaborated this exchange theoretic concept of emergence, emphasizing the need to "derive the social processes that govern the complex structures of communities and societies from the simpler processes that pervade the daily intercourse among individuals and their interpersonal relations" (p. 2). He outlined a three-step sequence of emergence, working up from lower levels to higher levels. Processes of social attraction result in the emergence of exchange; exchange results in the differentiation of status and power; and, finally, this differentiation results in two phenomena: legitimation and organization, on the one hand, and opposition, conflict, and change, on the other (pp. 7, 14). Even while grounding macrosocial phenomena in foundational psychological processes, Blau cautioned against Homans's psychological reductionism, claiming that it "tends to ignore these emergent characteristics of social life" (p. 3).

Such passages led some scholars (e.g., Archer 1979, 5–42; Buckley 1967, 143) to emphasize Blau's methodological differences with Homans in his 1964 work. Yet Blau's 1964 concept of emergence was different from the structuralist nonreductionism that he was to advocate later (1977, 1981), because it focused on social exchange between two individuals and argued that "more complex social processes evolve out of simpler ones and have their ultimate source in psychological dispositions" (1964, 7). Blau himself later noted that in his 1964 book he thought that "macrosociological theory should be built on the basis of microsociological theory" (1987, 99), and he gradually shifted from this more reductionist view of emergence to a more structuralist and sociologically realist view. By 1970, Blau had begun to reject his earlier attempts to ground macrotheory in microsociology (Blau 1970a, 338; also see 1977, 1987), and he concluded that there could be no such foundation because "the major terms of macrosociological theories refer to emergent properties of population structures that have no equivalent in microsociological analysis" (1987, 87). The reason why this is so is the large size and complexity of societies: "[I]t is impossible to trace and dissect the interpersonal relations of many thousands or millions of people, and neither would it be meaningful if all were described" (p. 97).

The philosophical account shows that Blau's invocation of emergence is incomplete. In 1981, Blau argued that emergent properties were irreducible by using Lewes's and Durkheim's nineteenth-century analogy: the properties of water emerge from those of hydrogen and oxygen. Yet the emergent properties of water have in fact been reductively explained by quantum mechanics. The philosophical account shows that a focus on emergent properties is not "inherently anti-reductionist," as Blau claimed (1981, 10).

These inadequacies lead to another significant weakness of Blau's account: He did not provide an account of how emergent social properties could have causal power. For Blau, social structure is not simply an abstract conceptual representation of the sociologist but possesses causal powers over actors (1981, 15–16; also see 1977, 2, 244). Several theorists have criticized Blau and other structuralists for proposing causal accounts that reify social structure such that society becomes ontologically autonomous from individuals (I. J. Cohen 1989; King 1999b, 270–1; Varela and Harré 1996, 316–19). If structure supervenes on individuals, then a theory that attributes to it causal force over those individuals must be careful to clarify its ontological foundations.

The weaknesses in Blau's account can be addressed by nonreductive individualism. Although emergence is not "inherently anti-reductionist," emergence conceived of in terms of multiple realizability and wild disjunction can ground nonreductionist claims. Nonreductive individualism provides a justification for Blau's claims that social properties can participate in causal laws. However, with each social property, whether it is realized with a wildly disjunctive supervenience base is an empirical question that can only be resolved through sociological study. Blau generally implies that such an empirical demonstration is unnecessary and that all emergent social properties are irreducible.

Roy Bhaskar's transcendental realism

It is only if social phenomena are genuinely emergent that realist explanations in the human sciences are justified . . . conversely, emergent phenomena require realist explanations. (Bhaskar 1982, 276)

In developing his argument for *transcendental realism*, Bhaskar appealed to emergence in arguing that social reality is ontologically stratified. Bhaskar referred to his thesis as "synchronic emergent powers materialism" and argued that although social structure is dependent on individuals' actions, it is irreducible to them and ontologically autonomous from them (1979, 37–44, 97–107). In sharp contrast with individualist emergentism, Bhaskar held that emergentism is identical with realism.[7] Although society emerges from individuals, it is ontologically autonomous from individuals: "There is an ontological hiatus between society and people" (p. 37). In arguing this claim, Bhaskar wrote, "People do not create society. . . . Rather, society must be regarded as an ensemble of structures, practices and conventions which individuals reproduce or transform, but which would not exist unless they did so. Society does not exist independently of human activity (the error of reification). But it is not the product of it (the error of voluntarism)" (p. 36).

---

[7] Other transcendental realist variants of emergentism include Collier 1989, 183–5, and Lawson 1997, 63. Occasional rhetorical similarities with structuration theory are misleading; Giddens has explicitly rejected emergentism and social realism (see Chapter 7). As Ira J. Cohen (1989) wrote in his overview of structuration theory, a practice orientation "entails dispensing with all arguments for the emergence of social patterns" (pp. 76–7).

Bhaskar implicitly accepted supervenience as an account of the relation between higher- and lower-level properties. He held that there is only one substance in the universe; synchronic emergent powers materialism "does not require the postulation of any substance other than matter as the bearer of the emergent powers" (1982, 282). He accepted the supervenience claim that societies "are unilaterally, existentially dependent on" the material world such that "any social change entails a natural change" (p. 281) – one of the implications of supervenience.

The philosophical account of emergence is incompatible with several elements of Bhaskar's account. For example, Bhaskar claimed that emergence applies not to properties of events but to entities (1982, 277), and on other occasions he referred to these entities as "mechanisms" ([1975] 1997, 47) or "things" (p. 51).[8] This seems to entail a rejection of token event identity and the property focus of the philosophical account; yet this would also entail a rejection of supervenience. This would be hard to reconcile with Bhaskar's many claims that suggest that society is supervenient on individuals.[9]

Like Blau, Bhaskar (1979) connected emergence with social causation (p. 39). But how can social entities have causal autonomy from individuals when they are supervenient on these individuals? Several critics have noted that Bhaskar did not present an account of causality that is grounded in his conceptions of generative mechanisms (Keat and Urry 1975, 243; Suchting 1992, 25; Varela and Harré 1996, 316) and that his concepts of structure, causal power, and generative mechanism remain unclear. In part because Bhaskar never articulated in detail the nature of the supervenience relation between lower- and higher-level properties, his argument does not successfully accomplish its realist goal.

Bhaskar did not present an account of causality and its relation to his conceptions of laws or regularities. He rejected the covering law model in arguing that science is not about laws but is about generative mechanisms, yet he did not propose an alternate account of causality. He did not say what causal "powers" and "tendencies" are; they seem to be properties of entities (and explicitly not properties of events, because Bhaskar

---

[8] Collier's (1989) reading of critical realism also speaks of the emergence of *entities* rather than properties, unlike in the philosophical account (p. 183).

[9] At times Bhaskar seems to want it both ways, arguing on some occasions that societies are supervenient on individuals and on other occasions that societies are ontologically distinct entities. For example, Bhaskar was not ready to accept the form of mental supervenience accepted in nonreductive materialism, suggesting that humans may possess some "paranormal" substance that bears these irreducible causal powers (1979, 98). Bhaskar's tendency to reject materialist monism led him to claim scientifically insupportable allies: various forms of dualism and immaterialism, including vitalism, Alexander's spiritualist version of emergentism, and Bergson's dualism (Bhaskar 1982, 278).

insists that science is about entities, not events: He stated that "the objects of scientific investigation are structures, not events," 1982, 277, and as already noted he referred to these entities as "mechanisms" or "things"). But Bhaskar never articulated in detail what the relation between lower- and higher-level properties are, as philosophers of mind did in arguing for nonreductive materialism.

In sum, Bhaskar failed to sufficiently develop his theory of emergence. This left him open to the charge that his theory hypostatizes or reifies society (cf. King 1999b; Suchting 1992; Varela and Harré 1996) in spite of his many statements that society is supervenient on individuals.

Margaret Archer's morphogenetic dualism

There is a glaring absence of bold social theories which uncompromisingly make "emergence" their central tenet. (Archer 1995, 135)

During the course of her career, Archer's account of emergence has shifted from methodological collectivism to sociological realism. Prior to 1995, Archer held to a nonrealist form of emergentism, accepting the supervenience assumption "that groups are made up of nothing more than individuals and the relations between them" (1979, 6). Although accepting ontological individualism and rejecting sociological realism, Archer used emergence arguments to reject methodological individualism in favor of "explanatory emergence" (p. 6, following Brodbeck [1958] 1968, 301–3). Archer claimed that social science had demonstrated the intractable complexity of the composition laws that might allow us to explain collective phenomena in terms of individuals; therefore, explanatory emergence is the only methodological option currently available to sociologists (p. 9). She also agreed with the philosophical account in claiming that resolution of the emergence question requires empirical research and granting to individualists that "such emergent organizational properties may ultimately prove susceptible of reduction" (p. 31).

In 1982 and 1988, Archer further elaborated her theory of emergence in her account of *analytic dualism,* an alternative to Giddens's inseparability of structure and action (see Chapter 7). Archer appealed to Blau's 1964 version of emergence to resolve the individual-collective problem: Emergence is embedded in interaction, and emergent properties are relational. As in 1979, she explicitly rejected sociological realism: "[T]here is no suggestion that we are dealing with separate entities, only analytically separable ones and ones which it is theoretically useful to treat separately" (1988, xiv). Archer's emphasis on time (1988, xxii, and elsewhere) and her claim that current structural conditions were not created by the current actors but by actors in the past are foundational to her emergentist accounts of morphogenesis (1988, 1995).

In 1995, Archer changed her ontological stance. As in her earlier work, she accepted a part-whole concept of supervenience (1995, 173–4), and she argued that emergent properties are "irreducible group variables" (p. 251), but in contrast to her earlier methodological stance, she argued that emergence entailed realism and endorsed Bhaskar's realist conception of causal powers (p. 90). Social properties emerge from individual properties that are anterior to the emergent properties; once a property has emerged, it has "relative autonomy" from properties at the emergence base, and "such autonomous properties exert independent causal influences in their own right" (p. 14). This social realism accepts "ontological emergence" (p. 15) and claims that emergent social properties are just as real as their lower-level supervenience base (p. 63).[10]

Yet this shift to realism resulted in internal contradictions. She continued to make non-realist statements like "what is being defended is not philosophical dualism but the utility of analytical dualism" (1995, 180). She acknowledged that individuals are the only causal forces in social life, and that this raised a problem for her claim that emergent structures can also bear causal powers (p. 195). Although realist, she denied that her position reified structure (p. 148). Her continued usage of her older term "analytical dualism," along with her failure to explicitly note contrasts with her prior writings, makes the exact nature of her social realism unclear.

Archer argued that it is emergence over time – morphogenesis – that makes emergent structural properties real and allows them to constrain individuals (p. 183). Current social structures emerged from the past actions of individuals such that they cannot be explanatorily reduced to actions of current individuals (e.g., p. 148). Yet emergence over time does not provide an ontological argument for social causation, as the philosophical account makes clear (this is similar to the critique of Archer in Healy 1998). For example, Kim (1999) emphasized the distinction between reflexive downward causation and diachronic downward causation and noted that the diachronic case – the one corresponding to Archer's argument – was not problematic for reductionists because it is consistent with a supervenient causation in which the causal powers are entirely associated with the lower-level realization (also see Mendonça 2002; Pihlström 2002; Rueger 2000; Stephan 1998; Symons 2002). Even

---

[10] Note her acceptance of Brodbeck's "explanatory emergence" in 1979 and her explicit rejection of it in 1995 (p. 27).

though social property $S(t)$ is emergent from a process that occurred at $t - 1$ and before, it must nonetheless be supervenient on individual properties at time t, owing to token event identity. Rational choice and complexity accounts also require temporality; just because structure represents the consequences of past actions does not mean that it is real or autonomous from contemporary actions or agents. As Symons (2002) argued,

While the diachronic case will meet with few objections, the real prize is the synchronic case. Arguing for a robust form of emergentism requires that we demonstrate the significance of relations to the causal powers of a system. . . . As Kim's analysis makes clear, the only way to do so in a way that avoids reducing the power of emergent properties to those of their constituents is via the synchronic case. (pp. 195–6)

Realist versions of social emergence require a synchronous account of reflexive downward causation.

Thus Archer provided an inadequate foundational argument for the ontological independence of emergent properties and how they could exert downward causation. If one accepts supervenience, the causal power of $S(t)$ must inhere in its individual-level supervenience base at time t; one cannot ground sociological realism in a temporal conception of emergence, even though an explanation of how $S(t)$ came to be may require examination of what Archer (1982) called the "analytical history of emergence" (pp. 475–6).

Douglas Porpora

Although emergently material social relations are generated by cultural constitutive rules, those relations independently affect the ways in which situated actors think and act. (Porpora 1993, 213)

Like Bhaskar and Archer, Porpora is a critical realist. Porpora rejected covering law explanations and held that the task of sociology is to uncover the generative mechanisms underlying observed social phenomena (1983, 1987, 1993). Porpora (1993) argued that social theory must be extended with the concept of *emergently material social relations*. For Porpora, emergently material social relations "are generated by cultural constitutive rules [in Winch's (1958) sense]"; however, those relations then "independently affect the ways in which situated actors think and act" (p. 213). Porpora rejected the Marxian position that the material is primary and determines social relations; instead, "material social relations are generated by cultural constitutive rules and thus are ontologically dependent on those rules" (p. 217). He did not clarify his concept of "material," which for him seems to refer to symbolic cultural products and not to what Marx meant by the term. (In fact it is unclear in what sense the position is specifically Marxian; Porpora's position is essentially a version of structural sociology.)

Social relations are emergently material phenomena that "have an ontologically objective and socially consequential existence, whether or not any actors are aware of them" (p. 222). To demonstrate his concept of emergence, Porpora presented the example of a chess game. The flow of each specific game is emergent from the "constitutive rules" of the game and from the successive actions of the two players. Yet soon after the game begins, objective relationships become established, as pieces begin to occupy positions with strategic relationships "which emerge only in the context of the rules but which exist, nevertheless, whether or not the players are aware of them" (p. 223).

Porpora's position shares similarities with nonreductive individualism. They both support a social realism in which emergent social properties are real. However, whereas Porpora rejects covering laws, nonreductive individualism supports a notion of social causation that is consistent with deductive-nomological explanation. The identification and description of the mechanisms of social emergence is an important part of sociology (see the final section of this chapter); however, nonreductive individualism shows that this task is compatible with the potential existence of emergent social properties that participate in causal laws. In contrast to the critical realists, many social mechanists have argued that lawful explanations are not in conflict with mechanistic explanations (Bunge 1996, 1997, 2004; Elster 1998; Sawyer 2004a).

Kyriakos Kontopoulos

A new convergent [robust emergentist] model has emerged – a nonreductive, nonequilibrium, multilevel conceptualization of phenomena. (Kontopoulos 1993, 4)

The Logics of Social Structure (Kontopoulos 1993) is an enlightening survey of sociological theory within an emergentist framework. Kontopoulos's argument for *heterarchical emergence* shares some overall features with nonreductive individualism. Heterarchical emergence is defined as "underdetermination of the macrostructure(s) by the given microparts and as semiautonomous emergence of higher-level phenomena out of lower level phenomena" (p. 12). He noted parallels between heterarchical emergence and philosophical arguments for nonreductive materialism (pp. 12–13). Like Bhaskar and Archer, he argued that "diachronic reduction" is in principle possible whereas synchronous reduction is in principle impossible (p. 30).

Kontopoulos distinguished among three distinct emergentist positions that fall between reductionism and holism: compositional emergence, heterarchical emergence, and hierarchical emergence. Compositional emergence corresponds to what I have called "individualist emergentism," and the latter two correspond to collectivist emergentism. The main problem rests with his distinction between his two forms of collectivist emergentism: heterarchical emergence and hierarchical emergence (nonreductive individualism falls somewhere in this gray area). He associated hierarchical emergence with methodological holism and rejected it in favor of heterarchical emergence. His distinction results in some confusion about the ontological status of emergent higher levels and the nature of social causation. He seemed to reject social realism and downward causation, equating it with transcendence (Kontopoulos 1993, 23). His counterproposal, for "semiautonomous" causation, is confusing: He elsewhere wrote that there is both upward and downward influence at once in a heterarchical level structure (e.g., pp. 29, 239), "privileging neither a methodologically individualist nor a methodologically collectivist mode" (p. 301). Ultimately his defense of semiautonomous emergent levels is incomplete because he did not address the supervenience counterargument of the individualist emergentists (as the wild disjunction argument does).

These unresolved issues can be addressed by the argument presented earlier for nonreductive individualism and by appeal to third-wave complexity concepts. Although it shares some features with nonreductive individualism, Kontopoulos's account is not based on the philosophical concepts of supervenience and multiple realizability, and it does not draw on third-wave systems theory. His complexity metaphors are inspired by the nonequilibrium thermodynamics of Prigogine and chaos theory (p. 26), placing him in the second wave of social systems theory (see Chapter 2). Nonreductive individualism could extend Kontopoulos's account by clarifying its treatment of social causation; it can support social realism and holism yet is not necessarily functionalist. And third-wave systems theory could extend Kontopoulos's account by elaborating the mechanisms of emergence.

The five theorists discussed in this and the preceding sections used emergence to defend an antireductionist position, one that holds that the social level of analysis results from individual actions and yet takes on an independent existence. I argued that each of these theories of emergence was incomplete. None of the five used the term "supervenience" nor built on philosophical discussions of supervenience; however, each of them implicitly accepted an ontology consistent with supervenience: only individuals exist, social properties and entities are nothing more than the individuals that compose them, and social properties cannot change unless the constituting individuals change. Along with these theorists (and some of their critics), I agree that these assumptions are necessary to avoid the undesirable positions of ontological dualism and social reification. However, supervenience alone cannot support sociological realism. The five theories are incomplete because they fail to deal with the fact that supervenience entails that causal powers be grounded in the supervenience base, and they fail to make an antireductionist and socially realist argument that is consistent with supervenience. I have argued that one can address these problems by drawing on philosophical extensions of supervenience that originated in the philosophy of mind. One can build on these theorists and accomplish antireductionist goals by using the multiple realizability and wild disjunction arguments; these can provide both an antireductionist account of social properties and an antireductionist account of social causal laws.

Critical responses

A few social theorists have explicitly rejected socially realist arguments based on emergence. These include the structuration theorists Giddens and Cohen as well as King (e.g., his hermeneutic and Marxian critique). These critics make some valid points about the weaknesses of collectivist emergentists, but their critiques can be addressed by extending collectivist emergentism with the foundational account of nonreductive individualism.

Structurationist critiques of social emergence

Emergence is central to the debate between structuration theory and structural sociology (Archer 1982, 1995; see also Chapter 7). Ira J. Cohen, for example, claimed that structuration theory "postulates no emergent properties for patterns of interaction" (1989, 93), and Giddens repeatedly criticized Durkheim's concept of emergence. Giddens's concept of the "duality of structure" was an attempt to accomplish the theoretical functions of this dialectic without falling into the ontological dualism of structural sociology. Structuration theory argues that only in social praxis can one identify processes that reproduce the social order.

Giddens explicitly rejected the notion that objective social structures could emerge from individual action, holding instead that "structure is not 'external' to individuals: as memory traces, and as instantiated in social practices, it is in a certain sense more 'internal' than exterior" (1984, 25). As Cohen wrote in his overview of structuration theory, a practice orientation "entails dispensing with all arguments for the emergence of social patterns ... *the routine repetitions of institutionalized modes of interaction between agents is not something apart from the patterns they form*" (1989, 76–7, original italics).

There are no independent social phenomena; "structure" instead refers to rules and resources; "systems," or patterns of relations, are always dependent variables – never independent – and are thus epiphenomenal (cf. Porpora 1993, 219). Thus, in structuration theory, nothing actually emerges. Because structure is inseparable from agency, "*there is no sense in which it can be either emergent or autonomous or pre-existent or causally influential*" (Archer 1995, 97, original italics). Structuration theory's major failing is that it cannot resolve the question of the apparent causal power of structural phenomena (cf. Archer 1982, 1995). Although Giddens held that social relations are simply abstractions and have no causal efficacy, structuration theorists nonetheless often refer to the causal effects of relations (cf. the critiques of Archer 1982; Porpora 1993, 220).

The structuralists have been criticized for reifying and objectifying social structure such that society becomes ontologically autonomous from individuals (I. J. Cohen 1989; King 1999b, 270–1; Varela and Harré 1996, 316–19). Cohen (1989) argued that structural sociologists pull a fast rhetorical move: First they say that their proposals for emergent social structures are merely analytic abstractions, then they propose that those structures guide behavior, exert pressure on individuals, and resist change. But analytic abstractions cannot do these things; only real phenomena with causal power can have such impacts on individuals. Cohen argued that emergence versions of structural sociology have not adequately theorized downward causation. He noted that those theorists that claim that emergent structure has causal power seem to be hypostatizing that structure – in other words, proposing a multi-layered ontology of the social world such that social structures seem to exist independently of their individual participants (p. 71). Likewise, Varela and Harré (1996) concluded that only agentive human beings can be the source of social causation (p. 316). But then in what sense is there social causation at all?

King's critique of critical realism

King's (1999a, 1999b) separate critiques of Bhaskar and Archer pointed out weaknesses in their accounts of emergence, but King's concerns can be addressed by nonreductive individualism. King argued that society is nothing more than individuals and their relations and that we should reject any notion of autonomous social structure. Like Archer (1995), he opened up the temporal scope and proposed that social facts at any given moment are emergent from individuals and their actions at prior moments in time. Unlike Archer, he used this observation to reject social realism: If we expand the scope of explanation to include all space and time, social facts are nothing but the actions of individuals. He agreed with Archer that for any given individual the structure may be essentially autonomous and may appear to have independent causal force, although the analyst could reduce this causation to the original causal force of the past individuals that gave rise to that social fact. Thus King disagreed with the realist claim that emergence results in social phenomena with autonomous, real existence. Only individuals exist, and social phenomena can always be reduced to individuals, so long as one includes all individuals in the social system, both at present and in the past.

King's (1999b) position is straightforward methodological individualism: "The concept of structure becomes wholly superfluous to the description of social life which can be adequately accounted for by reference only to individuals, their practices and relations" (p. 278).[11] An institution is nothing more than "complex networks of individuals, whose daily interactions and practices, constitute the institution." Thus an institution, although not reducible to any one individual, "is and cannot be more than all the individuals who work in it." So, "by claiming that some aspects of social reality become more than all of the individuals involved in them, emergence falls exactly into this error of reification which fails to recognize that the properties of networks of interacting individuals, while certainly more than any individual in them, coheres exactly with those networks." Thus, social reality "is not 'emergent' from those individuals" (p. 272).

King claimed there were unresolvable contradictions in Bhaskar's writings: "Bhaskar implicitly recognizes that society is always reducible to other individuals" (p. 273) because he accepts that social structure, although irreducible to the presently living and acting individuals, is reducible to the intentional actions of people in the past. "Since society can only exist through individuals either in the past, present or future and society can never be autonomous of all of these individuals, it is more accurate to argue not that individuals recreate emergent social structure but rather that, through their interactions, they maintain, transform and renegotiate social relations with other individuals" (p. 274). King argued

---

[11] He preferred to call his position "interpretivism," although it is not clear why (cf. Archer 2000); see my discussion of interpretivism in Chapter 10.

contra Bhaskar that it is not possible for society to be both dependent on individuals and yet independent of them (p. 270); he was so concerned with this apparent contradiction in Bhaskar's writings that he called it "embarrassing" (p. 278).

King's error was to assume that supervenience implies an antirealist position with respect to the higher level. But this is partly due to the incomplete theories of emergence in Bhaskar and Archer (see the earlier discussion of their views). King's critiques show the need to buttress theories of social emergence by appeal to nonreductive individualism. Nonreductive individualism shows that even though society is supervenient on individuals, social properties and social laws may not be reducible to individual properties, even if all individuals present and past are included. In nonreductive individualism, any given token instance of an emergent social property could perhaps (depending on complexity considerations) be reduced to the individual supervenience base, but if that social property is disjunctively realized, then its type cannot be so reduced.

Unresolved Issues

I began this chapter by presenting an argument for nonreductive individualism based on the current nonreductionist emergentist consensus in the philosophy of mind. I then reviewed two opposed ways that emergence has been conceived by sociologists: first, in a reductionist fashion by methodological individualists, and second, in an antireductionist fashion by methodological collectivists and sociological realists. I used the philosophical account to evaluate each of these, and I concluded that each has flaws or internal inconsistencies that make its conclusions suspect: reductionist conclusions in the case of individualist emergentists, and realist conclusions in the case of collectivist emergentists. Thus several unresolved issues are brought into focus by the philosophical perspective. In the following, I identify four issues facing theories of social emergence: realism, causation, mechanism, and characteristics of irreducible systems.

Realism

One of the major contrasts between reductionist and antireductionist accounts of sociological emergence is whether or not they are realist concerning the social. Individualist emergentists acknowledge the existence of emergent social properties but nonetheless maintain that these properties are not real but are merely analytic constructs and thus require an explanation in terms of individuals and their interactions. In contrast, collectivists argue that emergence entails a stratified ontology and supports social realism. They accept the supervenience of the social on the individual, yet claim that social entities and structures are ontologically autonomous. Not all nonreductive materialists make realist claims concerning higher-level entities; there remains considerable debate about whether or not nonreductive materialism entails that mental properties are real (e.g., Clarke 1999; Kim 1993a). Sociological realists can draw on these debates to develop an account of how social properties can be both supervenient on individuals and yet ontologically independent of them.

Individualists often criticize sociological realists for proposing a dualist ontology, a world in which both individuals and social entities are autonomous realms of reality. They can potentially gain some support for this critique from the philosophical account. However, for the most part individualists go too far in drawing reductionist methodological conclusions from the fact of ontological individualism. Although society is supervenient on individuals, social properties and social laws may be real, have causal power over individuals, and be irreducible to individual properties and laws. The philosophical account demonstrates that ontological individualism is not necessarily opposed to social realism.

Higher-level realism has not been reconciled with supervenience, as the philosophy of mind debates demonstrate. Sociologists who accept social-individual supervenience and yet intend to make socially realist claims must show why reduction to individuals is not possible even though groups consist of nothing more than individuals. Multiple realizability and wild disjunction can potentially provide this argument. Many social properties are multiply realized by wild disjunctions of individual beliefs and dispositions, including "being a church," "being a collective movement," and "being an act of discrimination." Social laws that contain such social properties are likely to be irreducible to individual laws.

Causation

Closely related to the realism issue is the issue of social causation. Collectivist sociologists propose causal laws in which social properties are the causal antecedents. Social causation has been a definitional assumption in many nonindividualist sociological theories, from Durkheim's social fact (Chapter 6) to Archer's irreducibly emergent properties. Methodological individualists reject the possibility of such laws in principle.

Realist emergentists defend social causal laws by holding that emergent social entities or properties are ontologically autonomous. If the social is ontologically autonomous, then its causation is not problematic, but this leads to the problems associated with realism – ontological autonomy is difficult to reconcile with supervenience. Yet if the higher level is not ontologically autonomous, then how can it have causal power? Due to such concerns, the status of mental causation is hotly debated in contemporary philosophy of mind (e.g., Andersen et al. 2000; Heil and Mele 1993). If emergentists reject a dualist ontology and at the same time argue that social properties have causal force, the argument must root that causal force in their emergence from lower-level components. The position suggested by nonreductive individualism is supervenient causation: There can be social causal laws that are not lawfully reducible to individual terms and laws even though in each token instance the causal power of the social property lies in its individual supervenience base (Sawyer 2003e).

Note that the token event identity assumption that underlies the supervenience thesis entails that the causal power of an emergent property cannot be attributed to events that occurred in the past, as Archer (1995) did in arguing that social properties are not supervenient on simultaneous individual properties because their "emergence depended upon the activities of previous 'generations'" (p. 169). Although the explanation of a social property's emergence will require an account of how it developed over time – as even individualist emergentists agree – that social property's (ontological) causal power must inhere in its supervenience base in the present. The fact of temporality cannot be used to defend social property realism; note that artificial society and rational choice models also model emergence processes over time and yet do not entail any realist claims about the properties that emerge.

Collectivist emergentists simultaneously consider two directions of causation: emergence of the higher-level property from the lower level, and downward causation from the higher level to the lower level. Individualist emergentists are reductionist in emphasizing only the first of these processes. Most nonindividualist sociological theorists have emphasized this dialectic process, including the otherwise opposed theories of Giddens and Archer (Chapter 7). Yet nonreductive individualism is subtly different from either position; social causation is a lawful relation between a social property and an individual property, even though in any given token instance the causal force of the social property inheres in its individual-level supervenience base. In this sense, social properties constrain individuals, but at the same time they are supervenient on the actions and interactions of those very same individuals.

Mechanism

Both individualist and collectivist emergentists agree on the empirical importance of analyzing processes of emergence through time. In this, they are consistent with the focus on mechanism and generative explanation in third-wave systems theory (Sawyer 2004a). Theories of emergence mechanisms held by individualists and collectivists are remarkably similar. Archer's (1995) diagrams of the morphogenetic cycle (e.g., pp. 156–8) emphasize that social properties must be explained in terms of the "analytical history of their emergence" from their individual supervenience base (p. 167). Similarly, Bhaskar (1979) claimed that the realism of synchronic emergence is compatible with "diachronic explanatory reduction," where higher-order entities are explained in terms of the processes of formation from their composing elements (p. 98). In practice, this is hard to distinguish from artificial society models of emergence processes (see Chapter 8) or from Coleman's (1990) rational choice method, which examines a three-stage process of "the macro-to-micro transition, purposive action of individuals, and the micro-to-macro transition" (p. 19). Although methodologically individualist, Coleman nonetheless accepted that accounts of the macro-to-micro transition could be valuable in sociology (e.g., "the transmission of information from the macro level to individual actors can greatly affect the actions they take and thus affect system behavior," p. 21). But ultimately macrophenomena should be explained in terms of "micro-level actions, their combinations, the feedback from those combinations that affects further micro-level actions, followed by further combinations, and so on" (p. 20).

In their empirical methods for studying the mechanisms of emergence, individualist and collectivist emergentists have the potential to find common ground. Both individualists and collectivists agree that some social properties are reducible; others are not reducible, owing to complexity considerations; and the only way to determine which is which is to engage in empirical studies of the temporal mechanisms and processes of emergence that give rise to social properties. Artificial society simulations have great potential to address these issues because they focus exactly on temporal mechanisms and processes of emergence (Chapter 8).

For both individualist and collectivist emergentists, interaction is central; higher-level properties emerge from the interactions of individuals in a complex system. Thus the empirical study of emergence mechanisms requires a focus on symbolic interaction (see Chapter 9 for further elaboration of this claim). Most sociological theorists working in this area have not connected their theories of emergence to the close empirical study of symbolic interaction in groups. In general, theorists of the micro-macro link have not provided an adequate account of symbolic interaction (cf. Collins 1981; Giddens 1984; Rawls 1990). Many individualist emergentists radically simplify interaction into the formalisms of exchange theory, game theory, or rational choice theory. At the same time, collectivist emergentists typically focus on much broader timescales and do not study microinteraction. The types of emergence that are observed in human social systems are likely to result from the unique fact that the participating entities are symbol-generating and -interpreting agents. The same sorts of emergence will not necessarily be found in systems that do not consist of symbol-exchanging elements. Due to this unique feature of social systems, general systems theories that attempt to explain all levels of complex dynamical systems using the same formalisms (e.g., Holland 1995; Kauffman 1995) may have limited applicability to social systems. (I elaborate this argument in Chapter 9.)

Characteristics of irreducible systems

Collectivist emergentists accept that not all properties of collectives are emergent and irreducible. The average height of a population is an aggregate and can easily be reduced to properties of individuals even though it is a property of the collective.[12] At the same time, individualist emergentists accept the possibility that "some large social facts are simply too complex for a full reduction of them to be feasible" (Watkins 1957, 107n1). These qualifications point the way toward a common ground between these versions of emergentism.

The philosophical account of wild disjunction shows how a higher-level property could be supervenient on and yet not reducible to its lower-level base. However, the sociologist cannot assume that any given social property manifests wild disjunction; it must be demonstrated to be wildly disjunctive through empirical study. Philosophical accounts (e.g., Bechtel and Richardson 1993; Fodor 1974) accept that the issue of whether a reductionist or holist approach is appropriate for any given higher-level property or phenomenon is an empirical issue that can only be resolved via scientific inquiry. Before engaging in such study, we cannot know which social properties can be explained through methodological individualism, and we cannot know which are not explainable or predictable in terms of individual-level descriptions. Thus both individualist and collectivist emergentists face an empirical question with regard to any given sociological property: How must we combine lower- and higher-level explanation in developing a complete scientific explanation of that property?

A significant problem facing collectivist emergentists is that very few have clearly and explicitly defined the properties of systems that are likely to have irreducible higher-level emergent properties. Failure to resolve

---

[12] Such distinctions have been widely noted in sociological theory; see Lazarsfeld and Menzel 1969; Liska 1990.

this question has contributed to the confusion that has allowed emergentism to be adopted in contradictory fashion by both methodological individualists and by social realists. Fortunately, there are several suggestions along these lines from complexity theory. In the 1980s and 1990s, complexity theorists began to identify the characteristics of systems within which wild disjunction was likely to hold between system-level properties and the properties of the system's components.

Nonaggregativity   Wimsatt equated emergence with nonaggregativity and consequently argued that it is not necessarily incompatible with reductionism (1986). Aggregative properties meet four criteria, and most social properties do not satisfy them. First, the system property is not a product of the way the system is organized; the parts are *intersubstitutable* without affecting the system property. In social systems, individualists and collectivists alike agree that individuals and subsystems are not intersubstitutable because the network of relationships among individuals is significant. Second, an aggregative property should remain qualitatively similar despite the addition or removal of a part of the system. Third, the composition function for the property remains invariant under operations of decomposition and reaggregation of parts. Individualists and collectivists agree that these conditions do not hold of many social systems; for example, many social movements manifest threshold phenomena such that the addition or removal of the Nth individual may result in a qualitative change in the system even though the addition or removal of individuals $N - 1$ and before did not. Fourth, there are no cooperative or inhibitory interactions among the parts; thus, the relation between parts and whole is linear (Bechtel and Richardson 1993, 266). Again, individualists and collectivists agree that this condition does not hold for most social systems because relationships among individuals are often cooperative or inhibitory.

Most social properties are not aggregative and thus are emergent. But under this definition of emergence, a property could be emergent and nonetheless be reducible; even for a nonaggregative property there must exist some composition function that relates the emergent property to a decomposition of the system into parts with relationships. This is why individualists can easily accept that social systems are not aggregative. The disadvantage of Wimsatt's account is that it is so general that essentially all properties of complex systems will be nonaggregative (as was acknowledged by Wimsatt 1997, S382), and because it does not address the issue of reducibility, it fails to speak to the essence of the sociological debate, which centers on whether an account in terms of individuals and their interactions will be sufficient. Nonetheless, the characteristics associated with nonaggregativity are likely to contribute to the difficulty of reducing a given system property.

Near decomposability   Decomposable systems are modular, with each component acting primarily according to its own intrinsic principles. Each component is influenced by the others only at its inputs; its function (processing of those inputs) is not itself influenced by other components (Simon 1969). In such a system, the behavior of any part is *intrinsically determined*: it is possible to determine the component's properties in isolation from the other components despite the fact that they interact. The organization of the entire system is critical for the function of the system as a whole, but that organization does not provide constraints on the internal functioning of components.

In contrast, in nondecomposable systems, the overall system organization is a significant influence on the function of any component; thus, component function is no longer intrinsically determined. Dependence of components on each other is often mutual and may even make it difficult to draw firm boundaries between components (Bechtel and Richardson 1993, 26–7). Systems that are not nearly decomposable are likely to have emergent system properties that are wildly disjunctive at the level of description of the components, and such systems are thus less likely to submit to reductionist explanation.

Localization   A system is localizable if the functional decomposition of the system corresponds to its physical decomposition and if each property of the system can be identified with a single component or subsystem. If system properties cannot be identified with components but are instead distributed spatially within the system, that system is not localizable (Bechtel and Richardson 1993, 24). Many social properties are not localizable. For example, "being a church" cannot be localized to any of the individuals belonging to the church, nor to any subnetwork of those individuals. Higher-level properties that are not localizable are likely to have wildly disjunctive descriptions at the level of their components and are more likely to be irreducible to components (Bechtel and Richardson 1993, 228).

The brain is generally agreed to be nonlocalizable in this sense, and much of the theory about localizability has been inspired by connectionist models of brain function in cognitive science (Cilliers 1998; see also Chapter 4). Connectionist models suggest that the density of network connections is related to localizability and decomposability of the system. Likewise, social systems with a high dynamic density are less likely to be decomposable or localizable and consequently are more likely to manifest social properties that are wildly disjunctive at the individual level of description. In modern societies, dynamic density increases as communication technology and transportation technology advance, increasing the number and frequency of network connections among individuals (cf. Durkheim [1895] 1964, 114–15; see Chapter 6).

Complexity of interaction   In complexity theory, notions of emergence are based on interactions and relations among the component parts. For example, the criteria of nonaggregativity, nondecomposability, and nonlocalizability described in the preceding three sections are all defined in terms of the complex systemic relations among components. Consequently, several emergence theorists have suggested that the complexity of each interaction among components may be another variable contributing to emergence. Darley (1994) proposed that emergence is a function of both the number of units and the complexity of the rules of interaction, and Baas (1994) suggested that emergence occurs when "the interactions are nonlinear" (p. 522). The additional complexity of human symbolic interaction is another characteristic that contributes to the irreducibility of social properties.

Individualist emergentists and collectivist emergentists agree that interaction is central to micro-macro process accounts, although they have differing models of interaction. In mechanical and biological systems, component relations are relatively well understood and well defined. Because they are inspired by such systems, complex dynamical systems models of social and economic phenomena tend to assume extremely simple interactions. Yet as I noted earlier in this section, although human communication is qualitatively more complex, emergentists have not connected their theories to the study of symbolic interaction in groups. If there is a qualitative difference in the complexity of this communication and that in natural complex systems, then social theories of emergence may need to incorporate a theory of symbolic interaction; this issue is the topic of Chapter 9.

Conclusion

Like alcohol, [the theory of emergence] is a stimulant only in proper doses: many who have used it have gotten drunk in the attempt to apply it to everything. Sociology, however, is one field in which it has yet not been applied to full advantage. (Ablowitz 1939, 16)

The concept of emergence has been repeatedly invoked in sociological theory. However, emergence has proven to be a slippery concept; several prominent theorists have subtly shifted their positions on emergence throughout their careers. Homans's earlier emergentism was holist (1941, 1950), but in his canonical 1958 paper he had begun a shift toward psychological reductionism, and by 1964 he explicitly claimed that emergence was compatible with reductionism. During the same period, Blau shifted from an individualist form of emergentism (1955) to a less reductionist form (1964), which yet later led to an explicitly collectivist account of structural sociology (1970a, 1977). This confusing situation had not changed by the 1990s. Coleman's 1990 book elaborated a methodologically individualist account of emergence, and Archer's 1995 work presented a realist and nonreductionist account of emergence. Like Homans and Blau, Archer shifted her stance on emergence during the course of her career, from a methodological conception of emergence (1979, 1982, 1988) to a realist one (1995).

In this chapter, I have attempted to clarify these competing accounts of emergence by reference to several decades of analogous theory in the philosophy of mind. Borrowing directly from this tradition, I defined the concepts of supervenience, multiple realizability, and wild disjunction that have been used to argue for nonreductive materialism – the position that mental properties are supervenient on the physical brain and yet not reducible to physical properties. Likewise, causal laws concerning mental properties may not be reducible to causal laws concerning physical properties.

I used the parallel argument of nonreductive individualism to show that social properties may be supervenient on individual properties and yet not reducible to those properties. This account of emergence suggests that methodological individualists cannot argue a priori that all social properties and laws are reducible to individual properties, relations, and laws and at the same time suggests that methodological collectivists cannot argue a priori that a given social property is not so reducible. Whether or not a social property is reducible to individual properties, or a social law reducible to individual laws, is an empirical question that can only be resolved through empirical study. Nonreductive individualism suggests a theoretical stance that is partially compatible with both positions and suggests an empirical program that can help sociologists to resolve these competing claims.

The balance of my argument leans toward a nonreductionist and realist account of emergentism; after all, the philosophical argument originated to counter physicalist reductionism. Most social properties seem on the face of it to meet the criteria of nonreducibility described in the preceding sections: Most social properties are nonaggregative, many social systems are not decomposable, most are not functionally localizable, and all depend on symbolic communications that use the full richness of human language. For these reasons, wild disjunction holds for many social properties, and these nonreductionist arguments are applicable to sociology.

6   Durkheim's theory of social emergence

> There can be no sociology unless societies exist, and ... societies cannot
> exist if there are only individuals.
>
> Émile Durkheim

In what sense do social phenomena exist? Durkheim was the first to argue that this question was foundational to sociology. He argued that if only individuals exist, "Sociological laws can be only a corollary of the more general laws of psychology; the ultimate explanation of collective life will consist in showing how it emanates from human nature in general" ([1895] 1964, 98). As we saw in Chapter 3, most philosophers of the nineteenth century held to either utilitarian atomism (in which sociology is ultimately reducible to psychology) or metaphysical organicism. Durkheim proposed a third path: a scientific sociology that could not be connected in any systematic way to psychological phenomena. To many of his contemporaries, this seemed to be an unresolvable dilemma: One was either a scientist and accepted that society was reducible to individuals, or else one was proposing a metaphysical dualism. In this chapter I present a new perspective on how Durkheim resolved this dilemma. I interpret Durkheim as a theorist of social emergence, the first sociologist to elaborate Comte's original insights (see Chapter 3). I argue that the central guiding premise that unifies all of Durkheim's work is the attempt to account for both the emergence of the social from the individual and downward causation from the social to the individual.

Although many sociologists have acknowledged in passing that Durkheim was an emergence theorist (e.g., I. J. Cohen 1989, 71–6; Giddens 1984, 169–74; L. J. Goldstein [1958] 1973, 281; Porpora 1993, 222; Schmaus 1994, 51–3), none has substantively engaged this thread of Durkheim's work. Durkheim's emergence argument has been widely misunderstood, starting with his contemporaries and continuing through the twentieth century. Many contemporary sociologists have read it to be an unresolvable dilemma and have dismissed his discussions of this theory as metaphysical, unscientific, or logically incoherent, particularly in his 1895 book *The Rules of Sociological Method*, where this argument is made most forcefully. These scholars have argued that the *Rules* is an odd, almost embarrassing misstep that Durkheim quickly abandoned (T. N. Clark 1969; Fenton 1984; Giddens 1977; Lukes 1973; Parsons [1937] 1949; Pickering 1984, 288; cf. Berthelot 1995; Gane 1988; Turner 1995, 2). I argue that such interpretations result from a failure to understand Durkheim's theory of social emergence. This failure has led to a wide range of misunderstandings of Durkheim that are fairly entrenched, including the perceived weakness of the *Rules*, the notion that one can separate Durkheim's theoretical and empirical work, and the suggestion that there were "two Durkheims," with a fundamental break in his work after the 1897 publication of *Suicide*.

This failure to understand Durkheim's theory of emergence is a manifestation of a broader bias in American sociology: a bias toward individualist sociological theories (cf. Hinkle 1960). I use the term "individualist" in Mayhew's (1980) broad sense, to include sociological theories that fundamentally require a theory of the individual, whether that theory is objectivist or subjectivist. Durkheim's theory of emergence, in contrast, is largely a structuralist theory; an emergentist reading of Durkheim lends support to those who claim that Durkheim was a structural sociologist. Beginning with Parsons's ([1937] 1949) influential voluntarist reading of Durkheim, many sociologists have emphasized the voluntarist elements of his theory, and this individualist emphasis has contributed to a misunderstanding of his theory of emergence.

Since the 1960s, philosophers of mind have examined emergence processes in the context of the mind-brain debate, resurrecting a philosophical tradition of emergentism extending back to the 1920s (see Chapter 3). Like Durkheim, these philosophers view emergence as a third path: in their case, between neurophysical atomism and metaphysical dualism. To date, these recent philosophical debates have not filtered into sociology. In the first half of the chapter, I build on the discussion in Chapter 5 of contemporary emergence thinking in philosophy, and I revisit Durkheim as an emergence theorist through the lens of this recent work. In the second half of the chapter, I draw on the contemporary philosophy of emergence to identify several unresolved issues in Durkheim's emergence theory. Reconstituted as an emergence theorist, Durkheim points the way toward a resolution of the atomism-holism dilemma that is compatible with both individualism and macrosociological theory.

Emergence in contemporary philosophy

In Chapter 4, we saw that emergence has been extensively discussed by philosophers of mind, psychological theorists, and cognitive scientists because these fields are increasingly threatened by the potential of reduction to neuroscience. The threat – analogous to the threats of methodological individualism facing sociology – is that these disciplines will be reduced to explanations and analyses of neurons and their interactions. These conceptions of emergence have been inspired by computational models of emergence processes, including connectionism (T. N. Clark 1997), artificial life (Brooks and Maes 1994; Langton 1994), and multi-agent models of social systems (Gilbert and Conte 1995; Prietula, Carley, and Gasser 1998; see also Chapter 8). In this recent formulation, *emergent systems* are complex dynamical systems that display global behavior that cannot be predicted from a full and complete description of the component units of the system.

For many complex systems, reductionist explanations of emergent phenomena are elusive. Complexity theory has long noted that complex systems display an unusual sensitivity to initial conditions. The system's behavior follows general laws, but because the effect of a small change in initial conditions is so large, predictability from the laws can be undecidable or noncomputable (Chapman 1987; Meyer and Brown 1998). Thus, in sufficiently complex systems, higher-level emergent patterns may not be predictable from laws at the lower level. By this reasoning, some philosophers have argued that the human mind, as an emergent phenomenon, cannot be reduced to neurophysical explanations, even though it is emergent from neuronal interactions. This position is known as *nonreductive materialism* (see Chapter 5).

Computer simulations of social systems are based on emergence assumptions (see Chapter 8). Many of these models derive from artificial life technologies, such as the work associated with the Santa Fe Institute (e.g., Epstein and Axtell 1996); other social modeling work is based on multi-agent systems technologies (Gilbert and Conte 1995; Lesser 1995). In multi-agent simulations, the system is designed to be self-organizing through emergence processes. Global conventions emerge from the simulation, even though each agent is autonomous and has access only to locally available information. Such simulations remain essentially reductionist and assume the utilitarian-atomist conception of the individual that most sociologists thought had been convincingly put to rest a hundred years ago (cf. Parsons [1937] 1949). Durkheim, who rejected the utilitarian atomism of Spencer, is not an emergence theorist in this sense. To understand Durkheim's notion of emergence and how it is compatible with his theory of the individual, we need to draw the philosophical theories of emergence introduced in Chapter 5.

Philosophers of mind turned to emergence beginning in the 1960s, following the cognitivist rejection of behaviorism. By the 1980s, the consensus position of *nonreductive materialism* had become established. The nonreductive materialist argues that there are strong grounds for believing that reduction of higher level laws is not possible even though there is nothing in the universe other than physical matter. Because there is only physical matter, there are only physical events; thus, psychological events are the same events as neurophysiological events. However, descriptions of these events within different scientific languages may be incommensurable, and the higher-level description may on occasion be a better description.

Philosophers have staked out a nonreductionist position that is not found in contemporary sociology. In Chapter 5, I identified analogies between these arguments for the independence of a mental level of analysis and arguments for the independence of a sociological level of analysis. The analogous position in sociological theory is nonreductive individualism: nothing but individuals exist, yet some social properties may be real and have causal power over individuals. This form of social emergence is compatible with the science of the lower level, unlike the nonreductionism of many structuralist sociologists, who refuse on principle to connect sociology to the science of the individual (more on this later).

Durkheim's concept of *sui generis*

Society is not a mere sum of individuals. (Durkheim [1895] 1964, 103)

Social things are actualized only through men; they are a product of human activity. (p. 17)

These seemingly contradictory quotations epitomize Durkheim's dilemma. In the *Rules*, Durkheim seemed to bounce between two incompatible ontological positions: Society is not just a sum of individuals, yet social facts arise out of the joint activity of individuals. Society emerges from individuals in interaction, yet social structure then becomes autonomous and external to individuals and exerts causal power over those individuals ([1893] 1984). Contemporary interpreters of Durkheim have typically read these as unresolvable contradictions or as unfortunate ambiguities, requiring either a dismissal of Durkheim's theory or a radical reworking (e.g., J. C. Alexander 1982; Giddens 1977; Lukes 1973).

These apparent dilemmas can be resolved by interpreting Durkheim as an emergence theorist. Durkheim's theory of emergence is presented most explicitly in the *Rules* and in the essay "Individual and Collective Representations," and its empirical demonstration is the explicit purpose of *Suicide*. He presented his work in terms of emergence throughout his career, from the beginning, where *Division of Labor* presents an emergence theory of morality and of the individual, to *Elementary Forms*, which uses the theory of social emergence to develop a sociologically based epistemology.[1]

The concept of social emergence did not originate with Durkheim but rather was an active current in nineteenth-century French thought. From Renouvier, Durkheim borrowed the axiom that the whole is greater than the sum of its parts; from Boutroux, the idea that each level of analysis is irreducible to the lower levels because of the "contingency" of natural laws (Boutroux [1874] 1916; Durkheim [1907] 1982, 259; 1909–1912, 326). Durkheim was also influenced by an early year spent in Germany, where organicism was dominant; this experience cautioned Durkheim to avoid the metaphysical assumptions and the excessive biological analogies of organicism (see Giddens 1970). Perhaps more than any other source, Durkheim was influenced by Comte's antireductionism. Comte also struggled with social emergence and is misunderstood on this point as often as Durkheim.[2]

Durkheim's theory of emergence contains several components, including most of his key theoretical concepts: social facts, collective representations, social currents, dynamic density, social milieu, social substratum, and *sui generis*. Durkheim never used the term "emergence"; rather, his phrase "*sui generis*" was used in a sense synonymous with contemporary uses of the term "emergent." Following common usage in the nineteenth century, Durkheim also used the terms "synthesis" and "association" when referring to emergent systemic phenomena that resulted from nonadditive combinations of elements.[3] To demonstrate

---

[1] See Rawls's (1996) argument that *Elementary Forms* presents a sociological epistemology. Her interpretation is compatible with my presentation here, although she does not draw on the concept of emergence. The emergence basis of Durkheim's epistemology is stated most explicitly in the introductory and concluding chapters of *Elementary Forms*.

[2] See the discussion of Comte in Chapter 3. Durkheim himself may have been confused by these ambiguities. In the *Rules*, Durkheim read Comte as a reductionist ([1895] 1964, 99), even though one of his professors, Émile Boutroux, thought Comte was a nonreductionist (Boutroux [1893] 1914, 193); by 1903, Durkheim had decided that Comte was not a reductionist ([1903] 1982, 178; [1907] 1982, 259).

[3] Note Durkheim's ([1900] 1960) critique of Simmel's concept of "association," which demonstrates that Durkheim's usage of this term is emergentist.

his concepts of synthesis and association, Durkheim ([1897] 1951) drew analogies with chemistry:

There is nothing more in animate nature than inorganic matter, since the cell is made exclusively of inanimate atoms. To be sure, it is likewise true that society has no other active forces than individuals. . . . Of course the elementary qualities of which the social fact consists are present in germ in individual minds. But the social fact emerges from them only when they have been transformed by association since it is only then that it appears. Association itself is also an active factor productive of special effects. In itself it is therefore something new. (p. 310)

Both *social facts* and *collective representations* are emergent social phenomena. Both are *sui generis* properties of a social system, emerging from the association of individuals.[4] Durkheim famously defined the social fact to be both *external* and *causal*. His central claim was that sociology could not be an independent science unless its objects of study could be shown to have causal powers: "All that [sociology] asks is that the principle of causality be applied to social phenomena" ([1895] 1964, 141). This is the same position that several contemporary philosophers of mind have come to: that "mind" is a meaningless construct and psychology an unnecessary discipline unless there can be "mind-brain" downward causation (Chapter 4).

In fact, in "Individual and Collective Representations," Durkheim anticipated the key elements of contemporary philosophical arguments that intelligence and consciousness can be analyzed as emergent from the interactions of the neurons of the brain. Durkheim ([1898] 1953) noted that "[Individual minds] are compounds" (p. 320) and that "Not without reason has it been said that the self is itself a society" (p. 111). He noted that mental emergents are caused by neuronal activity and that they also exert downward causation on those neurons: "They are caused, but they are in their turn causes" (p. 4). Otherwise, "Ideas have no power" (p. 10). Reductionist analysis is inappropriate because the combining elements are changed by their association (p. 11). Durkheim's argument here is analogous to nonreductionist theory in contemporary philosophy of mind, which holds that mental phenomena are emergent from neuronal interaction yet are not epiphenomenal, in that they can be said to be causal antecedents.

Durkheim, of course, was interested in the emergence of mind only indirectly: as a way to argue by analogy that an emergentist theory of sociology was just as scientific as psychology. Durkheim realized that

---

[4] The preface to the second edition of *Rules*, first published in 1901, makes clear that collective representations are social facts; the essence of both concepts is their *sui generis* nature (see also [1912] 1915, 263–4).

analogous threats of reductionism faced both sociology and psychology; he argued that if psychological phenomena exist, then so must social phenomena:

Each mental condition is, as regards the neural cells, in the same condition of relative independence as social phenomena are in relation to individual peo- ple. . . . Those, then, who accuse us of leaving social life in the air because we refuse to reduce it to the individual mind have not, perhaps, recognized all the consequences of their objection. If it were justified it would apply just as well to the relations between mind and brain. ([1898] 1953, 28)[5]

The central theme of the essay is based on this emergence argument. Just as individual representations have no necessary link to the science of the neuron, collective representations have no necessary link to the sci- ence of the individual. Thus, "there is between psychology and sociology the same break in continuity as between biology and the physiochemical sciences" ([1895] 1964, 104). Collective representations are of a quali- tatively different nature than individual representations because they are emergent social facts. In opposition to this emergentist reading, some crit- ics argue that Durkheim used Renouvier's term "representation" because he intended the concept to have a psychologistic connotation (e.g., Jones 1995, 30–3; Schmaus 1999; Turner 1995). For example, Schmaus (1999) wrote that "Durkheim originally conceived collective representations as a type of mental entity shared by the members of a society" (p. S315). Such readings are hard to maintain in light of Durkheim's 1898 essay (as was also argued by Némedi 1995, 48–50).

Like today's complexity and systems theorists, Durkheim realized that his emergence argument required him to focus on networks of people and their interactions: "*The first origins of all social processes of any importance should be sought in the internal constitution of the social group*" ([1895] 1964, 113, original italics). Durkheim referred to this "internal constitution" using the terms "social milieu" and "social substratum," with the latter term replacing "milieu" in *Suicide* and thereafter.[6] In *Rules*, Durkheim defined the milieu as an emergent system: It is characterized by its *size*, or the "number of social units," and its *dynamic density*, or "degree of concentration" – the number of individuals who have "social relations" ([1895] 1964, 114). Although the milieu includes only physical things

---

[5] Compare this passage to the following by Simmel (1950): "It is perfectly arbitrary to stop the reduction, which leads to ultimate real elements, at the individual. For this reduction is interminable" (p. 7).

[6] Durkheim also used the term "substratum" to describe, by analogy, emergence at other levels of analysis: thus, his discussions of psychic and physiological substrata. For a similar take on "substratum," see Némedi 1995, 45–6.

and persons, neither can be seen as the causal origin of change; rather, "as an active factor, then, the human milieu itself remains." The source of system change lies in properties of the network connections among the units of the system itself. Durkheim defined the substratum in the same terms as the milieu; the substratum was defined by the size and space of the land occupied, the number and density of the population, "secondary groupings" such as population centers, and technologies influencing the density of connections such as roads, walls, and architecture ([1900] 1960, 360–1).

The concepts of material density and dynamic density are structuralist notions and serve the same theoretical function within a theory of emergence. Both notions foreshadow the emphasis on density of connections in today's social simulations.[7] As dynamic density increases, the conditions for emergence also increase: "[Social life] is thus the more intense the more the reactions exchanged between its component units are themselves more frequent and energetic" ([1893] 1984, 277). But this frequency and energy cannot originate from within individuals because they are themselves a product of society. Instead, it depends on the "number of individuals who have entered into relationships, and . . . the volume and density of society" (Durkheim [1893] 1984, 278).

Durkheim realized that not all social systems manifest the same degree of emergence: "Social facts lend themselves more readily to objective representation in proportion as their separation from the individual facts expressing them is more complete" ([1895] 1964, 44). In his definition of the social milieu – the substratum of society – Durkheim identified the same variables currently considered to contribute to emergence: The social milieu manifests emergence to the extent that it has a sufficient number of units and a sufficient density of interconnections. Similarly, today's connectionists and artificial life researchers hold that emergence is likely to be found in systems with two characteristics: large numbers of components interacting and a complex communication system among the components (see Chapter 5).

---

[7] In *Division of Labor* Durkheim's emergence argument was based on material density, whereas in *Rules* he elaborated this notion into the theoretically more powerful concept of dynamic density. Durkheim felt that his shift in terminology was a rather minor adjustment, and this claim is not problematic from the perspective of emergence theory, which requires a focus on the density of connections (as in both Alife and multi-agent systems models), not only on the geographic proximity of agents. Some critics have interpreted his shift from material density to dynamic density as a substantive theoretical shift, but such interpretations result from the imposition of a voluntaristic action perspective onto Durkheim, as I discuss below. For example, Jeffrey C. Alexander (1982, p. 220) misinterpreted the concept of dynamic density, reading it as "a moral and emotional fact," and claimed that it was evidence of a shift toward idealism.

The exploration of which systems will manifest emergence has been a central concern of contemporary complexity theory (Bechtel and Richardson 1993; Sawyer 1999, 2004a). For example, Bechtel and Richardson (1993) argued that emergent systems do not demonstrate many of the characteristics of reducible systems: direct localization, near decomposability, functional and physical independence of units, and linearity. In contemporary terms, social systems with a high dynamic density are less likely to be decomposable or localizable. Like today's connectionists, Durkheim argued that mental phenomena do not display direct localization nor near decomposability: "If we concede that ideas can be decomposed into parts, we should have to admit further that to each of the parts corresponds a particular neural element. . . . Such a geography of the brain belongs to the world of the novelette rather than to that of science" ([1898] 1953, 12).

Reading Durkheim as an emergence theorist clarifies an ambiguity in Durkheim's concept of the individual. His emergence arguments seem to posit a utilitarian conception of the individual (associated with Spencer) that he has already rejected ([1893] 1984, 286); yet he argued that the individual is constituted by society.[8] Although some scholars (e.g., Giddens and Alexander) view this as a contradiction, this dialectic is found in all complex systems with emergence and downward causation. For example, mental phenomena emerge from neuronal interaction, yet via mental causation neurons can be affected by mental phenomena. The causal power of mental phenomena does not require a "theory of the neuron"; rather, it is theorized in what sociologists would consider to be essentially structural terms – in terms of the networks of connections, the density of the network, and the nature of the communication among neurons.

In sum, Durkheim, *avant la lettre*, outlined a theory of complex systems, one that he believed applied not only to the social level but also to the chemical, biological, and mental levels. Only through the recognition of this fact can his many analogies with these other sciences be substantively understood.

Critiques of Durkheim's theory of emergence

Many Durkheim interpreters who have commented on his theory of emergence do so only to dismiss it. I will briefly comment on the interpretations of Parsons, Giddens, Lukes, and Alexander.

---

[8] This opposition is subtly different from the "homo duplex" issue also noted by Durkheim: the opposition between man's physical and social/moral aspects (Durkheim [1914] 1960).

Parsons ([1937] 1949, 354) was disturbed by Durkheim's many analogies to nonsocial realms (ants, chemicals) because these analogies imply that what Parsons thought was important – subjective action – is not important. Whenever Durkheim's theory failed to correspond to Parsons' voluntaristic theory, Parsons selectively (mis)read Durkheim, and this is why he misunderstood Durkheim's focus on emergence.

Parsons homed in on the emergence problem: Social reality is only found in the individual representations of it (p. 361). All we can examine is the individual's representation of it, not the thing itself; otherwise it would be "a metaphysical assumption with no scientific justification." What Parsons intended to do was to reject the positivistic introduction of "a foreign element," namely, social facts, and instead pursue this implication of Durkheim's, that what's really critical is the individual's representations of society (p. 362). Parsons took the usual interpretivist path, rejecting the "emergence" Durkheim and arguing that social reality is really nothing other than the individual's subjective representations of it.

But in his own conclusion (p. 737) he made the same move that he criticized Durkheim for: He argued that we must treat a unit act as a scientific unit as long as we can conceive of it existing from the other parts (of that system). "Action systems have properties that are emergent only on a certain level of complexity in the relations of unit acts to each other" (p. 739). How to determine which properties are emergent? Parsons appealed to methodological observation; if we find that the different levels vary in value independently of one another, then it can be scientific to analyze the higher level. He stated unequivocally that the emergent is just as real as the elementary; to claim priority for the elementary he called "metaphysical atomism." "There is no mysticism whatever about this concept of emergence. It is simply a designation for certain features of the observable facts" (p. 749). Parsons wrote his sections on Durkheim first (1970, 875n8); this perhaps explains why he didn't notice that he had contradicted himself when he made a very similar emergence argument in his own Conclusion, which must have been written many years later.

Parsons misquoted Durkheim as saying that society consists only of "ideas and sentiments" (p. 442). Durkheim's theory is more complex, for it claims that individuals and society require each other: "[S]ociety cannot do without individuals any more than these can do without society" ([1912] 1915, 389). The problem here is a more general misreading by Parsons; he failed to see the implications of Durkheim's emergence argument, instead believing that the way to resolve the apparent contradiction in Durkheim was to focus on individuals' subjective representations of society. He then attributed that belief to Durkheim, making it appear that Durkheim participated in his "theoretical convergence."

Although Giddens represents a radically different sociological perspective than Parsons, he also dismissed Durkheim's emergence argument in a few brief pages (1984, 169–74), saying that the *Rules* "is the weakest of Durkheim's major works" (1977, 292). Giddens's dismissal of Durkheim's theory of emergence was based on his claim that Durkheim alternated between two incompatible conceptions of the individual. He argued that Durkheim's notion of emergence was based on an assumption that human actors exist in separation from one another and then come together "*ex nihilo* to form a new entity by their fusion or association," just as hydrogen and oxygen molecules come together to form water (1984, 171). Giddens argued that the analogy with chemical emergence "only works for those very types of perspective Durkheim set out to criticize, such as utilitarian individualism. If individuals, as fully formed social beings, came together to create new social properties by the fact of their association, as in contract theories of society, the analogy might hold; to support Durkheim's case, it does not" (1979b, 51).

However, the theory of emergence does not require a Spencerian notion of the presocial individual; Durkheim's emergence theory was meant to apply regardless of one's conception of the individual. These apparent ambiguities in Durkheim's concept of the individual do not substantively impact his emergence argument. Of course, Giddens was committed to an interpretivist view of individual agency in sociological theory, one that prevented him from considering any sociological theory that did not take individual subjectivity into account and that equally prevented him from granting any independent status to social structure. As Cohen wrote in his overview of structuration theory, a practice orientation "entails dispensing with all arguments for the emergence of social patterns . . . *the routine repetitions of institutionalized modes of interaction between agents is not something apart from the patterns they form*" (1989, 76–7, original italics; also see Chapters 7 and 10).

Within Giddens's structuration theory, Durkheim's two concepts of the individual represent a substantive ambiguity, but within Durkheim's own emergence theory, there is no substantive issue, because the individual's subjectivity is not relevant to the emergence argument. Durkheim acknowledged the importance of studying how individuals internalize social facts – in this, he granted more to individualism than today's structural sociologists. Nonetheless, the emergent social fact is independent of any individual's internalization of it or subjective orientation toward it. Note again that the nonreductive materialist argument holds regardless of one's model of the neuron.

In another critique of Durkheim, Lukes – who, instead of the term "emergence," used Durkheim's term "*sui generis*" – was dismissive of Durkheim's argument and, like Giddens, addressed this aspect of Durkheim only in isolated passages. Lukes correctly noted that the dichotomy between the social and the individual was "the keystone of Durkheim's entire system of thought" (1973, 22), but his dismissal of the emergence argument led him to underestimate the overall coherence of Durkheim's project and, again like Giddens, to perceive ambiguities that were not substantive for Durkheim (pp. 20–1). Regarding the possibility of a *sui generis* sociology, Lukes referred to Durkheim's "shaky argument" by analogy with mental phenomena (p. 233) and called Durkheim's writings on the point "indecisive," "highly ambiguous" (p. 228), and "conceptually confused" (p. 20), concluding that the project was misconceived and "must remain frustrated" (1982, 23). Lukes believed that Durkheim's analogies with chemical and mental phenomena were not drawn for substantive theoretical reasons but rather from a misguided desire to seem more scientific. But emergence theory makes clear that these were substantive analogies; in fact, recent philosophy of biology has also drawn on the concept of emergence in developing the now mainstream position of *physicalist antireductionism* (Bechtel and Richardson 1993; Hoyningen-Huene and Wuketits 1989; Rosenberg 1997).

Jeffrey C. Alexander, in volume 2 of his *Theoretical Logic in Sociology* (1982), failed to mention emergence or *sui generis*, and this neglect led him to misunderstand Durkheim's theory of the social fact. Alexander, like Giddens, noted an ambiguity in Durkheim's concept of the individual. Is it the utilitarian atomism of Spencer? Alexander attributed this perspective to the early Durkheim. Is it a voluntaristic notion, as in Parsons's ([1937] 1949) seminal reading? Alexander read the Durkheim of the *Rules* as indicative of a shift to a voluntaristic action theory of the individual and as advocating that social facts are subjective and internal (1982, 217, 464n35). When Durkheim described the emergence substrate of social facts as "religious denominations, political, literary, and occupational associations," Alexander interpreted these terms to refer to subjective individual factors, when in an emergence account these terms have a classically structuralist meaning; they refer to properties that affect the dynamic density of the social milieu. Similarly, he cited Durkheim's use of the term "collective sentiment" in support of his voluntarist reading; yet in an emergence account, this term refers to a uniquely structural and nonindividualist fact (e.g., "[I]f each individual consciousness echoes the collective sentiment, it is by virtue of the special energy resident in its collective origin," Durkheim [1895] 1964, 9). Among Durkheim scholars, Alexander proposed one of the most individualistic readings of Durkheim's *Rules*, saying that "[t]he critical point is that each of these examples of structure... is subjectively formed... from the stuff of human emotions" (1982, 218–9). However, the language of "emotions" that Alexander quoted are intended by Durkheim to refer to properties of collectives and not to properties of individuals.[9]

Durkheim frequently used the apparently psychologistic terminology of emotions, sentiments, and ideas to refer to social facts. These psychologistic terms have often led readers to assume that Durkheim was making psychological claims when in fact he was describing strictly social facts. As I argued above, many scholars have made the same mistake regarding Durkheim's extension of Renouvier's term "representation" to refer to both collective and individual phenomena. Durkheim was fairly explicit on this point through *Elementary Forms*: "This synthesis [*sui generis* emergence] has the effect of disengaging a whole world of sentiments, ideas, and images which, once born, obey laws all their own... these combinations are not commanded and necessitated by the condition of the underlying reality [individual consciousnesses]" ([1912] 1915, 471).

In a theory of social emergence, one can logically speak of the emotions, sentiments, and ideas of a collective without implying anything about the participating individuals. It would have been less ambiguous had Durkheim coined completely new terms to refer to the emergent properties of collectives, but this was not his choice. The terms he did use perhaps makes it easier for those with a voluntarist orientation to misinterpret Durkheim's emergence argument, reading into Durkheim ambiguities that are issues within a voluntarist theory of action but not within a theory of emergence.

Resolving Durkheim's dilemma

I have argued that emergence processes are central to Durkheim's empirical and theoretical projects and that sociologists have neglected this aspect of Durkheim's work. As we saw in Chapter 5, several contemporary sociological theories have appealed to the concept of emergence in arguing for the independence of a social level of analysis, including the structuralism of Blau (1981), the morphogenetic dualism of Archer (1982, 1995),

---

[9] Alexander was aware of competing interpretations; see the two-page extended footnote (1982, 469–70n82). Yet here his dismissals of structuralist readings of Durkheim are directed not at emergence interpretations but at materialist readings of Durkheim that compare him to Marx.

the social realism of Bhaskar (1979), and the Marxian concept of social structure proposed by Porpora (1993). These theorists used emergence to accomplish the same theoretical function as Durkheim's concept of *sui generis*: to explain how a social level of analysis could result from individual actions and yet take on a seemingly independent existence. In the following sections, I show how Durkheim's writings on emergence can contribute to this line of contemporary sociological theory.

How do social facts have causal powers independent of individual agency?

Causation is a major theme in Durkheimian scholarship, from concern with the implementation mechanisms whereby collective representations constrain individuals to concern with the epistemological underpinnings of Durkheim's statistical method (e.g., Némedi 1995; Porter 1995; Schmaus 1994; Turner 1986, 1996). The emergentist reading provides a new perspective on Durkheim's concept of causation. Many sociologists believe that Durkheim presented a mechanistic and deterministic sociology. Indeed, in the *Rules* Durkheim described the causal force of social facts primarily in coercive terms. After the publication of *Rules*, several critics attacked this notion of coercion, including an unfortunate misreading by Tarde, who interpreted coercion strictly in terms of explicit power relations.[10]

In response to criticisms of the *Rules*, Durkheim further clarified his meaning of "constraint" ([1897] 1951, 307–20; [1901] 1964, liii–lvi). Yet in spite of his repeated attempts at clarification, Durkheim is still criticized for providing ambiguous senses of coercion (Giddens 1977, 280–2; Lukes 1973, 20–2; cf. Rawls 1996, 471n23). Giddens argued that Durkheim's notion of social fact conflates two types of constraint: factual constraints deriving from the material world and moral obligations (1977, 280–2). Because Giddens's theory is based on subjectivist elements, these two forms of constraint seem radically distinct, yet Durkheim always maintained that this distinction was superficial because all forms of constraint share the key property that they derive from emergent collective phenomena. In the *Rules*, for example, Durkheim distinguished between the coercive force of the social fact and the individual's psychological

---

[10] Tarde read Durkheim to be implying that an explicit coercive relationship – like the relationship of a battle's victor to the vanquished – is highly social, whereas the spontaneous conversion of a people to a new religion is not social because it is not coercive. Tarde found this to be ridiculous: "The error is so palpable that we must wonder how it could arise and take root in a mind of such intelligence" (1969, 118). Of course, this was never Durkheim's concept of coercion.

internalization of it: "Inhibition is, if you like, the means by which social constraint produces its psychological effects; it is not identical with this constraint" ([1895] 1964, 102). Giddens's perceived ambiguities only appear if one attempts to read Durkheim through the eyes of an individualist.[11]

Although he used the terminology of coercion, Durkheim realized that social constraint occurred within a dialectic between downward causation and emergence processes. Within an elaborated emergence theory, Durkheim's concept of constraint can be reformulated as downward causation, a form of constraint that is simultaneously undergoing processes of emergence. In this sense, social facts constrain individuals but at the same time emerge from the actions and interactions of those very same individuals. Even in the 1912 book *Elementary Forms*, Durkheim remained focused on this dialectic: "Social life, just like the ritual, moves in a circle. . . . On the one hand, the individual gets from society the best part of himself. . . . But, on the other hand, society exists and lives only in and through individuals. . . . [S]ociety . . . cannot do without individuals any more than these can do without society" ([1912] 1915, 389).

As Durkheim observed in 1898, arguments for mental causation in the philosophy of mind can be used to develop an account of social causation that does not require a theory of the individual, subjectivity, or agency (see Chapter 5). Emergent social structure may constrain individuals, apart from any consideration of the subjective states of actors, even though that structure emerges from those very same individuals.

Social dynamics as emergence processes

Durkheim's social dynamics was an emergentist version; this becomes clear in his critique of prior social theories of historical stages. Comte, Spencer, and Marx attributed the onset of each new stage to causal factors in the prior stage. In response, Durkheim argued that causality cannot proceed directly from one historical stage to the next: "It is impossible to conceive how the stage which a civilization has reached at a given moment could be the determining cause of the subsequent stage" ([1895] 1964, 117). Causation does not work from the past to the present; it must be between two co-occurring factors. Thus, Durkheim argued that sociology must explain contemporary social facts by reference to "concomitant circumstances." Drawing on his emergence insight, Durkheim proposed that new stages emerge from lower-level, simultaneous factors: the *social*

---

[11] Turner (1986) made this same point regarding the criticisms of Lukes and Giddens (pp. 126–7).

milieu. Durkheim held that the social milieu was the "determining factor of collective evolution" and argued that without incorporating such factors "sociology cannot establish any relations of causality" ([1895] 1964, 116). In the Conclusion of *Rules*, Durkheim again emphasized that sociological explanation must proceed from social milieu to social phenomena: "We have shown that a social fact can be explained only by another social fact; and, at the same time, we have shown how this sort of explanation is possible by pointing out, in the internal social milieu, the principal factor in collective evolution" ([1895] 1964, 145).[12]

This emphasis on emergence from the social milieu – or what he later called the social substratum – remained central to Durkheim's method for the rest of his career (cf. Turner 1986, 142–3). However, Durkheim never developed this perspective into a full-fledged processual-dynamic view of social emergence. He reasoned that many social facts were stable structures – institutions like law and government – that had emerged long ago; consequently, the processes of their emergence could not be directly studied. Thus Durkheim's empirical studies, in both *Suicide* and *Elementary Forms*, took as a given the social structures that had emerged and focused on their reproduction and their causal powers over individuals.

This was Durkheim's concern with the "problem of order": how social structures, once emerged, were reproduced and maintained over time. Because of this focus on the reproduction of social order rather than change, conflict, or transformation, Durkheim is often considered to have focused on social statics to the neglect of social dynamics. However, Durkheim's thinking on the problem of order was fundamentally grounded in his emergence theory of structural etiology. Many interpreters have been misled by Durkheim's focus on reproduction – reading him as locating the source of order in individual internalizations of social facts, following Parsons's voluntarist reading and the general individualism of American sociology. If one's theory of reproduction is grounded in a theory of structural emergence, then that theory does not necessarily require a theory of individual agency, as suggested both by analogy with the philosophy of mind and by the existence of computer simulations of society in which macro-social order emerges and then is maintained over time via the same emergence processes.

---

[12] Durkheim did not deny the possibility of history, but he argued that history as science would be indistinguishable from sociology because it would incorporate analysis of the concomitant substratum factors that give rise to social facts. This is what underlay Durkheim's claim that there could not be historical causal laws (see [1898–1899] 1960, 345–8).

For Durkheim, emergence processes were central not only to the origin of social structure but also to its continued maintenance and reproduction. The role of emergence processes in reproduction has been quite confused in contemporary sociological theory. In her seminal 1982 critique of structuration theory, Archer criticized structuration theory for conflating two types of mechanisms and calling both of them "reproduction": the stable replication of existing social order and the genesis of new social forms (p. 479). In this case, structuration theory has the more Durkheimian insight: both mechanisms involve a dialectic between emergence processes and downward causation.

If Durkheim had retained his earlier focus on the processes whereby social structure emerges from the individual level, it would have complemented his empirical focus on the downward causation of the social structure, and this combined theory could better account for dynamics such as change and conflict over time. It remains unclear how Durkheim would have developed a more sophisticated emergence approach to social dynamics.[13] One can hardly fault Durkheim for failing to resolve this complex and challenging issue, for it remains unresolved.

Emergence in microinteraction

The theory of emergence helps us to understand two Durkheimian concepts that have been widely misunderstood: the notions of *social currents* and *crystallization*.[14] Social currents are social facts that are not yet crystallized. "All sorts of currents come, go, circulate everywhere, cross and mingle in a thousand different ways, and just because they are constantly mobile are never crystallized in an objective form" ([1897] 1951, 315). Durkheim's examples of social currents include joyous confidence, individualism, philanthropy, and cosmopolitanism. "But because this part of collective life has not enough consistency to become fixed, it none the less has the same character as [material social facts]. *It is external to each average individual taken singly*" (p. 316, original italics). Durkheim felt that social currents were not qualitatively different from fixed, objective social

---

[13] Turner (1986, p. 160) also noted that Durkheim never successfully identified laws of this type, apart from *Suicide*.

[14] For example, Lukes wrote that *Suicide* is not about social currents, even though Durkheim presented it in these terms (Lukes 1973, p. 36); Lukes dismissed terms like "current" and "crystallization" as "distinctly inappropriate analogical language" (p. 215). In his Introduction to the 1982 translation of *Rules*, Lukes suggested that the term crystallization be replaced with "institutionalization" (Lukes 1982, p. 5), and "social current" is translated as "social force" (e.g., p. 82). My interpretation in this chapter should make it clear why I use the 1938 translation by Solovay and Mueller.

facts, such as types of architecture, communication and transportation networks, and technology (e.g., [1895] 1964, 12, 45).

An example from linguistic anthropology is instructive. Certain ways of talking and the speech styles of a people constitute a social current. Over time, a stable oral tradition may emerge from such linguistic behavior, resulting in performance texts that have a high degree of stability even though they are never written down. These oral traditions are crystallized social currents. When such a performance takes on an objective material form – for example, by being transcribed into a ritual text or by becoming designed into the architecture of a ritual space – Durkheim called it a *materialized* social fact. Durkheim argued that the nature of the crystallized social fact is the same whether or not it is materialized; thus, whether or not such an emergent performance text is ever written down is not relevant to the sociologist ([1897] 1951, 313–16).

Regardless of the validity of this theoretical claim, Durkheim believed that the only scientific methodology available to sociology was to study materialized social facts. Ultimately, sociology would also be a science of social currents, but Durkheim could not conceive of a scientific methodology that would allow their study. Thus Durkheim never extended his methodology to micro-sociological processes. However, because social currents are not qualitatively different from crystallized social facts, the study of the latter can indirectly provide us with an understanding of the former:

Social life consists, then, of free currents perpetually in the process of transformation and incapable of being mentally fixed by the observer, and the scholar cannot approach the study of social reality from this angle. But [a current can crystallize] without ceasing to be itself. . . . Since, on the other hand, these practices are merely social life consolidated, it is legitimate . . . to study the latter through the former. ([1895] 1964, 45)

Given that one of Durkheim's theoretical goals was to study emergence processes – how interactions among individuals within the substratum (or social milieu) give rise to social currents – the only way to study these directly would be to closely study symbolic interaction. This study requires technological devices that were not available to Durkheim – the technology to record social interaction, including audio and video recording devices. Unlike in Durkheim's time, video and audio recordings now allow us to study the emergence of social currents from symbolic interaction in the social milieu. The microprocesses of emergence can be studied with contemporary micro-sociological methods, including those of ethnomethodology, conversation analysis, and symbolic interactionism (I advocate their use in Chapter 10).

Communication among individuals has changed dramatically with new media technologies, including radio, television, and, more recently, the Internet. The mass media play a significant role in the formation, maintenance, and documentation of social currents. Through the mass media, large-scale social currents – communication among individuals in the social milieu – leave traces that can be directly analyzed. The emergence and maintenance of these social currents could be studied using methods from communication research and cultural studies.

It is unclear why Durkheim maintained that social currents did not change substantively once they were crystallized. He provided neither theoretical argument nor empirical evidence in support of this claim. There may be qualitative differences in emergence and downward causation involving social currents, crystallized currents, and materialized currents. To develop a complete theory of emergence, we need to extend Durkheim by theorizing how emergence leads to both intersubjectively shared social emergents (social currents) and objective, material social emergents; this is the task I begin in Chapter 10.

Durkheim hinted at the need for the close study of symbolic interactional processes in *Elementary Forms* in his discussions of "collective effervescence" (e.g., [1912] 1915, 250–60). Durkheim stated that the "religious idea" is born out of participation in ritual activities. In these events, "the collective life has been able to attain its greatest intensity and efficacy" (p. 251). Durkheim suggested that these events result in a "pseudo-delirium" that especially contributes to the creation of collective representations (p. 260). New ideas and new gods emerge during periods of "creative effervescence" (p. 475), and rituals are a way of reliving these emergence events. To identify what makes these interactional performance events particularly social requires a theory of symbolic interactional processes.[15]

Social ontology

Despite his explicit denials, Durkheim has often been read to be proposing that society is a distinct ontological entity. In the *Rules*, Durkheim perhaps went further than necessary in claiming an existence for social facts.[16] After the 1895 publication of *Rules*, Durkheim was widely

---

[15] Rawls (1996, 477–8) also argued that Durkheim perceived symbolic interaction to be central to his broader theory. Compare Stone and Farberman 1967.

[16] In part, this was to distinguish his argument from Comte's position, which was an epistemological argument for the necessity of sociology rather than an ontological one. Although Comte famously wrote, "A society therefore can no more be decomposed into individuals, than a geometric surface can be resolved into lines, or a line into points"

attacked for seeming to hypostatize structure; Tarde perceived this as his weakest point and called it Durkheim's "ontological illusion" (1969, 115). In response to these criticisms, Durkheim backed down from his initial statements (e.g., in the Preface to the second edition of *Rules*).

Downward causation, Durkheim realized, is an essential property of society if sociology is to avoid reduction to psychology. However, many emergents do not have causal effects; they are only epiphenomenal. The V-shape of the bird flock does not exert any downward causation on the birds; they are aware only of the local interactions with other birds. This was Tarde's attack: How can an emergent exert downward causal force if it is merely epiphenomenal? In response to Tarde's attacks, Durkheim clarified his position; he did not think that societies existed apart from individuals. "There is nothing substantival or ontological about this substratum [all the individual consciences in union and combination], since it is merely a whole composed of parts" ([1897] 1951, 319). Yet throughout his career Durkheim maintained that social facts have causal powers over individuals. In *Elementary Forms*, he argued that "the collective consciousness acts upon individual consciousness" ([1912] 1915, 254) and that society contains "forces outside of and superior to the individual" (p. 257).

Durkheim never completely resolved how society could have causal powers over the individual, and this led him to continue to make ambiguous statements about the existence of the social. Again in *Elementary Forms*, there are passages that seem to hypostatize the social ("[S]ociety is not made up merely of the mass of individuals who compose it . . . but above all is the idea which it forms of itself," p. 470) and passages that deny the social exists apart from individuals ("The collective force is not entirely outside of us . . . since society cannot exist except in and through individual consciousnesses," p. 240). Although he maintained that social structure did not actually exist apart from the composing individuals, he never explained how structure could have causal powers; thus the common criticism that Durkheim reified or hypostatized structure and the concern among Durkheim scholars with social causation.

The argument for nonreductive individualism presented in Chapter 5 shows that even if social facts are supervenient on individuals and their interactions, one could nonetheless argue against the possibility of reduction of social laws, concepts, and theories to individual laws, concepts, and theories. Yet ultimately this irreducibility has to be empirically

([1854] 1966, 153), he also believed that "the day may come" when sociology could be reduced to biology, and when it was, "biology will be seen to afford the starting-point of all social speculation" ([1842] 1854, vol. 2, 81, 112).

demonstrated for each candidate social fact. There are points at which Durkheim seems to acknowledge that science might eventually be capable of a reductionist explanation of some social facts: "If this exteriority should prove to be only apparent, the advance of science will bring the disillusionment and we shall see our conception of social phenomena change" ([1895] 1964, 28).

Durkheim's arguments for social emergence were incomplete, and he left himself open to the charge of proposing a dualist social ontology. Today's collectivist emergentists are struggling with the same issue, with many arguing for the complete irrelevance of any science of the individual level (e.g., Mayhew 1980) and likewise being accused of hypostatizing social structure (see Chapter 5).

A theory of social emergence does not have to argue for a dualistic ontology to make the argument for structural sociology and against individualism. Archer (1982, 458) took an epistemologically nonreductionist position in proposing that sociologists must accept an "analytical dualism" when considering both structure and action. Nonreductive materialism is materialistically monist, yet its advocates argue that psychological terms, laws, and concepts may never be reducible to the terms, laws, and concepts of neurobiology. Similarly, Durkheim argued that although only individuals exist, the science of society may, of necessity, always be independent of the terms, laws, and concepts of the sciences of the individual.

Integrating the individual and social structure

Unlike Marx, Durkheim did not think that sociology would make psychology obsolete. Durkheim even suggested that psychological study would be helpful for a budding sociologist ([1895] 1964, 111). But although Durkheim did not deny a place for psychology, he repeatedly argued that there could be no systematic relationships between phenomena at the two levels. Many of Durkheim's critics have regarded this as his major theoretical failing (e.g., Lukes 1973, 228). These critics argue that Durkheim's lack of concern for the individual led him to alternate between two conceptions of the individual: a utilitarian, instrumentalist conception that is borrowed from Spencer and a more idealistic, voluntaristic, subjectivist conception (J. C. Alexander 1982, 220; Giddens 1977, 283–9; Parsons [1937] 1949, 367–8). In *Division of Labor*, Durkheim criticized Spencer, arguing that the individual himself was created by society, and thus Spencer's utilitarian atomism could not be correct: It could not be the case that presocial individuals came together and created society ([1893] 1984, 286). His main theoretical claim in *Division of Labor* was that the individual was a product of social organization, not a cause of it (e.g., p. 277). The onset of the division of labor and the resulting organic solidarity require a transformation of the individual (p. 284). Society was created – through emergence processes that Durkheim largely attributed to the structural properties of the social milieu, its size and dynamic density – and then it created the individual. Many interpreters of Durkheim have argued that his rejection of Spencerian atomism implies a subjective, voluntaristic agent.

Durkheim acknowledged that emergence requires individuals. He frequently commented on the dual nature of man, most explicitly in 1914: "It is, therefore, quite true that we are made up of two parts. . . . the one purely individual and . . . the other social" ([1914] 1960, 337). However, Durkheim did not resolve the dialectic between social structure and the newly emergent, modern individuals; this dialectic requires that the theory of emergence become a dialectic theory that explains the emergence of social from presocial individuals, downward causation (or "constraint") from the social to the individual, and how the emergence of social individuals results in modified emergence processes. Although Durkheim acknowledged in several passages that this dialectic occurs ([1893] 1984, 285, 287, 288n16), he never fully developed a theory of it, perhaps out of fear of yielding too much to psychological reductionists such as Tarde. Thus there is continuing debate among Durkheim scholars concerning the role of intentional states of individuals and their internalizations of social facts and collective representations.

This dialectic – of the emergence of the social order, downward causation to individuals, and the continued reproductive emergence of order – is extremely complex, and a complete analysis of these historical processes is a difficult task. Durkheim completed portions of this analysis in all of his empirical works. In his first work, *Division of Labor*, Durkheim first identified the emergence processes that gave rise to social differentiation – the material density of the society – and then explored the processes of downward causation whereby that social differentiation created the modern "cult of the individual." Similarly, in his last work, *Elementary Forms*, Durkheim proposed an epistemology that explained the origin of Kantian categories in the social structure. The primary empirical focus of this work was to delineate the processes of downward causation: how religion, and the very categories of thought, were caused by different social structures. "[The categories] should depend upon the way in which [the group] is founded and organized, upon its morphology" ([1912] 1915, 28). To empirically demonstrate this, Durkheim conducted a comparative study that showed how different social organizations are regularly correlated with different religious forms. The missing component of this last study was the documentation of emergence processes themselves: How did the different social structures originate? Durkheim implicitly assumed the emergence theory of the *Division of Labor.* The social structure emerges from the dynamic density of the social milieu. For example, in his Conclusion, Durkheim proposed that "international life" is now resulting in "universalizing religious beliefs" (e.g., [1912] 1915, 474, 493). Durkheim seemed to suggest that the size and the dynamic density of society had expanded to encompass all of humanity, resulting in a maximum, thus a logical endpoint of historical development.

What remains missing from Durkheim's empirical accounts is an analysis of the continuing process of this dialectic once the individual has resulted from society. What are the detailed, objectively observable mechanisms and processes whereby individuals create societies and societies create individuals? How does the emergence of this new type of individual result in further, and probably more complex, forms of emergence? How do emergence processes themselves change once individuals have been transformed by the creation of these categories of thought?

Conclusion

Society has a creative power which no other observable being can equal. (Durkheim [1912] 1915, 495)

I have argued that Durkheim must be read as an emergence theorist and that such a reading helps to clarify several difficult and confusing aspects of his work. Throughout his career, he can be seen as consistently arguing for a sociology of emergence. Even as he focused on the problem of order – how structures are maintained and reproduced over time – his underlying theoretical perspective on these processes was essentially an emergentist one.

Drawing on the philosophical material in Chapter 5, I discussed several commonly misunderstood aspects of Durkheim's theory. When Durkheim's sociological project is unified around the concept of emergence, the *Rules* becomes a central, seminal text, and there is not a fundamental shift from an early to a late Durkheim.

Thus we return to Durkheim's dilemma: Do social phenomena exist? There are two nonemergentist responses associated with the traditional philosophical positions of atomism and holism. Sociological holists, including today's structural sociologists, assume that collective phenomena exist, that they have causal powers over individuals, and that they cannot be reduced. The problem, of course, is that many sociologists and nonsociologists alike do not believe that this assumption is valid. In contrast, they hold that collective phenomena are nothing more than the actions of participating individuals; such positions include sociological behaviorism, exchange theory, rational action theory, and multi-agent–based models of society.

Subjectivism is a variant of individualism in that it argues that the only way to understand social life is to focus on subjective mental states: intention, agency, meaning. Action-theoretic frameworks derived from Weber and Parsons emphasize the role of intention and subjectivity in action; the dominance of such perspectives in American sociology has contributed to misreadings of Durkheim. From the viewpoint of structural sociology, to focus only on mental states is a variant of individualism; yet to posit that these are internalizations of external social structures returns us to the realm of emergence theory.

A sociological theory of emergence provides us with a path between individualism and collectivism. Contemporary emergence theory allows us to retain many of the most useful insights of Durkheim's emergence theory while elaborating them to be more relevant to contemporary issues in sociological theory. A complete emergence theory would have to distinguish among several different forms of social emergence – forms that Durkheim tended to conflate:

1. The crystallization of social phenomena from social currents
2. The historical emergence of a social stage from a social milieu
3. The emergence of collective representations from the social milieu (Durkheim [1898] 1953, 30–1)
4. The emergence of "second-degree" collective representations from those that originally emerged from the social milieu (p. 32)
5. The emergence of larger social groups from combinations of smaller groups[17]
6. The emergence of "secondary groups" from the interactions of individuals with those first-order emergent societies (p. 24)

Without reading Durkheim as an emergence theorist, it is difficult to properly understand the similarities and differences in these passages. These different types of emergence would have to be distinguished and clarified to fully elaborate a theory of emergence. All of these types of emergence can be theorized so that they are amenable to empirical study. One promising approach is to use techniques of video analysis developed in late twentieth century social science, including ethnomethodology and

---

[17] As discussed in Durkheim [1895] 1964, 81–6. For example, "The constituent parts of every society are societies more simple than itself" (p. 81). Note that this is also Comte's conception of emergence: The individual is not the basic unit of emergence, rather it is the family. See the discussion of the "element" of society in Turner 1986, 113–15.

conversation analysis, but also linguistic anthropology, cultural studies, and sociolinguistics. Likewise, for each type of emergent phenomena, the moment-to-moment processes of downward causation could be documented by this sort of empirical study, as I argue in Chapter 10.

An elaborated theory of social emergence drawing on Durkheim's works and on recent philosophy of mind has several implications for sociological theory. First, one does not need to propose a dualistic ontology to argue against individualism; emergence is consistent with the claim that social properties are supervenient on individual properties. Second, socially emergent properties may have causal powers even though those properties are supervenient on complex systems of individuals. Third, one may not need a theory of agency or subjectivity to theorize the causal power of the social, nor to theorize the maintenance and reproduction of the social order. Fourth, sociology can partly proceed without a theory of the individual – as structuralists claim – but can also benefit from integration and coordination with the theory of the individual. To the extent that the individual is theorized as one moment in a dialectic of emergence, this theory of the individual will always remain a sociological concern and not part of psychology.

In this chapter I compare the emergentist view of the social world with a contemporary alternative: elisionist theories, including both Anthony Giddens's structuration theory and socioculturalism in contemporary psychological theory. Elisionist theories share two foundational theoretical assumptions: They assume a *process ontology*, and they assume the *inseparability* of individual and social levels of analysis. A process ontology holds that only processes are real; entities, structures, or patterns are ephemeral and do not really exist. As for inseparability, the assumption is that the individual and the social cannot be methodologically or ontologically distinguished; thus the name "elisionism" (coined in Archer 1995). For example, socioculturalists in education argue that the individual learner cannot be meaningfully separated from the social and cultural context of learning, and they reject a traditional view of learning in which the learner is presumed to internalize knowledge presented from the external world. Rather than internalizing knowledge, the learner should be conceived of as *appropriating* or *mastering* patterns of participation in group activities. Learning involves a transformation of the social practices of the entire group and thus cannot be reduced to an analysis of what any one participant in the group does or knows.

In comparing social emergence with elisionism, I summarize two independent debates: the contemporary sociological debate between Anthony Giddens and Margaret Archer and internal debates within sociocultural psychology. In social theory, Archer's position is representative of emergentism, and Giddens is representative of elisionism. Giddens's *structuration* model is founded on a process ontology and on inseparability. Archer rejects both assumptions, has criticized Giddens's model for conflating the individual and the social, and has proposed an emergentist model characterized by an *analytic dualism* between individual action and social context. This sociological debate demonstrates the incompatibility between theories that argue for a process ontology and inseparability and those that do not. In sociocultural psychology, an isomorphic debate has taken place, with some theorists holding to elisionist positions and others holding to emergentist positions. I examine the various stances toward a process ontology and toward inseparability held by several prominent sociocultural theorists, including Michael Cole, Jean Lave and Etienne Wenger, Barbara Rogoff, Richard Shweder, Jaan Valsiner, and James Wertsch. Both debates demonstrate that elisionism has insurmountable problems and suggest that the only way forward is a sociology of social emergence.

Two theoretical assumptions of elisionism

Anthony Giddens's work is well known to most sociological theorists. In contrast, the theoretical writings of the socioculturalists are not – perhaps because they conduct their work in departments of psychology and education. Socioculturalism continues a long tradition of attempting to study culture and psychology together (Cole 1996). Within socioculturalism, I include cultural psychologists, Vygotskian educational theorists, and those studying situated action and cognition (Bruner 1990; Cole 1996; Forman, Minick, and Stone 1993; Lave and Wenger 1991; Rogoff 1990; Stigler, Shweder, and Herdt 1990; Suchman 1987; Valsiner 1998b; Wertsch 1998). This is a "big tent" definition, as these groups hold subtly different theoretical positions, but for sociological purposes they can be placed together because they generally accept elisionism: They emphasize a process ontology and methodology, and they claim that the individual and the social are inseparable both in reality, or *ontologically* (distinct entities do not really exist), and in practice, or *methodologically* (the analyst cannot meaningfully distinguish between what is internal to the individual and what is external context).

Socioculturalists who accept inseparability reject two approaches to the study of human action associated with traditional psychology. First, they reject methodological individualism. Among socioculturalists, the term "methodological individualism" refers to the typical approach in experimental psychology of operationalizing variables and constructs associated with individual human subjects (note the contrast with the meaning of "methodological individualism" in sociology). The objects of sociocultural study are events, activity, and practice, and they are considered to be irreducible to properties of individuals. Second, they reject the ecological or "social influence" approach that conceives of the individual as acting in and being influenced by an external context or environment. Such attempts to incorporate social context into psychology assume that the individual and the context can be analytically isolated and the interaction between them then studied. Inseparability is incompatible with conceptions of the relation between individual and sociocultural context that assume that the individual acts "in" a context or that the individual is "influenced by" the context; such conceptions implicitly accept the possibility of methodological separability between individual and situation (cf. Rogoff 1982, 1990, 1998). The theoretical assumptions of the socioculturists lead to a distinctive methodology: a rejection of the individual subject as the unit of analysis in favor of an *action* or *event* unit of analysis (comparable to Giddens's emphasis on practices). As a result, the socioculturists favor close empirical study of symbolic interaction in naturally occurring micro-social situations using ethnographic and qualitative methods.

I show that sociocultural theory is quite similar to the elisionism of Anthony Giddens, even though socioculturists are largely unaware of Giddens's work.[1] The similarities arise because sociocultural theory grows out of many of the same theoretical traditions that inspired Giddens: the pragmatism of Dewey and Mead, the ethnomethodology of Garfinkel, and various strands of twentieth-century Marxian social theory, including the Soviet school of psychology today associated with Vygotsky. The theoretical connections of socioculturalism to both Marxian theory (through Vygotsky) and to pragmatism have been widely noted (e.g., Cole 1995b, 112). The pragmatists Dewey and Mead elaborated the process ontology of Whitehead and Bergson, contributing to the sociocultural emphasis on practices and processes. They were also influenced by Cooley, who may have been the first to argue the inseparability claim that "'society' and 'individuals' do not denote separable phenomena" (1902, 1–2). Most contemporary practice theories in sociology are likewise based on a Marxian framework (e.g., Giddens 1979a, 4). Thus, the parallels I identify in the following are not incidental but derive from broad historical currents.

Structuration theory

Process ontologies reject the terms of the debate between individualists and collectivists. Only process is real. Entities and objects – including individuals and groups – are not the fundamental categories of being; rather, process is fundamental, and entities are derivative of or based in process: "[T]he ultimate atoms of social reality are *events* . . . they are the

---

[1] Several socioculturalists have briefly acknowledged parallels with Giddens. Barbara D. Miller (1995, 72, 77) commented on Giddens's process ontology and its relationship to socioculturalism; Lave and Wenger (1991, 50–4) noted similarities with Giddens, Bourdieu, and Bauman. Cole (1996, 358n10) also noted his "close affinity" with Giddens, although I challenge this in the following.

only elementary ontological objects" (Sztompka 1994, 275). Abbott, following Mead, argued that "the world is a world of events" (Mead 1932, 1) and that the fundamental entities of sociological inquiry are "events, instantaneous and unique" (Abbott 1995, 863).

Arguments for a process ontology and for individual-society inseparability have been most thoroughly developed in Anthony Giddens's structuration theory. Giddens's focus on practices is a form of process ontology. Giddens argued that practice is the fundamental category of being: "The basic domain of study of the social sciences ... [consists of] social practices ordered across space and time" (1984, 2). Giddens noted the close connection to the inseparability thesis: "I regard social practices ... as crucial mediating moments" between "the dualism of the individual and society" (1979a, 4). One must reject a focus on either society or the individual as entities in favor of "the analysis of *recurrent social practices*" (1989, 252). In place of the individual-society dualism, Giddens proposed the *duality of structure*: "[S]tructure is both medium and outcome of the reproduction of practices" (1979a, 5). Social structure exists only in the activities of human agents (1989, 256); inseparability implies not only that social structure cannot be analytically isolated but also that properties of individual activity (reasons, intentions, mental states) cannot be analytically isolated (1979a, 40, 56). Thus Giddens rejected a methodological individualism that would reduce analysis of social systems to individual psychology (1979a, 94–5). As early as 1979, this theory had led Giddens to a sociocultural conception of development: "Socialization is never anything like a passive imprinting of 'society' upon each 'individual'. From its very earliest experiences, the infant is an active partner in the double contingency of interaction. ... [T]he socialization involved is not simply that of the child, but of the parents and others with whom the child is in contact" (1979a, 129–30).

Individual and group cannot be analytically separated because "the notions of action and structure *presuppose one another*" (1979a, 53). Thus Giddens rejected the language of the micro-macro debate because it presupposes that the individual and the social are two distinct ontological realms that causally interact with each other. In a process ontology, the relation between individual and group "is distinct from that involved in the relation of 'parts' and 'wholes'" (1979a, 71). Giddens rejected forms of sociology in which social structure is conceived of as an external constraint on individuals (1984, 16) because "structure exists ... only in its instantiations in [reproduced social] practices and as memory traces orienting the conduct of knowledgeable human agents" (1984, 17). Enduring social patterns that sociologists have conceptualized as external structures – race, class, cultural institutions, power asymmetries – are instead conceived of as "deeply-layered practices constitutive of social systems" (1979a, 65).

Giddens argued that inseparability entails a rejection of social causation and social laws (1984, 172–9, 343–7). Consequently he rejected structuralism (1979a, Chap. 1) and structural sociology (1979a, 59–65; 1984, Chap. 4), both theories that posit irreducibly collective entities that have lawful causal influences over individuals. Instead, Giddens described actors that consciously choose among available options rather than being unknowingly forced to act by external structure. He preferred to speak of structure as "enabling" rather than constraining, and this focus led to an emphasis on agents' knowledgeability or *practical consciousness*.

The implications of Giddens's inseparability claim have been widely criticized by sociological theorists (Archer 1988, 1995; Craib 1992; Layder 1987; J. W. Smith and Turner 1986; Thompson 1989). Giddens took a strong stance on inseparability in rejecting "dualism"; however, somewhat paradoxically he retains a notion of "duality." Many critics have argued that Giddens's notion of a duality that is not a dualism is not theoretically substantive (e.g., Layder 1987, 31); if "duality" means there are two analytically separable elements, then why isn't this a dualism? Duality is problematic because inseparability implies that structure and agency "cannot refer to separate processes or separate structures" (Layder 1981, 75). Archer likewise noted that

If someone were to insist in the Elisionists' defence that an amalgam still has two constituents, it nevertheless remains the case that for them we are compelled to see the two only in combination and constrained to regard this combination of being of a particular kind. . . . [I]ssues surrounding the relative independence, causal influence and temporal precedence of the components have been eliminated. (1995, 93–4)

Archer observed that structuration analyzes the social world by "considerably flattening out the ontological depth of the social world by denying the existence of emergent properties which pertain to a 'higher stratum' when they do not obtain at a 'lower' one" (1995, 94; also Craib 1992, 145–55).

Giddens's ontology of practice is similar to the socioculturalist's focus on situated or mediated action and on events as irreducible units of analysis. Both individual and society exist only in instantiated practices, and these social practices are the ultimate constituents of social reality. People only become real by drawing on structural properties in social practices; structure only becomes real when instantiated by human action. Because social practices are the central concern, we cannot examine "heterogeneous constituents of social life" but rather are concerned with "one homogenous though Janus-faced entity," social practices (Archer 1995, 104). Thus, "'inseparability' precludes just that examination of the interplay between structure and agency upon which practical social theorizing depends" (p. 64). Archer claimed that such a stance is empirically and theoretically untenable and "is always an error in social theory" (p. 101). Similarly, Layder proposed that social theory retain a dualism of individual and social structure that "does not necessarily imply opposition or unrelatedness" (1987, 31); such a mutually constitutive dualism achieves the same theoretical goals at lesser cost than inseparability (p. 32; cf. Craib 1992, 165).[2]

Contextual influences

Inseparability does not allow the sociologist to account for social emergence, for the constraining power of external social forces, for macrosociological patterns, for history, or for material conditions: "The ontology of praxis constantly comes up against an interface with another level of social reality whose features cannot be construed as practices themselves, their unacknowledged conditions or unintended consequences" (Archer 1995, 116). These features "are properties emergent from social relations which constitute a distinct stratum of social reality" (p. 117). Archer noted that inseparability even requires a dismissal of material entities as potentially constraining; yet a famine exists and has social consequences regardless of anyone's instantiated practice (p. 98). Layder likewise argued that Giddens "does not properly account for the collectivist or objectivist moments of social reality" (1987, 26).

In contrast, Archer proposed a socially emergentist form of social realism in which emergent properties at both the collective and the individual level are "*distinct* from each other and *irreducible* to one another. . . . [T]he different strata are *separable* by definition precisely because of the properties and powers which only belong to each of them and whose emergence from one another justifies their differentiation as strata" (1995, 14). Layder also emphasized that power structures are historically emergent and thus not simply a property of agency (1985, 134, 143). Theories of sociological emergence have a long history in sociology (see Chapters 3 and 6), and both Archer and Giddens agree that such theories are incompatible with inseparability.

---

[2] Other critics who note that structuration is not a resolution of the structure-agency problem but simply a "dissolution" of it include J. W. Smith and Turner 1986; Thompson 1989.

However – in part demonstrating the theoretical incoherence of the elisionist position – Giddens at times used emergentist language; for example, he accepted a conception of structure as "structural properties" of human action, the same claim made by emergentists (1979a, 64–6; 1984, 17, 19, 185–91), and he acknowledged that "a range of unintended consequences of action feed back to reconstitute the initiating circumstances" (1984, 27). He cited Schelling's (1971) checkerboard simulation of neighborhood segregation (1984, 10, 13), a classic example of social emergence. Yet inseparability denies that the analyst can identify emergent social properties (Archer 1995, 133). In rejecting any role for structural explanation, Giddens proposed to explain emergent social properties solely in terms of individuals' motivations: "[N]o explanatory variables are needed other than those which explain why individuals are motivated to engage in regularized social practices across time and space, and what consequences ensue" (Giddens 1984, 14); ultimately "all [structural] explanations will involve at least implicit reference . . . to the purposive, reasoning behavior of agents" (p. 179). Such passages make it exceedingly difficult to distinguish Giddens's position from methodological individualism, in spite of his many protests to the contrary.

Inseparability allows structuration theorists to transcend individual-social dualism. However, what is lost are "any autonomous features which could pertain independently to either 'structure' or 'agency'. Otherwise such features could be investigated separately. . . . [and then] dualism would once more be the name of the game" (Archer 1995, 97). Because of this inseparability, structure cannot be emergent or autonomous nor have any causal powers over individuals. Layder likewise argued that Giddens cannot account for the causal role of social structures in individual action because he rejected a conception of "constraint" as external to social action (1987, 39); however, "there is no such thing as social constraint unless it is constituted outside the realm of human agency" (p. 41).

The theory of the individual

I have claimed that Giddens's position often veers quite close to methodological individualism. But it cannot be methodological individualism, because structuration prevents one from acknowledging that individuals have properties and requires one to deny the possibility of individual psychology. The self can only be formed through social practices; yet which practices form which people? Inseparability prevents one from answering this question. Separability allows different individuals to have different properties that influence the social practices they are drawn to and can participate in; inseparability does not allow this because it holds that all individual properties are socially mediated, and to analyze different properties of different individuals would imply separability between the individual and the social. "The success of the Elisionists' enterprise depends upon their being able to eliminate any reference to selfhood which is independent of social mediation, for otherwise a stratum of individual features (personal psychology) would have to be acknowledged and its interplay with social properties would then require examination" (Archer 1995, 121). In structuration, there can be no individual experience that is not socially mediated; the self is purely sociological (Archer 1995, 122, 126). Thus structuration rejects that action is motivated by internal intentions; intentions and reasons for actions are not properties of individuals but are "instantiated in that activity" (Giddens 1979a, 40). Note that this implication is not reconcilable with Giddens's focus on motivations in other passages, contributing to the incoherence of structuration theory (Giddens 1984, 14; see the discussion earlier in this section). In sum, structuration cannot explain specific instances of human behavior because inseparability rejects explanations either in terms of internal motivation or in terms of structural influences.

Tensions in sociocultural theory

Like structuration theory, many versions of socioculturalism are based on both a process ontology and the inseparability of the individual and the social. In the preceding section, I discussed the centrality of these claims to Giddens's structuration theory. I then summarized several of the criticisms of these two claims, focusing on those of Margaret Archer.

In this section, I discuss a range of sociocultural statements of these two foundational assumptions. Although almost all sociocultural theorists can be found making claims for inseparability and for a process ontology, these claims take many diverse forms. The debate between Giddens and Archer suggests that some of these claims are mutually incompatible, resulting in unresolved tensions.

Process ontology

Developmental psychologists in some sense are always interested in process because they focus on change over time. Socioculturalism differentiates itself from this general developmental orientation by making a stronger ontological claim: Process is not only a guiding orientation but is the fundamental nature of reality. This results in one of the unifying features of the paradigm: The unit of analysis is situated social practice rather than the bounded individual, as in traditional psychology (Hatano and Wertsch 2001, 79). I begin by summarizing the strongest and most explicit statements of process ontology and gradually move toward more nuanced and weaker statements.

Hutchins makes one of the most explicit statements of the process ontology underlying socioculturalism: "Culture is not any collection of things, whether tangible or abstract. Rather, it is a process . . . and the 'things' that appear on list-like definitions of culture are residua of the process" (1995, 354). Learning is conceived as a property of the group, not the individual participant, and this *distributed cognition* perspective was a central feature of Hutchins's 1995 study of ship navigation teams. However, Hutchins found it difficult to maintain this stance consistently; he also made entity-implying statements like "humans are processors of symbolic structures" (p. 369) and "symbols are in the world first, and only later in the head" (p. 370), suggesting that individuals, symbols, and symbolic structures exist as entities in some sense.

Lave and Wenger (1991) also made strong collectivist claims for learning in their "social practice theory of learning" (p. 35). Learning is the process of reproduction of the social structure as embodied in the participatory practices of the community (pp. 54–8). Unlike most socioculturalists, Lave and Wenger acknowledged debts to Giddens, Bauman, and Bourdieu, all practice theorists in the Marxist tradition (pp. 50–4).[3] They claimed that a focus on practice "suggests a very explicit focus on the person" (p. 52); this claim is in tension with their collectivist claims, because when focusing on the person, structural, institutional, and cultural factors are often neglected.[4]

Like Hutchins, Lave and Wenger demonstrated that a process ontology is difficult to maintain consistently in empirical practice. They discussed individuals as if they were analyzable entities, observing that "legitimate peripherality provides learners with opportunities to make the culture of practice theirs" and that "apprentices gradually assemble a general idea of what constitutes the practice of the community" (1991, 95). They defined a person as "a member of a community of practice," implying a

---

[3] Archer criticized Bauman's (1973) theory of mutual constitution on much the same grounds as she criticized Giddens (Archer 1988, 72–96).

[4] Although such passages are explicit about the individualist orientation of socioculturalism, most socioculturalists claim to reject methodological individualism. One exception is Shweder, who explicitly acknowledged that the action orientation of his cultural psychology is methodologically individualist (1995) because intentionality is "action responsive to and directed at mental objects or representations" (1990, 26) and culture is "an intentional world composed of conceptions, evaluations, judgments, goals, and other mental representations" (1990, 26). Note that (1) Shweder also claimed that Wertsch's theory of mediated action is methodologically individualist and (2) his definition also seems to apply to Giddens's focus on subjective intentionality.

stratified ontology of entities, with individuals being members of larger entities called communities (p. 122). Such statements are inconsistent with a process ontology, in which there can be no such entities and no relation of membership (cf. Giddens 1979a, 71).

Other socioculturalists advocate an empirical focus on situated practice but without making strong claims for a process ontology. For example, Wertsch advocated a focus on *mediated action*; all action involves an individual in a social situation using cultural tools. Although Wertsch was not explicit on this point, he implied that individual agency cannot be analytically separated from the mediational means that individuals use in practice: "[A]gency cannot be reduced further than that of 'individual(s)-operating-with-mediational-means'" (1993, 170). Yet his own discussions of "mastery" and "appropriation" often imply an analytic dualism, with entities called individuals appropriating entities called mediational means. Wertsch (like the socioculturalists more generally) did not propose a theory of how specific mediational means are organized and structured into larger complexes that others have called cultures, discourses, institutions, or social structures; like other practice orientations, including structuration theory, this results in a neglect of macrostructural forces.

Like Hatano and Wertsch (2001), Cole perceived the unifying thread of socioculturalism to be its focus on "cultural practices" (1995b, 105). Yet as Cole notes, there is no consistent theoretical conception of what "cultural practices" are – they are variously interpreted as activity, context, event, and situation (1996, Chap. 5). Cole's implicit process ontology, unlike Giddens's, suggests that there may be multiple processes that somehow interact: "[A]ny psychological phenomenon emerges from interaction of processes" (1995a, 191). Such language is problematic because it risks treating distinct processes as entities; a true process ontology is holistic and cannot distinguish between distinct processes that interact without risking a return to entification. Giddens is consistent on this point, even holding that the analyst cannot identify discrete actions because human action is "a continuous flow of conduct" (1979a, 55). A few other socioculturalists also refer to multiple interacting processes, but none has presented a corresponding ontological theory nor a causal theory of how processes could interact.

This discussion reveals several distinct stances toward a process ontology and raises several issues. First, an empirical focus on practice does not require a process ontology. One could accept the traditional "entity" view that individuals and groups both exist and nonetheless argue that it is methodologically necessary to study situated practices. Wertsch and Cole take this approach, whereas Rogoff and Lave and Wenger take the stronger stance of assuming a process ontology. Second, how can one study socially situated practice without analytically distinguishing among individuals? Most socioculturalists study individuals and their relations and make analytic observations about them that are disallowed in a strong inseparability theory (more in the following section). Third, whose practice is being analyzed? Which individuals and in which communities or societies? Answering this question requires an analytic identification of distinct entities known as individuals, communities, and societies. A process ontology rejects the existence of such entities, making it difficult to theorize difference, heterogeneity, cultural tension, and conflict.

Inseparability

Inseparability is a second paradigm-defining feature of socioculturalism. Socioculturalists maintain a wide range of theoretically incompatible stances on inseparability, and this has resulted in an ongoing theoretical debate. All socioculturalists argue that the individual must be studied in social context, but their stances range from a "weak social interaction" view (Valsiner 1991, 1998a; Wertsch 1993, 1994; Cole 1996), which accepts some form of separability, to a "strong" view, which holds to inseparability (Lave and Wenger 1991; Matusov 1998; Rogoff 1990, 1997; Shweder 1990). Valsiner further distinguished two types of weak social interaction, which he called "exclusive" and "inclusive" separation (1991, 314; 1998a). Exclusive separation corresponds to Rogoff's "social influence" view (1998): The social context is reduced to variables that are measured only in the ways that they impact individual behavior. Inclusive separation is the sociogenetic claim that individuals and sociocultural setting are separate but interdependent.

Vygotsky introduced the concept of *internalization* to emphasize the socially embedded nature of human development. In Vygotsky's theory, development involves a transfer of social patterns of interaction into the individual learner's mind: "An interpersonal process is transformed into an intrapersonal one" (1978, 57). Like Vygotsky, Lawrence and Valsiner (1993) proposed a view of development as internalization: "[W]hat was originally in the interpersonal (or intermental) domain becomes intrapersonal (intra-mental) in the course of development" (p. 151). As constructivists, they rejected a concept of internalization as transmission ("exclusive separation"), emphasizing Vygotsky's claim that internalization involves transformation (see also Valsiner 1989). Like all socioculturalists, this view rejects theories of development based on genetically predetermined stages and theories of development that are not foundationally based on social interaction.

However, many socioculturalists have begun to reject the Vygotskian conception of learning and development as internalization, even when conceived of as constructivist transformation, because it proposes that the "social and psychological planes are separate" (Matusov 1998, 329). Rogoff is one of the strongest advocates of inseparability; she was one of the first psychologists to view context and individual as "jointly producing psychological events" (1982, 132).[5] This early statement was not an inseparability claim because it accepted the value of "separating aspects of an event" (p. 132). By 1990, Rogoff had fully embraced the implications of inseparability, advancing a strong "mutual constitution" view: "The child and the social world are mutually involved to an extent that precludes regarding them as independently definable" (p. 28). Rogoff argued that "the boundary between individual and environment disappears" (1997, 267).[6]

However, in empirical practice Rogoff maintained a threefold analytic distinction between individual, group, and community, referring to these as "angles," "windows" (1990, 26), "lenses," or "planes of analysis" (1997, 267–8). These terms imply analytic separability although they avoid the ontological connotations of the conventional term "levels of analysis." Although "the three planes cannot be isolated," the analyst can nonetheless examine the individual or the social plane as a "current focus of attention" (1997, 269). In referring to these three as "perspectives" rather than entities, individuals and cultural contexts "can be considered separately without losing sight of the inherent involvement in the whole" (Rogoff 1992, 317). These perspectives are separable in practice and are in principle not reducible to each other (Rogoff 1997, 269n3). This acceptance of analytic separability is difficult to reconcile with theoretical claims for analytic inseparability, as Archer argued.

The central questions from Rogoff's perspective seem to imply that the individual can be analytically distinguished (cf. Valsiner 1998a): "What are the activities in which people participate? Why and with whom and with what?" (Rogoff 1997, 271). Sociocultural analysis "examines individuals' roles in the context of their participation" and "how they coordinate with others" (p. 279). Such questions require an analytic focus on specific individuals, on relationships between distinguishable individuals, and on specific individuals in distinguishable contexts, all disallowed by

---

[5] Like Rogoff, Lave and Wenger (1991) took a strong inseparability position: "[A]gent, activity, and the world mutually constitute each other" (p. 33). They rejected the term "situated learning" because it seems to separate learning from context; rather, "social practice is the primary, generative phenomenon, and learning is one of its characteristics" (p. 34).

[6] Rogoff has often commented on her own theoretical development (e.g., 1998, 687).

inseparability. For example, Archer (1995) pointed out that Giddens has to reject a notion that structural properties inhere in relations among people (pp. 106–7). If the individual is not analytically separable, then one cannot study relationships between individuals; the only available object of study is undifferentiated social group practices.

Recently, Matusov elaborated the inseparability stance of Rogoff and Lave and Wenger, making more explicit its incompatibility with Vygotsky's internalization theory of development. Matusov rejected Vygotsky's internalization model because it "leads to a chain of mutually related dualisms between the social and the individual, the external and the internal" (1998, 331). In opposition, Matusov advocated Rogoff's *participation antithesis*, asserting that "social and psychological planes mutually constitute each other and are inseparable" (p. 329).

Rogoff, Lave and Wenger, and Matusov took a strong stance on inseparability, but this strong inseparability is not shared by all socioculturalists, many of whom continue in the Vygotskian framework of inclusive separation. Wertsch, for example, took the Vygotskian view that "human action and sociocultural setting [are] analytically distinct, yet inherently interrelated levels of analysis" (1994, 203). Wertsch implicitly criticized inseparability claims: "If we must take all dimensions of the phenomena into account before we can examine any one of them, it seems that there is no manageable way to 'break into' the cycle of complex issues at hand" (203). Wertsch defined sociocultural research as the study of "the relationship between human mental functioning, on the one hand, and cultural, historical, and institutional setting, on the other" (1995, 56). Like Archer's analytic dualism, his view is that individual and society are "analytically distinct, yet inherently interrelated levels of analysis" (1994, 203), which stands in contrast to the position of strict inseparability theorists.

Although essentially Vygotskian, Wertsch argued that the term "internalization" is problematic because it presupposes a "dualism between the external and the internal" (1993, 168); he suggested that we can avoid this dualism by using the term "mastery" (p. 169). However, Wertsch did not reject analytic dualism: Development involves "transformations in individuals' understanding (i.e., their mastery) of the meaning of cultural tools such as language" (p. 170). His rejection of the term "internalization" should be viewed as a matter of emphasis rather than an ontological stance; he was concerned that the term implies a passive learner and may repeat the methodological individualist's error of neglecting the interaction of learner and social context.

Cole (1996, 226), in acknowledging Bronfenbrenner as an influence, accepted the ecological psychology approach that Rogoff rejected (e.g.,

Rogoff 1990, 26–8; 1998). Cole implicitly accepted that the "cultural system" can be analyzed as a structure analytically distinct from instantiation in human action; he referred to such cultural systems as *tertiary artifacts* (following Wartofsky 1979). A cultural system is "constituted jointly by artifact-mediated practices ... and by the nature of its ecological setting" (1995a, 197), but it can nonetheless be analyzed as independent (1995a, 198, Fig. 8.1). The experimental studies that he reported in (1996) are described as, for example, studies of "the impact of schooling on cognitive development" (p. 77), implying a causal relation between context and individual that Giddens explicitly rejects. He spoke of the cultural system being "appropriated" by individuals (1995a, 203) and of "individual children's ability to internalize the scripted roles" (1996, 281), and he analyzed cultural systems as distinct entities, as in a study with Nicolopoulou contrasting the library and the boys club settings of the Fifth Dimension (Nicolopoulou and Cole 1993). He defines cultural psychology as "the study of culture's role in the mental life of human beings" (1996, 1), implying that an individual psychology is possible, which inseparability must deny (cf. Shweder 1990).

Although socioculturalists disagree on inseparability, they rarely make these differences explicit. One exception has been Jaan Valsiner's critiques of inseparability (1991, 1998a; also see Carelli 1998, 358; Lave 1993, 17–20). Valsiner criticized Rogoff's inseparability claim in terms reminiscent of Archer's critique of Giddens: "[I]t is exactly the use of the fusion terminology that creates further obstacles for theory-building" (Valsiner 1991, 311). It prevents us from thinking about internal psychological functions: "[R]educing the domain of intrapsychological phenomena to the process of fusion with 'sociocultural activity' does not solve the fundamental problem of human psychology" (p. 312) and in fact makes psychology impossible.

Regarding social and cultural contexts, Rogoff has no theory about social structure nor about activity structure, and thus she cannot theorize about how different structures result in different activities; she reduces these structures "to an endless unstructured variety of everyday events" (Valsiner 1991, 313). This problem results from her inseparability claim: It is an unproductive "theoretical shortcut" to reduce "all intrapersonal psychological structure to external actions within socially supported contexts, and a similar reduction of the structure of the external social world to problem-solving settings" (p. 313).

Valsiner, like Wertsch, objected that "if any distinction between two parts of a whole ... is objected to as a 'dualism', then our knowledge construction may lead to overlooking the structure of the systems"

(1998a, 351–2). In contrast, Valsiner proposed an inclusive separation that distinguishes "the organism (person) from its environment (social world) *while maintaining their dynamic interdependence*" (352). Valsiner observed that Rogoff's own analyses analytically separate the individual; her empirical work focuses on "a person's *contribution* to *sociocultural activity, responsibility, ownership of the activity, relations* with other people," and each of these terms "entail inclusive separation of the participants and the field of participation" (1998a, 353; also see 1991, 312).

A resolution: The analytic dualism of social emergence

I began by identifying two theoretical assumptions held by many socioculturalists and by structuration theorists: They assume a process ontology and the analytic inseparability of individuals and sociocultural contexts. I briefly summarized the sociological debate surrounding these two aspects of structuration theory, revealing significant problems with both claims. I then used this debate as a backdrop for a discussion of the various positions held by socioculturalists. There have been only a few references to these distinctions in the literature, with most socioculturalists assuming more theoretical unity than there actually is. How to resolve these differences and move forward?

All socioculturalists reject methodological individualism in favor of a theory and a methodology that incorporates both the individual and the social as foundational elements. All avoid reduction of the social to the individual, and all avoid a social determinism because they are constructivists, emphasizing the child's creative role in transforming knowledge as it is acquired and in acting back on the social world. Most contemporary social theory likewise rejects the historical positions of both individualism and collectivism. Archer (1988, 1995) observed that contemporary attempts at unity have taken two forms: the inseparability and process ontology of Giddens's structuration theory and the emergentist and morphogenetic account of analytic dualism. Within socioculturalism, these two extremes are represented by Rogoff and Valsiner. Like Giddens and Archer, both Rogoff and Valsiner transcend the traditional theoretical positions of individualism and collectivism; this is what leads both to be identified as socioculturalists in spite of their theoretical differences.

Commenting on contemporary social theory, Archer noted that a "concern with *interplay* is what distinguishes the emergentist from the non-emergentist whose preoccupation is with *interpenetration*" (1995, 15). Many socioculturalists deny inseparability and analyze the interplay and are thus emergentist, while those who emphasize interpenetration and inseparability are structuration theorists. Archer's criticisms have not been successfully refuted by structuration theorists. If one accepts analytic dualism, one is required to theorize the nature of individuals, the nature of social environments, and the nature of their causal interaction. Socioculturalists who make strong claims for inseparability have naturally not developed such theories. Archer's critique of structuration sounds quite similar to Valsiner's critique of Rogoff: "[T]he central question is whether 'duality' merely throws a blanket over the two constituents, 'structure' and 'agency' which only serves to prevent us from examining what is going on beneath it" (Archer 1995, 102).

The inseparability hypothesis entails that psychology cannot exist as a discipline apart from sociology and anthropology, and some socioculturalists have made this explicit: "The mind, according to cultural psychology, is content-driven, domain-specific, and constructively stimulus-bound; and it cannot be extricated from the historically variable and cross-culturally diverse intentional worlds in which it plays a coconstituting part" (Shweder 1990, 13). These socioculturalists claim that there can be *no* universal laws or discoveries about human psychology, and they deny that there is a "central processing mechanism" that is essentially the same across cultures and environments (cf. Shweder 1990, 24). The inseparability claim implies that individual psychology cannot, in principle, exist apart from the study of situated practice. Although many socioculturalists are self-consciously oppositional to mainstream psychology, many still think of themselves as psychologists, and they may not be comfortable with the necessary logical implication of inseparability: There can be no role whatsoever for the study of individual properties apart from social practice. After all, this ultimately would require that socioculturalists affiliate with departments of sociology or anthropology rather than psychology.

There are even suggestions that inseparability is foundationally incompatible with developmental science. Archer (1995, 87–9) claimed that inseparability theories cannot in principle explain structuring over time because they require the analyst to focus on a timescale restricted to a small span around the present. And in fact many socioculturalists have focused on *microgenesis* rather than long-term development because it is indeed difficult to study the latter through a micro-sociological study of situated social practice. If Archer's argument is sound, this is a particularly vexing problem for developmentalists.

The theoretical problems associated with inseparability have not had serious empirical consequences, for two reasons. First, it has often been noted that structuration theory has no corresponding empirical program; second, socioculturalists – even those making inseparability claims in their theoretical writings – implicitly accept analytic separability. In fact, these theoretical tensions have been "a resource, not a shortcoming to be avoided" (Rogoff 1998, 697); the dialogue among views has allowed scholars to compare and evaluate different stances on the individual-society relation. Socioculturalists have done excellent empirical work demonstrating transformations in social group participation over time and documenting the intricate relations between individuals and contexts. Some of the most important empirical work has been done by those theorists who make the strongest inseparability claims, notably Barbara Rogoff and Ed Hutchins; this work has had a broad influence on developmental psychology and educational theory. However, this empirical work is successful because it implicitly accepts analytic dualism. By rejecting the inseparability claim in their empirical studies, socioculturalists have been able to study (1) properties of individuals, thus at times connecting their work to cognitive psychology; (2) properties of different contexts, such as different family arrangements, different activity frameworks in classrooms, and different peer group structures; and (3) the forms of micro-sociological practice that mediate between these two. But of course inseparability entails that such analytic distinctions are impossible to make. The short history of socioculturalism demonstrates the difficulty of applying Giddens's inseparability claim to empirical work (as argued by Domingues 1995, 35–8; Gregson 1989; J. W. Smith and Turner 1986, 126). Sociocultural methodology belies its strongest claims for inseparability, and it succeeds best when it adopts analytic dualism.

All of the socioculturalists discussed above agree that the individual and the group cannot be studied in isolation but only in situated practice and that they are inextricably linked. The theoretical differences relate to analytic, or methodological, separability, and there are two possible positions on this issue: Either individual properties and group properties of situated practice can be analytically distinguished, or they cannot. If they are inseparable, then theoretical consistency with a process ontology is assured; however, one is prevented from any form of empirical study that presumes that properties of specific individuals can be isolated, even when they are studied in context.

Yet the empirical studies even of strong inseparability theorists like Rogoff and Hutchins identify distinct properties of individuals and groups. If individual and group properties are analytically distinguished, then it becomes necessary to specify with some precision one's theory of how they are related. To be complete, a theory that accepts analytic dualism must include postulates about the two-way causal relationship between individual and social properties, including the internalization processes associated with development and the externalization processes whereby individuals affect social structure (Valsiner 1998b). These are the central concerns of social emergence theory. Does the individual deterministically internalize society? This extreme, accepted by many macrosociologists, is generally rejected by socioculturalists. Are individuals never constrained by social structures but rather "enabled" to act consciously and strategically? This extreme is held by structuration theorists and by interpretivists, including ethnomethodologists, and is implied by individualist psychologists as well. There are a wide range of potential positions between these two extremes, and I have shown that socioculturalists are spread throughout this hybrid territory. Theories of social emergence are focused on exactly these issues, and the resolution of these issues will involve a focus on social emergence. Although these theoretical tensions have generally not interfered with the progress of important empirical work, the situation is unstable; a field's theoretical framework should be consistent with its empirical practice.

Conclusion

An empirical emphasis on individual actions in small groups necessarily neglects the broader, larger-scale influences studied by macro-sociology. The process orientation inevitably focuses on human action to the neglect of social-structural factors. For example, inseparability theorists in sociology have frequently been criticized for their inability to account for power and differential access to power (as in Layder's 1987 critique of Giddens). The emphasis on small groups leads many socioculturalists into what sociologists call the "displacement of scope" error: assuming that theories developed from micro-sociological observation can be used to explain macro-sociological phenomena, or vice versa (Wagner 1964). The sociocultural version of this error is similar to that made by ethnomethodologists and other interpretivist schools in sociology: to assume that "society is simply the small group writ large" (Archer 1995, 8). Thus, we see socioculturalists examining small-group interaction, but neglecting to study large-scale patterns of macrosociology – social class, networks of role positions, institutions, long-term social history, or cultural symbol systems. Interpretivism has influenced Giddens and socioculturalism alike (see Chapter 10 for further critique of interpretivism), so it is not surprising that both share a similar interpretivist emphasis.

Neither socioculturalists nor structurationists have an adequate theory of social structure and how it constrains and enables individuals. Because most socioculturalists are psychologists or anthropologists, it is not surprising that they neglect macro-social concerns in favor of a focus on individual action and small-group behavior. Socioculturalists have rarely drawn substantively on sociology, political science, or history – disciplines that argue for the irreducibility of macro-level entities or structures such as social class, educational level, geographic region, race and ethnicity, social networks and institutional structures, and social power and its forms.

I have argued that the best way to resolve the theoretical tensions surrounding inseparability and process ontology is to reject strong inseparability and accept analytic dualism. This resolution would allow socioculturalism to better connect with individual psychology, on the one hand, and macrosociology, on the other. Socioculturalism could then more fully participate in the major theoretical issues of contemporary social science: What is the best theory of processes, individuals, and groups? What is the nature of the regularities holding between individuals and groups? To what extent does this relationship require psychology to incorporate theoretical models from sociology and require sociology to incorporate psychological models of individuals?

Many of Giddens's critics have argued that structuration theory is difficult to translate into an empirical program. Sociocultural psychology is the most thoroughly developed empirical version of the structuration theory associated with Giddens. Although the socioculturalists rarely cite Giddens, and sociologists likewise are ignorant of sociocultural studies, their intellectual influences date back to the same time frame and represent the same theoretical assumptions: the interpretivism and ethnomethodology of 1960s and 1970s sociology, which grew out of early twentieth century Chicago-school sociology – scholars like Cooley and Mead, who emphasize the close focus on small-group interaction. Many socioculturalists trace their approach to the 1920s Soviet psychologist Lev Vygotsky; but although Vygotsky's works have been frequently cited by socioculturalists, his ideas never would have been taken up if the audience had not already been prepared by familiarity with these deeply rooted American intellectual traditions.

The theoretical debate about the merits of Giddens's structuration theory no longer has to remain theoretical. The socioculturalists have been struggling to implement an empirical research program founded on the same theoretical assumptions since the 1980s. In the future, the sociological debate about structuration theory should draw on this empirical work. This exploration will reinforce sociological criticisms of inseparability theories and will contribute to the empirical study of social emergence.

The solution to the unavoidable theoretical problems associated with inseparability is to explicitly theorize social emergence. A theory of social emergence retains the advantages desired by the socioculturalists: It is consistent with a focus on situated practice, it is consistent with a close focus on the dynamics of interaction (see Chapter 10), and it emphasizes the continuing dialectic interrelationship of society and the individual.

8   Simulating social emergence with artificial societies

In this chapter, I examine a new computer simulation technology that has increasingly been used to simulate social emergence: *multi-agent systems (MASs)*. Until the development of MASs in the 1990s, computer simulations of social phenomena primarily used analytics, or *equation-based modeling (EBM)*. Examples include the utility functions of rational choice theory (e.g., Coleman 1990) and the system dynamics of macrosociological and organizational models (e.g., Forrester 1968). In EBM, the model is a set of equations (typically differential or difference equations), and the execution of the simulation consists of evaluating the equations (Halpin 1999; Parunak, Savit, and Riolo 1998).

Social simulations using MAS technology are known as "artificial societies." An artificial society contains a set of autonomous agents that operate in parallel and communicate with each other. The earliest implementation of an artificial society was the famous checkerboard simulation of racial segregation of Schelling (1971). Like Schelling's early simulation, artificial societies allow researchers to run *virtual experiments*, setting up a series of simulations to address a specific research question. The simulation consists of activating all of the agents and observing the macrobehavior that emerges as the agents interact. In the 1990s, computer modeling techniques and computational power evolved to the point where MAS technology became a viable simulation tool for sociologists and economists. This approach to social simulation has rapidly gathered momentum among computer scientists; several edited collections have appeared (Conte, Hegselmann, and Terna 1997; N. Gilbert and Conte 1995; N. Gilbert and Doran 1994; Moss and Davidsson 2001; Sallach and Macal 2001; Sichman, Conte, and Gilbert 1998), and a journal was founded in 1998, the *Journal of Artificial Societies and Social Simulation* (http://jasss.soc.surrey.ac.uk/, accessed 2 April 2005).

By allowing a rigorous exploration of the mechanisms of social emergence, artificial societies provide new perspectives on contemporary discussions of social emergence, focusing on three of its aspects: micro-to-macro emergence, macro-to-micro social causation, and the dialectic between social emergence and social causation (cf. J. C. Alexander et al. 1987; Archer 1995; Knorr-Cetina and Cicourel 1981; Wiley 1988).

Multi-Agent Systems

MASs are computer systems that contain more than one computational agent. The agents are *autonomous* – they have control over their own behavior and can act without the intervention of humans or other systems. Interest in MASs among computer scientists was first driven by the development of multi-processor computers in the 1980s and then by the rapid expansion of the Internet in the 1990s. The Internet is a type of MAS because it is constituted by thousands of independent computers each running autonomous software programs and each capable of communicating with a program running on any other node in the network. Other contributing factors are (1) the proliferation of powerful desktop computers resulting from the declining costs of computation and (2) the research field of *ubiquitous computing*, which attempts to embed very small autonomous agents in many household objects, such as a shirt or a carton of milk, and to network them using wireless technology. As these technologies have evolved, there is an increasing need for more sophisticated formalisms that can better understand, manage, and predict the performance of complex systems that are composed of many computational agents.

The term "agent" does not carry the same connotations as it does in sociological theory. To understand the term's connotations, a brief history of MASs is helpful. MASs emerged in the mid 1990s and grew out of precursor systems with multiple interacting processes but in which the processes were not autonomous. The earliest precursor of MAS technology was *object-oriented programming (OOP)*. In OOP, an object is a single computational process – an operating program – maintaining its own data structures and its own procedures. Objects communicate with each other using *message passing*. Each object has a defined set of messages that it is capable of receiving and responding to. When a message arrives at an object, the corresponding procedure, called a "method," is executed.

By 1990, artificial intelligence researchers had begun to use OOP to build *distributed artificial intelligence (DAI)* systems (O'Hare and Jennings 1996). Whereas objects had typically been rather simple programs, DAI objects each contained sophisticated software to represent intelligent behavior. Unlike the AI systems of the 1970s and 1980s – which focused on isolated agents – the interaction of the group of agents was an essential aspect of each agent's intelligence and of the overall behavior of the system. In most DAI systems, the individual processing units were not autonomous; instead, the units were hierarchically organized around a single centralized controller (Connah and Wavish 1990, 197; Conte, Gilbert, and Sichman 1998, 1). Gradually, researchers began to experiment with decentralization, designing distributed systems without any centralized controller and with each object having autonomy.

This shift to autonomy was foundational and led to the use of the term "agent." An agent is situated in an environment and is capable of autonomous action in that environment (Wooldridge 1999, 29). The notion of action in an environment is critical and in part developed out of research in situated robotics (Agre 1995). Because real-world environments are nondeterministic – constantly changing and not fully known by the agent – agents that interact directly with the environment must be capable of autonomous action. Because agents do not have complete knowledge of the environment, the same action performed twice – in two environments that seem identical to the agent – may have different results owing to unperceived yet important features of that environment. In particular, an agent's action may fail to have the desired effect.

Autonomous agents have control over their behavior and their internal state. Agents, unlike objects, can decline to execute the request of another agent or can respond by proposing to negotiate the parameters of the task. Thus, MASs raise a wide range of issues related to coordination and cooperation. The introduction of agents with autonomy has forced computer scientists to consider what sociologists have long called the *problem of order*: Why and under what conditions do individuals yield autonomy to social groups? How do social groups emerge and reproduce over time?

Developers of artificial societies have increasingly realized that one of the key challenges facing them is to develop effective theories of social emergence. Because MASs have no central control, they are complex systems in which the aggregation of agents' autonomous actions results in the global behavior of the system. MAS developers have discovered that the global behavior of these systems cannot always be predicted or derived from the properties of the component agents; the behavior can only be known by running the simulation (N. Gilbert 1995, 150). The global behavior can then be observed as it emerges from the agents and their interactions.

MAS developers begin by modeling individual agents and their interactions. The simulation is then run to see what macropatterns and processes emerge as the agents interact with one another. The emergent macropatterns are then compared to the empirically observed patterns of the society. Thus, artificial societies are *microsimulations*, simulations based on the properties of lower-level units such as individuals, in contrast to "macrosimulations" of the system dynamics variety, which attempt to directly model emergent macrophenomena. As microsimulations, MASs allow the exploration of what Coleman (1990) referred to as the foundation of sociology: the micro-to-macro relation.

Emergence has been widely discussed by artificial society developers (Axtell 2002; Conte et al. 2001; N. Gilbert 2002; Moss 2001, 10). Most of these developers are individualist emergentists (Chapter 5); methodological individualism has been a universal theoretical assumption underlying agent-based social models (Axelrod 1997, e.g., 4; Conte et al. 2001; Epstein and Axtell 1996, e.g., 6–20; see Macy and Willer 2002). In complexity theory in general, "emergence" is often used in an implicitly reductionist fashion: "[T]he laws at the higher level derive from the laws of the lower-level building blocks" (Holland 1995, 36; also see Bedau 2002), although nonlinear interactions can make this derivation difficult to discover (Holland 1995, 15). Note also that the artificial society community often speaks of "emergence," but they use the term in the reductionist sense associated with economics, rational choice, and game-theoretic frameworks. Consistent with these paradigms, many agent modelers believe that group properties are best explained by first modeling the participating individuals, then modeling their interactions, and then running the simulation to examine the processes whereby collective properties emerge from the microsimulation (Conte et al. 2001).

The MAS community is loosely divided between those who focus on *cognitive* agents and those who focus on *reactive* agents (cf. Brassel et al. 1997; Moulin and Chaib-Draa 1996). Cognitive agents have beliefs about the state of the environment, knowledge about actions and plans of actions, and knowledge about how their actions will affect the environment and the other agents. Cognitive agents have explicit goals, and they are capable of reasoning about how to achieve their goals; thus, they are also known as *intentional* or *deliberative* agents. Cognitive agents communicate using *agent communication languages (ACLs)*. Speech act theory is the explicit theoretical foundation for the two dominant industry-standard ACLs: FIPA (http://www.fipa.org, accessed 2 April 2005) and KQML (http://www.cs.umbc.edu/kqml/, accessed 2 April 2005). The widespread acceptance of these ACLs allows agents designed by different research teams to communicate.

Unlike cognitive agents, reactive agents do not contain any internal representation of the world – neither of the environment nor of the other agents. They do not have explicit goals and do not reason about goals and plans. Instead, reactive agents are driven by simple condition-action rules in which the "conditions" are certain features of the local environment of the agents. Reactive agents are also sometimes called *behavioral agents* because they respond directly to stimuli from the environment, unmediated by internal states. These agents have been used to model learning in configurations of neurons (Bechtel and Abrahamson 1991), flow in sandpiles (Breton, Zucker, and Clément 2000), and activities of social insect colonies (Drogoul, Corbara, and Lalande 1995; Sumpter and Broomhead 1998). Reactive agents are similar to the model of the individual proposed in behaviorist versions of exchange theory (Emerson 1972; Homans 1958). Whereas cognitive agents evolved from the DAI tradition, reactive agent systems evolved from the *artificial life (Alife)* tradition (Adami et al. 1998). Somewhat independently of DAI, Alife research has continued to influence artificial society simulations.

Computer scientists have explored the possibility of using MASs for a wide range of applications, including industrial process control, combinatorial auctions and electronic marketplaces, channel-allocation schemes for cellular phone networks, and network routing (for examples, see International Foundation for MultiAgent Systems 2000). As the MAS community expanded rapidly in the 1990s, several computer scientists and economists realized the potential of using MASs to model social systems. This line of work has been given various names, including "agent-based social simulation" (ABSS), "multi-agent–based simulation" (MABS), and "artificial societies," the term used here.

MAS technology and EBM differ in several ways, and each has a different scope of applicability. Several of these contrasts were first noted by economists, who have used MASs to allow them to relax some of the assumptions built into neoclassical theory (Epstein and Axtell 1996; Moss 1998); others have been noted by computer scientists interested in modeling social phenomena (Parunak, Savit, and Riolo 1998; N. Gilbert 1999b):

- In an artificial society, the model consists of a set of agents that simulate the behaviors of the various entities that make up the social system, and execution of the model involves emulating those behaviors. In EBM, the model is a set of equations, and execution of the model involves evaluating the equations.
- System dynamics makes extensive use of macrolevel observable variables (macrosimulation), whereas artificial societies define agent behaviors in terms of microlevel individual factors (microsimulation). Thus, artificial societies are better suited to domains where the natural unit of decomposition is the individual; system dynamics may be better suited to domains where the natural unit of decomposition is the macrolevel observable variable rather than the individual.

- Economic models of utility functions assume the rational actor of economic theory. Economists have long realized that such an actor is not very realistic, but the mathematical methods of EBM make it difficult to relax this assumption. MASs, by drawing on cognitive science, allow the representation of actors that use a wide range of decision strategies, both rational and nonrational. For example, MASs allow consideration of the internal representations of agents and their processes of plan construction and implementation, thus avoiding the behaviorist tinge of most rational choice theory. The role of an agent's internal models of social obligations, commitments, and responsibilities can be simulated, thus allowing an exploration of different theories of the sociological actor.
- In most EBM methods, agents are represented as homogeneous, and agent behavior does not change during the simulation. In economics theory, a representative actor is modeled; in system dynamics simulations, highly aggregate models of individuals are used to model social processes. (Some simulations allow highly constrained forms of agent variation, such as assigning a distribution of trait values to agents.) MASs, in contrast, allow the modeling of populations of radically heterogeneous actors, and these actors may modify their behavior during the simulation.
- Much of sociology (structural functionalism, network theory) has been concerned with static equilibria and has neglected social dynamics. After the structural-functional consensus faded in American sociology, sociological theories – most notably, conflict theory – became more concerned with social dynamics. System-dynamics EBM also support the exploration of social dynamics (Hanneman 1988); but MASs provide a methodology to study the mechanics of the micro-macro relations underlying social dynamics.

Social emergence in artificial societies

In the remainder of this chapter, I discuss specific artificial societies, grouping these examples according to their relevance to three aspects of social emergence: micro-to-macro emergence, macro-to-micro social causation, and the dialectic between emergence and social causation.

Social emergence

The ability to simulate social emergence is perhaps the most distinctive feature of artificial societies. In the artificial societies that I describe below, structural phenomena emerge, attain equilibrium, and remain stable over time. Thus, artificial societies provide sociologists with a tool to explore social emergence. In the following, I provide examples of artificial societies that represent two types of social emergence: the emergence of social structure and the emergence of norms.

The emergence of social structure Several artificial societies have been created in which there is no social structure initially and differentiated and hierarchically structured groups emerge during the simulation. An early example of such a simulation is Schelling's (1971) checkerboard simulation of residential segregation, which showed that almost total segregation can result from even rather small tendencies toward like neighbors. In the following, I give examples of simulations of the emergence of opinion clusters, the emergence of clusters of commitment surrounding supranational states, and the emergence of hierarchically structured and differentiated groups.

The emergence of opinion clusters has been observed in a simulation by Nowak and Latané (1994) in which agents behave according to Latané's theory of social impact. In this theory, the impact of a group of people on an individual's opinion is a multiplicative function of the persuasiveness of the members of the group, their social distance from the individual, and the number of the group members. At any moment during the simulation, each agent's opinion is determined by a multiplicative rule that derives the agent's opinion from the opinions of the agent's neighbors. The outcome of this simulation is that opinion clusters emerge and remain in dynamic equilibrium over a wide range of assumptions and parameters. The emergent equilibrium states contain multiple opinion clusters, and minority views remain active.

Axelrod (1995) used an artificial society to explore the emergence of new political actors: supranational entities that can regulate resource use at the global level. In his model, each agent represents a national state, and in repeat runs of the model, clusters of commitment emerge surrounding strong states. Thus, higher-level actors emerge from interactions among lower-level actors. This is a simpler version of Coleman's (1990) theory of how corporate actors emerge from the rational action of component members. Yet despite its simplicity, the simulation allows an examination of the unexpected effects of microtheoretical assumptions. For example, Axelrod's simulation reproduced historically observed patterns, such as *imperial overstretch*, when powerful empires are weakened by being dragged into fights involving weaker actors to whom they have developed commitments.

The purpose of the *Emergence of Organized Society (EOS)* project (Doran and Palmer 1995) was to investigate the growth in complexity of social institutions in southwestern France during the Upper Paleolithic period, when the archeological record indicates a transition from a relatively simple hunter-gatherer society to a more complex society with centralized decision making and several forms of differentiation, including division of labor, roles, and ethnicity. The EOS simulation was developed to explore various theories about the causes of this transition. For example, Mellars (1985) hypothesized that environmental change – resource deterioration as a result of the glacial maximum – led to the emergence of hierarchical, centralized decision making. The EOS researchers began by creating a virtual environment that simulated the environmental historical data from the known archeological record, such as the extent of glaciation in each year and the corresponding resource deterioration. They then created an artificial society composed of agents that operated within this environment.

When the simulation begins, agents do not have any knowledge of groups or of other agents. Each agent has the goal of acquiring a continuing supply of resources, and some of those resources can only be acquired through the cooperation of other agents. Thus, agents attempt to recruit each other to support their own plan of action. Based on these purely local rules of interaction, hierarchically structured groups emerge as the simulation is run. EOS supported Mellars's theory of this transition: Decreasing resources led to the emergence of more complex social structure.

The emergence of norms   A perennial issue for sociological theory has been what Parsons called the "problem of order": Why do autonomous, rational individuals come together to form groups? Why and under what conditions do individuals yield autonomy and power to macrosocial entities? MAS developers, by introducing autonomy into their computational agents, have been faced with a similar problem: how to design systems of autonomous agents in which cooperation and coordination occur. MAS developers have often solved this problem by imposing norms on their agents.[1] An active area of theoretical work in MAS has been the study of *deontic logic*, which consists of extensions of the predicate calculus that provide operators for conventions, responsibility, social commitment, and social laws (e.g., Dignum et al. 2000). Because many MASs are designed with a specific engineering goal in mind, designers often explicitly design agents that are predisposed to coordinate with

---

[1] In this section, I use the term "norm" quite loosely, to also refer to what sociologists call "values," "conventions," and "laws." In the context of the micro-macro link as discussed here, the theoretical points are the same in each case.

other agents (e.g., Fitoussi and Tennenholtz 2000). Because there is no centralization in an MAS, such norms must be programmed individually into each agent.

In Parsons's structural-functional theory, the problem of order is also resolved by shared norms. The integration function of social systems is served by the propagation of shared norms and conventions via socialization of individuals into an existing social structure. Much of subsequent sociological theorizing about norms occurred within a functionalist framework in which norms were hypothesized to serve various systemic functions like integration and cohesion. Many sociologists have criticized the functionalist assumptions of this normative approach to the question of order. A commonly noted problem with structural-functional approaches is their inability to explain the dynamics of systems: How do norms emerge in the first place? For example, network theorists reject the functionalist view of norms, arguing instead that analysts should look for integration in the network of connections linking individuals (Burt 1982). This is a more objectivist approach because it focuses on observable behavior rather than subjective belief (Wellman 1983, 162). A range of artificial societies are relevant to these sociological debates, including both simulations that impose norms in structural-functional fashion and simulations in which norms emerge during the simulation.

Many artificial societies impose norms and examine the resulting changes in the macrophenomena that emerge, contrasting the behavior with that in utilitarian rational actor systems in which there are no norms. For example, an artificial society by Conte and Castelfranchi (1995) explored how the introduction of norms affected macroemergence in a simple society of food eater agents. The agents were placed in an environment with randomly scattered food. Eating food increased an agent's energy, whereas fighting with another agent to take that agent's food reduced both agents' energies. First, Conte and Castelfranchi ran the simulation with no norms and with all agents acting according to personal utility. Agents frequently attacked other agents to take their food. After the simulation reached equilibrium, the researchers calculated the average strength of all agents. In a second simulation, they introduced a norm designed to reduce the overall amount of aggression: "finders keepers," specifying that the first agent to find food has a right to that food and will not be attacked. The introduction of this norm dramatically reduced aggression among agents and resulted in a correspondingly higher average agent strength once the society had reached equilibrium. Conte and Castelfranchi also found that the normative society was more equitable, with a smaller variance in the strength of agents.

This simulation shows how artificial society methods can be used to explore the macroimplications of the introduction of norms. However, in this simulation, the norms were imposed by the designers rather than emerging from the agents themselves. Such normative agents are not truly autonomous because they do not create nor choose their own norms. Note the similarities between these artificial societies and variants of sociological functionalism in which cooperation and common interest always develop owing to the functional requirements of the system (cf. Castelfranchi and Conte 1996).

Although designer-imposed norms can be an efficient solution to many engineering problems, such systems do not address some fundamental theoretical problems raised by autonomous agents: How do norms emerge in the first place? Why does an agent agree to adopt the goal requested by another agent? Why yield autonomy to a group? In addition to these theoretical concerns, engineering considerations have also led MAS designers to explore how norms might emerge during a simulation. In some applications, not all system requirements are known at design time, and the goals of agents might be constantly changing in response to environmental changes; further, in very complex systems, designers may find it quite difficult to design effective social laws.

Thus for both theoretical and practical reasons, MAS developers became interested in exploring how norms might spontaneously emerge from the local interactions of individual autonomous agents. If autonomous agents seek to maximize personal utility, then under what conditions will agents cooperate with other agents? In game theory terms, this is a prisoner's dilemma problem (Lomborg 1996, 278, 284). Purely self-interested agents have no desire to invest the resources in collaboration because they don't know if the other agents will also cooperate. Many studies of cooperation in MASs have been implementations of the *iterated prisoner's dilemma (IPD)*, where agents interact in repeated trials of the game, and agents can remember what other agents have done in the past (Axelrod 1984, 1997). Many MASs have been developed to simulate variations of the IPD, including the introduction of noise and of bounded rationality (Cox, Sluckin, and Steele 1999; Lomborg 1992, 1996; Macy and Skvoretz 1998; Sullivan, Grosz, and Kraus 2000).

In IPD-based artificial societies, norms of cooperation emerge even though they are not preprogrammed. These emergent norms of cooperation are not propositionally represented anywhere in the system; rather, cooperation is a component of the utility function. Thus, IPD agents are not normative in the sociological sense of the term because norms are not internalized and shared by all agents. In the late 1990s, artificial societies were developed in which explicit internal norms emerged during the simulation. One of the first attempts was by Walker and Wooldridge (1995), who extended Conte and Castelfranchi's (1995) system of food eaters described earlier. In their extension, a group of autonomous agents reached a global consensus on the use of social conventions, with each agent deciding which convention to adopt based solely on its own local experiences. The designers found that global norms emerged in each of sixteen different simulations, each run with a different *strategy update function*. Once the global norm emerged, the system remained at equilibrium. For example, one strategy update function was a *simple majority* function: Agents change to an alternative norm if at that point they have observed more instances of it in other agents than instances of their present norm. In each of the sixteen simulations, a different amount of time transpired before all of the agents converged on a single norm. In each, there was also a different average number of norm changes; because changes in norm can be costly for an agent and can lead to overall inefficiencies in the system, it is preferable for designers to choose an update function that results in the fewest norm changes while attaining norm convergence as quickly as possible.

Steels (1996) implemented a series of simulations in which agents have the task of learning how to communicate with each other about objects in their environment. They begin without any shared names for these objects. Steels explored a range of artificial societies in which all agents attain global agreement on a lexicon for these objects by playing successive rounds of the *naming game*. In the naming game, a speaker attempts to identify an object to a hearer by pointing and using a name. The game succeeds if the hearer correctly guesses the object chosen. If a speaker does not yet have a name for the object, the speaker may create a new name. A hearer may adopt a name used by a speaker. Both players monitor use and success, and in future games, they prefer names that succeed the most. In Steels's artificial societies, all agents gradually attain global coherence: They all use the same name for any given object. The resulting lexicon is an emergent property of the system. Each agent engages only in local dyadic interactions, and no agent has any awareness of the overall state of the system.

Steels and Kaplan (1998) then extended the simulation to allow for changes in the agent population. After global coherence is attained, one agent (out of twenty total) is allowed to change in every N games. When $N = 100$, the language remains stable (although the global coherence measure drops slightly), with new agents acquiring the language of the other agents in the group. These new agents occasionally create a new word for an object, but this word quickly gets rejected, dominated by the preferred word of the rest of the group. When $N = 10$, however, the language disintegrates, and coherence cannot be maintained.

In the examples just described, structures and norms emerge from the interactions of autonomous agents. These simulations provide support for methodologically individualist accounts of social emergence and allow rigorous examination of theories concerning social emergence in the micro-to-macro transition. They also provide a perspective on a related problem in sociological theory: Once a macropattern has emerged, how is it maintained over time? Some sociological theorists have suggested that emergence and maintenance are similar processes (Giddens), others that they are analytically distinct (Archer). The artificial societies described show that emergence and reproduction of structure are not necessarily distinct mechanisms and may not require distinct theories. In these simulations, macropatterns emerge and then are reproduced through the same dynamic processes. These macropatterns are similar to the equilibrium states of economics – which emerge from independent rational action – and they are dynamically maintained; thus, they are demonstrations of the functionalist concept of dynamic equilibrium.

Artificial societies suggest how structural theory can be extended to model social change. Parson's structural-functional theory was widely perceived to be only capable of modeling societies that remained in homeostasis. Contemporary structural theories, such as network analysis, are criticized on the same grounds. Artificial societies model both stability over time (the problem of order) *and* social change. Thus artificial societies suggest a form of structural theory that can potentially explain processes of emergence, conflict, and change: Stability emerges from dynamic processes, and those same dynamic processes can result in future change in response to change in environmental conditions (as in EOS). The Comtean distinction between static and dynamic sociology is blurred.

In all of the artificial societies described in this section, stable macrostructures emerge, and these differ depending on the models of individual agents and their interactions.[2] This seems to suggest that the extreme structuralist position – that macrostructure is the only appropriate subject of analysis for sociology and that individuals do not need to be theorized (e.g., Mayhew 1980) – cannot be maintained (these issues are further explored later in this chapter in "The Mutual Relations of Individual Action and Macro-Social Structure"). These

---

[2] Although many artificial societies result in the emergence of stable, reproducing macropatterns, not all possible simulations will do so. Those that do not are generally considered uninteresting and are not reported in the literature.

simulations demonstrate the sorts of emergence hypothesized by Blau's early exchange theory (1964), which proposed that social differentiation emerged from exchange processes. These demonstrations are also consistent with the methodologically individualist claims of rational choice theory (Coleman 1990).

The influence of structural phenomena on individuals

MAS developers often find it convenient to think of the emergent properties of a system as influencing the actions of the agents (N. Gilbert 1995, 149). In any of the MASs in the preceding section, once the overall system has attained equilibrium, this equilibrium macrostate could be said to constrain individual agents from changing their behavior. For example, in Nowak and Latané's artificial society, the agents' collective actions resulted in the emergence of opinion clusters. Once the clusters emerge, it appears that they influence the local behaviors of the agents. New agents in Steels and Kaplan's (1998) simulation could be said to be constrained to adopt the emergent language already in use by the rest of the agents. In this sense, MASs demonstrate a kind of macro-to-micro social causation: As the simulation proceeds, the agents and their dynamics change, and at any given moment in simulation time, agents' behaviors are determined by their local context within the currently emergent global pattern. This has led some MAS researchers to claim to have modeled both directions of the micro-macro relation (e.g., Conte and Castelfranchi 1996; Kennedy 1997; Lomborg 1996).

This is the notion of social causation held to by methodological individualists – that social causal laws are mere shorthand for what ultimately goes on between individuals (Coleman 1990, 20; Elster 1989, 158). Artificial societies represent a pure form of methodological individualism; they provide explanations of social phenomena in terms of individuals and their interactions. Artificial societies are methodologically individualist when they contain only explicit representations of individual agents and of their interactions, and the macrobehavior that emerges is said to be explained by the simulation (cf. Conte et al. 2001). For example, there is no explicit mechanism by which Nowak and Latané's emergent clusters "cause" agents to do anything; agents do not perceive the clusters and are only affected by their local neighbors. Note that these are not macro-to-micro effects in the usual sociological sense because actors are affected only by local interactions with neighboring agents, not by the macroproperties of society (Castelfranchi 2001; Sawyer 2002b, 2003e). The causal and ontological status of these emergent macro-structural phenomena is unclear; they seem to have no independent causal power (Bedau 2002).

These models are consistent with the claim of methodological individualists that although social causal laws may be a useful shorthand, social properties are not "real" and do not actually have causal power over agents.

However, there are also several MASs that provide support for the arguments of structural sociologists – that macrophenomena can be scientifically studied without regard for the nature of the individuals occupying the society. This is because of the design necessity of specifying the network topology of the simulation before running the model; the network topology corresponds to the macroproperties of both network theory and structural sociology. In this section, I describe three simulations that demonstrate how a change in structural features – network topology, social groups, and size of the society – results in changes in the bottom-up processes of micro-to-macro emergence.

Axtell (2000) conducted a simulation experiment in which he kept every feature of the simulation constant except for the network of connections among agents. The purpose of the simulation was to reproduce an observed macro-economic pattern in retirement age. Economists have been puzzled by the fact that although the U.S. government changed the social security law in 1961, allowing retirement as early as 62, the mean retirement age of the population did not shift from 65 to 62 until almost 30 years later, between 1990 and 1995. In an earlier version of this experiment, Axtell and Epstein (1999) had developed a reactive agent simulation that reproduced this pattern. The agents are connected in random graphs – each agent is randomly connected to n other agents. The simulation contains three types of agents: *rational agents*, which retire at the earliest age permitted by law; *imitators*, which play a coordination game in their social network, shifting their preferred retirement age once a certain threshold percentage of their connected agents have done so; and *randomly behaving agents*, which retire with some fixed probability as soon as they are able.

The model reproduces the empirically observed lag time, with ebb and flow in the preferred retirement age, until the new social norm is established (retirement at 62). The lag time decreases as the percentage of rational agents is increased. Once the new norm is established, it remains quite robust; in no simulation does the retirement age rise again once the new norm of 62 has been established. Thus, as in the examples in the preceding section, the artificial society simulates both the emergence of equilibrium and the reproduction of the equilibrium state once it has emerged.

Viewing a visual representation of the network while the simulation is running, one can see that the new retirement age first becomes established among older cohorts (many years older than 65) and is then propagated to younger agents, eventually reaching the age 65 cohort and shifting their retirement age down to 62.[3] Thus the model behaves as if the retirement age were diffusing through the population from older to younger individuals.

Axtell (2000) then modified the network topology to be a lattice network (a checkerboard grid with each agent connected to all agents within n spaces) rather than a random graph, keeping all other aspects of the simulation identical. He found that this systematically altered the overall behavior of the society. In a lattice network, the new social norm arises more quickly, regardless of the percentage of rational agents. In addition, viewing the visual representation of the simulation shows the transition to have a different dynamic. In contrast to a propagation from older to younger individuals – as observed in the random network – the lattice network shows the new retirement norm beginning first with a few agents of age 65, then growing outward within that cohort, then gradually propagating to older agents as that cohort ages. The social change occurs via a different mechanism than in the random graph network.

These two models demonstrate that the macroproperties of the network – not themselves emergent – have causal influence on the micro-to-macro processes of emergence. In both cases, a new social norm of retirement at age 62 is established with a lag. However, the dynamics of the transformation are quite different in the two network topologies. In a random network, the new norm is first established among older agents and then propagates to younger agents; in a lattice network, the new norm is first established among an age 65 cohort and then propagates upward as that cohort ages. This sort of micro-macro study of social dynamics is almost impossible to analyze in any detail without artificial society methodology.

In a second example of macroeffects on emergence, the sociologists Macy and Skvoretz (1998) developed an MAS to explore the evolution of trust and cooperation between strangers. In prior simulations of the prisoner's dilemma, trust emerged in the iterated game with familiar neighbors, but trust did not emerge with strangers. Macy and Skvoretz hypothesized that if the agents were grouped into neighborhoods, norms of trust would emerge among neighbors within each neighborhood, and that these would then extend to strangers. Their MAS contained 1,000 agents that played the prisoner's dilemma game with both familiar neighbors and with strangers. To explore the effects of community on the evolution of prisoner's dilemma strategy, the simulation defined neighborhoods that

---

[3] Java and Quicktime animations of these models can be viewed at http://www.brook. edu/dybdocroot/es/dynamics/models/retirement/, accessed 2 April 2005.

contained varying numbers of agents: from nine agents per neighborhood to fifty. Different runs of the simulation varied the *embeddedness* of interaction: the probability that in a given iteration a player would be interacting with a neighbor or a stranger. These simulations showed that conventions for trusting strangers evolved in neighborhoods of all sizes as long as agents interacted more with neighbors than strangers (embeddedness greater than .5). The rate of cooperation among strangers increased linearly as embeddedness was raised from .5 to .9. Simulations with smaller neighborhoods resulted in a higher rate of cooperation between strangers: At .9 embeddedness, the rate of cooperation between strangers was .62 in the ten-member neighborhood simulation, and .45 in the fifty-member neighborhood simulation (p. 655).

Macy and Skvoretz concluded that these neighborhoods – characterized by relatively dense interactions – allow conventions for trusting strangers to emerge and become stable and then diffuse to other neighborhoods via weak ties. If an epidemic of distrusting behavior evolves in one segment of the society, the large number of small neighborhoods facilitates the restoration of order (p. 657). Like the Axtell experiment described previously, this simulation demonstrates that social structure can influence micro-to-macro emergence processes; cooperation with strangers emerges when agents are grouped into neighborhoods but not when they are ungrouped.

Several simulations (Cox, Sluckin, and Steele 1999; Ray and Hart 1998) show that the size of the network – a nonemergent macroproperty – affects the emergent macrobehavior. For example, Ray and Hart (1998) ran simulations in which they varied the number of agents in the simulation; they found that as size changes, the types of emergent macrophenomena change. In systems of agents operating with imitation algorithms, they found that in a small network, mob behavior can be severe, whereas in a larger network, the mob behavior is diffused. Thus, the same microsimulation, but with different group sizes, can give rise to different macrobehaviors.

Many sociologists make a distinction between small groups and more complex macrosocial structures. Blau, for example, proposed that small-group structures could be emergent but not large collective structures, "since there is no direct social interaction among most members" (1964, 253). Blau distinguished between microstructures (interacting individuals) and macrostructures (interacting groups): "Although complex social systems have their foundation in simpler ones, they have their own dynamics with emergent properties" (pp. 19–20). In contrast, artificial society methodology assumes that the dynamics of small and large groups are fundamentally the same, even though different properties may emerge in societies of different sizes. The computational power of MAS techniques provides sociologists with a tool to extend the interactional methods of Blau (1964) and of network exchange theory (e.g., Markovsky 1987; T. S. Smith and Stevens 1999) to larger social groups.

These experiments support some claims of structural sociologists: Network topology and size have a causal influence on the social dynamics of the population, and this influence is independent of the models of the individual agents. Such phenomena are consistent with structural sociology (Blau 1977; Mayhew 1980). For example, Mayhew (1980) argued that sociology should be concerned with structural phenomena that have effects regardless of the nature of the entities occupying the nodes of the network. Axtell's simulations also provide support to network theorists who claim that network phenomena cannot be explained by aggregating the properties of actors and that network analysis does not need to consider individuals as causal forces (e.g., Wellman and Berkowitz 1988). Artificial societies provide some support for this emphasis and are compatible with the network theory tradition.

In Axtell's pair of simulations, the macroproperty "random graph or lattice network" causally influences the bottom-up processes of emergence. Because Axtell's simulations contained only reactive agents – agents that have no internal social representations – this form of social causation occurs without internalization or subjectivity on the part of the agents. The fact that such social causation is observed even in artificial societies with reactive agents mitigates against subjectivist claims, such as those of Giddens, that social structures and systems cannot exist unless individuals have a sophisticated knowledge of social activities, which Giddens called "practical consciousness." Giddens claimed that "structure has no existence independent of the knowledge that agents have about what they do in their day-to-day activity" (1984, 26). Yet, reactive agent societies demonstrate the emergence and reproduction of social structure even though agents have no internal representations.

Artificial societies demonstrate that the interpretivist arguments of Giddens and others are based on a false assumption. Contra interpretivists, objective structures can emerge, and the existence of those structures can "constrain" individual agents (via changes in patterns of local interactions) even when agents have no internal representations. Structuration theory could be modified to be compatible with such simulations; after all, in both artificial societies and structuration theory, social structure is produced and reproduced by agents' continued situated actions, even as that structure constrains those constituting agents. Such an extension of structuration theory would have to become more objectivist, limiting the emphasis on individuals' practical knowledge while at the same time acknowledging some theoretical role for emergent social structure (cf. Contractor et al. 2005; Layder 1987; see Chapter 10).

Network analysts have traditionally used methods of matrix algebra and EBM that were originally developed in the 1970s and early 1980s (e.g., Burt 1982). Network analysis is ripe for the introduction of MAS methods because they allow the evaluation of several unresolved issues. For example, artificial societies could be developed that would allow an exploration and a reconciliation of the opposition between exchange theory and network analysis (Cook and Whitmeyer 1992). Artificial societies also allow network theoretical models to undergo dynamic simulation, addressing the frequent criticism that network analysis is overly static and structural (e.g., Burke 1997). Several artificial societies show how network structures can emerge from individual actions, such as the emergence of opinion clusters in Nowak and Latané (1994) and the emergence of groups in networks with both strong and weak links (Chwe 1999; T. S. Smith and Stevens 1999). These artificial societies show how structure emerges from individual actions and interactions and then is reproduced over time via the same dynamic processes.

The mutual relations of individual action and macrosocial structure

The dialectic of emergence and social causation remains one of the most pressing issues in contemporary sociological theory: How do macrosocial phenomena emerge from individual action and then in turn constrain or otherwise influence future action? Although artificial societies offer helpful perspectives on various components of this process, MAS developers are just beginning to address this most intractable aspect of the micro-macro link (cf. Castelfranchi 1998; Conte and Castelfranchi 1996; Sawyer 2001b).

In "Social Emergence," I presented examples of systems in which macrostructure emerged from individual action. These simulations are consistent with individualist sociological theory, such as exchange theory and rational choice theory. In the next section, "The Influence of Structural Phenomena on Individuals," I presented examples of how macrostructural properties influenced the actions of individual agents; these simulations are more difficult to reconcile with individualism, and to an extent they provide support to structural sociology and network theory.

However, note that in none of these simulations are both micro-to-macro and macro-to-micro processes modeled simultaneously. In those simulations in which macroproperties influence individual action, those macroproperties do not themselves emerge from the simulations but are specified in advance by the designers (cf. Castelfranchi 1998; Hales 1998). For example, in Axtell's simulation of retirement behavior, the network topology was prespecified by the designer; it did not itself emerge from the actions of the agents during the simulation. In natural sociological systems, in contrast, macrophenomena (network topology, group size, communication mechanisms, and group and institutional structure) result from processes of social emergence, and only after they have emerged do future agents modify their behaviors under the influence of these macrophenomena. These twin processes are foundational in most contemporary theories of the micro-macro link, including those of Habermas, Giddens, Bourdieu, and Archer. Such theories attempt to integrate theories of the individual, individual agency, situated symbolic interaction, and social structure.

In the system dynamics tradition, *multi-level* simulation languages (such as MIMOSE, Möhring 1996, and Lisp-Stat, N. Gilbert 1999a) allow modeling of both micro- and macrolevels and simulation of their interactions. Using these tools, individuals, groups, and societies can be modeled as nested objects, and equations can be specified to represent interactions among levels. Although advocates of multilevel simulation sometimes claim that they allow the representation of how individual actions can influence or modify macrovariables (e.g., Saam 1999), this is done using equations that connect individuals to macrovariables that have already been created by the programmer, and the micro-to-macro relation is limited to rather simple types of aggregation. Consequently, multilevel models do not allow exploration of how macrostructure emerges from individual action and interaction; there is no micro-to-macro emergence in the MAS sense, nor in Coleman's (1987) sense. This reflects the general tendency in sociological multilevel models to focus on the macro-to-micro relation (see DiPrete and Forristal, 1994).

There have been some intriguing first steps toward multilevel artificial societies. The relevant simulation tools include the CORMAS and SDML languages and several of the tools developed for *computational organization theory (COT)* (Carley and Gasser 1999; Carley and Prietula 1994). However, the macro-to-micro processes that are modeled do not originate from macrophenomena that themselves emerged from prior micro-to-macro processes. Instead, the macrofeatures of the system are preprogrammed, as they are in system-dynamics multilevel simulation languages. The interactions of the microunits are allowed to modify the macrolevel but within a predefined structure.

For example, Antona et al. (1998) used the CORMAS environment to simulate the management of renewable resources. The researchers first noted that the management of renewable resources may be based either on public interventions at the macroscopic level or on regulation of the microscopic level. They simulated two forms of microregulation: (1) direct interaction through local trade and (2) centralized exchanges through an auctioneer such that general equilibrium processes set a global price. In both, agent trade behavior was based on neoclassical economic theory: an internal computation of welfare associated with exchanges. At the macrolevel, the simulation allowed the imposition of either a global quota (which directly affects the stock of the resource) or taxes (levied on each selling agent as a proportion of the resource sold).

These two variables allowed a two-by-three experimental design: microlevel (local trade or centralized equilibrium) by macrolevel (no regulation, global quota, or taxes). Thus, the simulation allowed the examination of how macroscopic interventions affected microsociological interactions at the same time that those interactions were giving rise to an emergent pattern of trade and price formation. The designers first began the simulation without any macrolevel regulation and then waited for the global price to reach equilibrium. Then, they imposed one of the two macro-regulatory schemes and examined how the overall dynamics of the system behavior changed.

The benefit of such a CORMAS simulation, compared with a simulation using a system-dynamics multilevel simulation tool like MIMOSE, is that autonomous, heterogeneous agents can be modeled, their interactions can be asynchronous and complex, and the processes of emergence can be more complex than simple aggregation. Note, however, that as in MIMOSE simulations the macrointervention was imposed by the designer; it was not emergent from the actions of the agents.

Carley's computational organization theory (COT) (Carley and Gasser 1999; Carley and Prietula 1994) is an application of MAS techniques to the analysis of business organizations. COT simulations allow the explicit modeling of organizational structure, permitting the designer to enter parameters such as authority structures, organizational procedures (e.g., workflow), and skill requirements for different organizational positions (Carley and Gasser 1999, 310–12). Organizational structure includes not only the traditional hierarchical organizational chart but also the informal friendship networks among agents, the task structures (ordering among subtasks), the task-skill structures (defining which skills are required for which tasks), and the task-assignment structures (defining which types of agents are allowed to work on which tasks). In these models, agents are constrained by their organizational roles, although within these roles, agents are autonomous and make their own decisions. Researchers in the COT tradition have developed several modeling tools that allow the development of artificial societies with multilayered organizational structures.

For example, Radar-Soar (Ye and Carley 1995) allows the explicit modeling of organizational structure and resource access structure. However, agents themselves do not create the organizational structure through emergence processes (although a few such models allow the agents to modify aspects of the organizational structure).

Like CORMAS, COT tools are MAS variants of multilevel simulation languages. These models are typically descriptive at the individual level (individuals are described as boundedly rational or with cognitive biases) and normative at the structural level (the best organizational design is sought) (Carley and Gasser 1999, 323). Because the goal is to find the best organizational design to accomplish a given task, COT researchers are not as concerned with sociological issues of emergence; rather, they are searching for better ways to engineer organizations.

In their relevance to the sociological theory of micro-macro relations, these multilevel artificial societies suffer from two of the same problems as multilevel EBM. First, the macrostructures or macroproperties do not themselves emerge from the simulation but are imposed by the designer. Yet in actual societies, macrophenomena are themselves emergent from microprocesses. In "The Influence of Structural Phenomena on Individuals," we saw how network structure changes the behavior of the simulation, and in "Social Emergence," we saw examples of structures emerging in simulations of autonomous agents. To date, no artificial society has brought together these two phenomena: In an MAS, the network among agents does not emerge or change but is fixed by the designer (especially in reactive agent systems). But this is a key issue for sociological theory: How do individuals come together to form networks? What sorts of networks are created? How do these change over time? Note that these questions also tend to be neglected by network theory, which typically examines a static, unchanging network. Yet in "Social Emergence," we saw examples of several artificial societies in which structures spontaneously emerge from microsimulation. It would be instructive to extend artificial societies so that agents can choose their neighbors and the strength of their connections. Multilevel variants of such models could allow higher-level structural and institutional factors to influence the interactions and networking options available to agents.

A second problem in applying these multilevel artificial societies to sociological theory is that agents do not have any perception of the emergent collective entity (Castelfranchi 1998; Conte, Gilbert, and Sichman 1998; Servat et al. 1998). In the CORMAS simulation, agents do not know that they are being taxed, nor that a quota has been imposed. In the EOS simulation of group formation, hierarchically structured groups emerge during the simulation as environmental change is introduced.

However, although the social structure is visible to the human observer, it is not explicitly modeled by any agent (Doran and Palmer 1995, 106). Rather, groups are constructed from the agents' own "social models" such that, for example, agent A comes to perceive agent B as its leader and B thinks of A as its follower. The complete network of these bilateral relations forms a hierarchically structured society, but only the human observer is aware of these macrostructures. No agent has awareness of its own group as an entity, and agents that are not in a group have no way of recognizing that the group exists or who its members are. Consequently, these agents have no ability to reason about social groups.

Economic theory has long accepted this utilitarian conception of the agent, and artificial societies perhaps tend to use such conceptions because the approach has been influenced more by economics than by any other social science discipline. Yet most sociological theories long ago abandoned this utilitarian conception of the agent in favor of some combination of Parson's *voluntaristic agent* (an agent with internalized systems of global norms) and the *interpretive agent* (an agent with potentially unique and idiosyncratic perceptions of and orientations toward the macro-social order, as in the influential theories of Winch and Giddens). In human societies, people are capable of detecting, reasoning about, and acting on the emergent macrolevel properties of the societies that they are in. A major emphasis of contemporary hybrid sociological theories is that actors' subjective interpretations of social structural phenomena affect their behaviors (e.g., Archer, Bourdieu, and Giddens).

Although much of sociology has rejected the utilitarian conception of the actor, artificial societies are interesting in that they allow utilitarian atomistic conceptions of the actor to be pushed to a methodological limit. As we saw in "Social Emergence," artificial societies of simple agents have successfully reproduced many macrophenomena of interest to sociologists, including structure, norms, languages, and cooperation. These examples suggest that the complex individual of voluntarist and interpretivist sociological theory is not always necessary to explain macrosocial phenomena, contrary to the thesis that the only way to introduce the microlevel into collective theorizing is through a subjectivist theory of action (e.g., J. C. Alexander and Giesen 1987, 17). Nonetheless, the question remains to what extent these models can be considered accurate representations of true human societies; after all, even neoclassical economists acknowledge that such agents are not much like people (cf. Epstein and Axtell 1996, 1). Thus artificial society models can help to negotiate a reconciliation between the disciplines of sociology and economics.

A few artificial societies implement cognitive agents that are said to have "social knowledge"; some researchers refer to these as "social agents." There have been several recent special issues on this topic ("Social Intelligence," *CMOT* 5, no. 3 (1999); "Simulation Models of Social Agents," *Adaptive Behavior* 7, nos. 3–4 (1999); *Journal of Cognitive Systems Research* 2, no.1 (2001)). Yet even in these artificial societies, although social agents have knowledge about the knowledge or capabilities of specific other agents, they do not have knowledge about emergent macrophenomena (Brassel et al. 1997; Moulin and Chaib-Draa 1996). In agent simulations of the IPD, social knowledge is represented as memory about how another agent has behaved in past games. The social knowledge of EOS agents is limited to knowledge about which other agent is a leader and which other agent(s) are followers. And in COT models (e.g. Ye and Carley 1995), although agents are said to have knowledge about the organizational structure, that knowledge is always modeled in terms of locally applicable rules; no agent has an internal representation of macroproperties of these structures.

To some extent, artificial societies suggest that social theory can proceed without a theory of agency. This supports the arguments of structural sociologists that it does not make any difference whether you have reactive agents or cognitive agents; sociology should be the study of the networks and structures among agents and should leave the study of the agents to psychology (Mayhew 1980). However, artificial societies also suggest that it is not possible to make a strict separation between network structure and agent design. In the artificial societies discussed in this chapter, the micro-macro relation changes dramatically as the model of the agent is changed. For example, agents with social knowledge (even as simple as memory in IPD simulations) give rise to different macropatterns than agents without such knowledge, and agents with internalized norms give rise to different macropatterns than agents with no norms. These findings reproduce an early network theory simulation study by Markovsky (1987), which showed that changes in individual strategies affected the power and profit distributions that emerged in a three-actor exchange network. These findings support claims that structural sociology must incorporate a theory of the individual (cf. Whitmeyer 1994).

Conclusion: Implications of artificial societies for sociological theory

Artificial societies provide sociologists with a new tool for the examination of social emergence. By demonstrating the emergence of structure from micromodels of the individual actor, and the appearance of a sort of "social causation" even in such models, artificial societies demonstrate the plausibility of the methodologically individualist position. If macro-structural phenomena can be shown to emerge from a simulation only of individual agents and their interactions, then this suggests that sociological theory may be able to proceed without explicit modeling of the emergent macrolevel. These demonstrations provide support to the methodological individualism of rational choice and game theoretic models.

However, artificial societies do not provide unequivocal support for methodological individualism; several artificial societies provide support for the arguments of structural sociologists that network structures have causal effects on individual action. Thus artificial societies do not strongly support either methodological individualism or social realism, and they can be used as tools for theory development by advocates of both positions. Consequently, artificial societies can be viewed as implementations of hybrid sociological theories: theories that attempt to reconcile individual autonomy, on the one hand, and structural and network phenomena, on the other. Artificial societies allow an exploration of the role of the individual and of how different theories of the individual relate to different hypotheses about the micro-macro relation (J. C. Alexander and Giesen 1987, 14; Cook and Whitmeyer 1992, 116–18).

Current artificial societies have several features that limit their relevance to sociological theory. To realize their full potential as a tool for sociological simulation, artificial societies may need to be extended by including explicit modeling of emergent macrofeatures of the system. This would require a simulation that could dynamically create models during the run of the simulation so that the macrophenomena represented would have emerged from the microinteractions of the agents. The emergence of a macropattern would automatically result in the generation of a computational structure to be added to the model, which would then be perceived and internally represented by social agents (cf. Servat et al. 1998).

This could be accomplished by extending artificial societies in the direction of multilevel simulation tools, as done by COT researchers. The difference between these simulations and COT simulations would be that the macro-level phenomena would themselves emerge from microinteraction rather than being explicitly designed into the simulations. This would allow simulation of a new consensus in sociological theory (J. C. Alexander and Giesen 1987; Archer 1995): that macrostructures emerge from the actions and interactions of individuals and that once they have emerged those structures then constrain and otherwise influence the future actions and interactions of those same individuals.

Many sociologists argue against explicit theories or models of emergent macrophenomena, claiming that this would be a reification or hypostatization of such structures (Giddens 1984; King 1999a). Yet in the artificial societies described here, structural phenomena have effects even when only local knowledge is explicitly modeled. And it may be necessary to explicitly model macro-social properties in those cases where social properties are real and their ontological autonomy results in causal powers (see Chapter 5).

Such simulations could contain complex social agents that are capable of examining the entire structure of the simulation and internalizing representations of it (cf. Castelfranchi 1998, 2001). For example, agents could form and break network links and make decisions about whether to join groups after become consciously aware of what groups exist and what their missions and compositions are. However, in complex modern societies, it is impossible for each individual to directly perceive the entire social order. Instead, individuals' perceptions of macro-social phenomena are typically mediated by institutions such as the mass media, government agencies, and educational institutions. To adequately simulate complex modern societies, artificial societies may need to explore the roles of such institutions.

Artificial societies provide a novel perspective on social emergence. They partially support both individualist and collectivist extremes of sociological theory. Artificial society methodologies can be used to rigorously implement and test hybrid micro-macro theories. More complex sociological theories can be developed, and unexpected consequences and internal conflicts can be identified. In this way, artificial societies have the potential to substantively contribute to the study of social emergence.

9 Communication and improvisation

Most sociologists assume that communication is not central to sociology's main concerns and that its study can be safely tucked away into the subfield of microsociology (symbolic interactionism, conversation analysis, sociolinguistics). In general, sociology assumes that all social constraint must be institutional; the implicit assumption is that communication is epiphenomenal – that it has no causal consequences, either for emergent macrophenomena or for individuals. Instead, the ultimate causal forces in social life are either institutions, networks, and group properties (for the collectivist) or rational actions taken in the context of pairwise game-like encounters (for the individualist). Thus both of these opposed camps agree in their implicit assumption that communication is of only marginal concern to the sociologist (cf. Rawls 1987; Ritzer and Gindoff 1992).

In Chapter 10, I present a framework for the study of social emergence, and communication is central to that framework. This chapter sets the stage by providing several examples of how differences in communication result in different emergence processes and outcomes. In the first half of the chapter, I describe communication and emergence in three broad classes of artificial societies: those with reactive agents, cognitive agents, and collaborative agents. Differences among these artificial societies demonstrate that very specific features of the agent communication language have subtle and unintended causal effects on social emergence. In the second half of the chapter, I describe the important role of *metapragmatic communication* in creating the emergent dialogues of improvised conversations. These examples demonstrate that the design of the communication language has causal consequences and that a theory of communication must be a central component of any theory of social emergence.

Reactive agent societies

Reactive agents do not contain any internal representation of the world – neither of the environment nor of the other agents. Reactive agents are also sometimes called "behavioral agents" because they respond directly to stimuli from the environment, unmediated by internal states. Reactive agents are similar to the model of the individual proposed in behaviorist versions of exchange theory (Emerson 1972; Homans 1958). Whereas cognitive agents evolved from the artificial intelligence tradition, reactive agent systems evolved from the artificial life (Alife) tradition (Adami et al. 1998).

The communicative formalisms implemented in reactive agent societies are radically simple compared to sociological theories of communicative action. For example, in reactive agent societies, a communication can be as simple as exchanging one bit of information. The Sugarscape artificial society (Epstein and Axtell 1996) uses interaction rules like Example 9.1.

Example 9.1.   An agent interaction rule in Sugarscape.
Cultural transmission rule (tag-flipping):

For each neighbor (4 orthogonally contiguous agents), a tag (one bit in an 8-bit mask) is randomly selected;

If the neighbor's bit setting agrees with the agent's at that position, take no action; if they disagree, flip the neighbor's tag to agree with the agent. (p. 73)

Such rules, typical of reactive agent societies, are simple versions of the forms of interaction assumed by both exchange theory and rational choice theory. In exchange theory, for example, all sociologically relevant communication is modeled as a form of exchange (e.g., the exchange of valuable information for status). As with Coleman's rational choice theory, social communication is modeled as a type of exchange (e.g., a transfer of trust from one agent to another) (1990, chap. 8).

One of the reactive agent societies that I discussed in Chapter 8 was designed by Walker and Wooldridge (1995). In this simulation, a group of autonomous agents reached a global consensus on the use of social conventions, with each agent deciding which convention to adopt based solely on its own local experiences. Once the global norm emerged, the system remained at equilibrium. The designers found that global norms emerged in each of sixteen different simulations, each with agents using a different *strategy update function*. It turns out that most of the strategy update functions involved different communication mechanisms. The simplest strategy update function was a *simple majority* function: Agents change to an alternative norm if so far they have observed more instances of it in other agents than their present norm. Each agent must be able to communicate the strategy it is currently using. A more complex strategy was called *simple majority with communication on success*: When an agent reaches a certain threshold level of success with a given strategy, it communicates its memory of experiences with this strategy to all nearby agents. Each agent must be able to make decisions about when to communicate and must be able to communicate a chain of remembered past experiences.

Walker and Wooldridge found that each of the sixteen functions resulted in a different amount of time before all of the agents converged on a single norm, and each of the functions also resulted in a different average number of norm changes on the way to equilibrium. Because many of the strategy update functions involve different methods of communicating with other agents, these sixteen simulations demonstrate that different communication languages result in different processes and outcomes of emergence. The processes vary in that each simulation experiences a different number of norm changes before it converges on a norm, and the outcomes vary in that the final norm is slightly different with each function.

Reactive agent societies use extremely simple communication languages. But even with these simple languages, variations in sometimes subtle features of the language result in the emergence of different macroproperties and in different processes of emergence – the microgenetic, moment-to-moment evolution of the emergent macropattern.

Cognitive agent societies: Toward a speech act theory

In contrast to the simple interactions of reactive agents, many recent simulations have begun to model what are known as *cognitive agents*. Cognitive agents have beliefs about the state of the environment, knowledge about actions and plans of actions, and knowledge about how their actions will affect the environment and the other agents. Cognitive agents have explicit goals, and they are capable of reasoning about how to achieve their goals; thus, they are also known as "intentional" or "deliberative" agents.

Because of social emergence, an agent-level focus on cognition cannot completely explain cognitive agent systems (e.g., Castelfranchi 1998, 27n2, 33–4). Both Castelfranchi (1998) and N. Gilbert (2002) argued that emergence processes in systems of cognitive agents are qualitatively different than in reactive agent systems because cognitive agents are capable of observing and internalizing emergent macrofeatures of the system, a process that has been called "immergence" (Castelfranchi 1998) and "second-order emergence" (N. Gilbert 1995; Hales 1998) to distinguish it from conceptions of emergence in complex dynamical systems in physics or biology. Second-order emergence would require agents capable of recognizing the existence of groups that emerged from their own collective activity (see one proposal in Servat et al. 1998). This conception of immergence is consistent with a sociological theory extending back to Durkheim ([1893] 1984): that the modern individual is a historical product and itself the result of long-term social emergence processes.

The actions of cognitive agents are based not only on their representations of the external world but also on their internal beliefs and goals and their expectations about the outcome of possible actions (thus allowing some cognitive processing concerning likely future events). To be able to accomplish their tasks, cognitive agents must be able to think about the actions of other agents in the system because such systems are designed to model tasks that are inherently distributed. For example, on many occasions an agent's goal cannot be met without the assistance of another agent, and part of the plan to accomplish that action necessarily involves a request for support to the other agent, along with expectations about how likely that agent is to agree and how competent that agent is to satisfy the request.

Cognitive agent societies use communication languages known as *agent communication languages (ACLs)*. Developers realize that ACLs are "the centerpiece of today's multi agent systems" because they are "a prerequisite for implementing social action" (Serrano and Ossowski 2002, 92). Speech act theory is the explicit theoretical foundation for the two dominant industry-standard ACLs: FIPA (http://www.fipa.org, accessed 2 April 2005) and KQML (http://www.cs.umbc.edu/kqml/, accessed 2 April 2005). Following speech act theory, KQML messages are called "performatives." Performatives are defined in terms of the agent's *knowledge base*, which contains two types of knowledge: *beliefs* and *goals*. For example, the performative TELL is defined in Example 9.2 (following Labrou and Finin 1997).

Example 9.2. Definition of the TELL performative in KQML.

TELL (A, B, X): A states to B that A believes X to be true.

Precondition for performative: This performative occurs when A *believes* X, and A *knows* that B *wants* to *know* whether X is true.

Result of performative: A *knows* that B *believes* that A *believes* X. B *knows* that A *believes* X.

This model of communication is based on a theory of agency that is widely used in multi-agent systems: the *belief-desire-intention (BDI)* model (Rao and Georgeff 1995). The italicized terms in Example 9.2

represent beliefs and desires of agents. Before any communicative act occurs, the agent must first have goals and beliefs about how to accomplish those goals. An "intention" captures the notion of *commitment* to a plan of action; agents communicate only after committing to a plan of action. Since 1995, computation theorists have developed a formal logic of BDI systems using *modal logic*, which includes logical operators such as "BELIEVE(x, y)" and "DESIRE(x, y)" (Wooldridge 2000). Agents reason about other agents' actions, assuming that those other agents are also operating according to BDI principles. Beliefs about the BDI states of other agents play an important role in composing and interpreting messages (as in Example 9.2).

It is widely recognized among cognitive agent developers that the ACL design influences emergence processes. For example, the recently agreed-upon industry standard FIPA has already been repeatedly modified to make it more effective in specific multi-agent domains. There are special language extensions for argumentation-based negotiation (Sierra et al. 1998), team formation (Dignum, Dunin-Keplicz, and Verbrugge 2001), and decision support (Serrano and Ossowski 2000). Serrano and Ossowski (2002) went so far as to argue that each organizational structure may require its own distinct ACL.

These distributed phenomena result in the emergence of simple dyadic relationships as well as global system properties. Emergent dyadic phenomena include *interference* and *dependence* relations. There is interference between two agents when the actions of one agent interfere with the goals of another, and there is dependence between two agents when one agent needs an action or a resource controlled by another agent to fulfill one of its goals (Hannoun et al. 1998; Sichman and Conte 1995). These are emergent properties of the dyadic relationship because they are objectively observable and hold whether or not the two agents are aware of them. Castelfranchi (1998, 29) observed that when agents are given the capability to recognize and become aware of such relations, these objective relations are transformed through what he called "cognitive emergence": Recognition of an interference relation can lead to competition, aggression, or exploitation; recognition of a dependence relation can lead to relations of power, influence, and cooperation. For example, cooperation can result from mutual dependence (e.g., when two agents depend on each other to realize a common goal), and social exchange can result from reciprocal dependence (e.g., when two agents depend on each other for two different goals) (Sichman and Conte 1995). As with other internal representations of an agent, these representations of emergent properties can be the objects of beliefs, goals, and plans. The fact

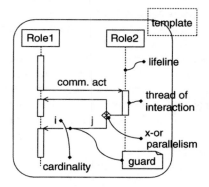

Figure 9.1. A sample protocol specification in AUML (from Pitt, Kamara, and Artikis 2001).

that agents can become partially aware of their collective effects results in additional, more complex emergent phenomena.

FIPA allows developers to create *protocols*, a sort of script or routine describing a regular pattern of interaction involving a sequence of communicative acts (FIPA 1999; see Figure 9.1). A protocol is an abstract template for a *conversation*, a sequence of communications among agents (Nowostawski, Purvis, and Cranefield 2001). Protocols were added to FIPA because in many real-world applications successful coordination among agents was difficult without them and because they increase the efficiency of distributed tasks that recur frequently; they represent a compromise in the continuing engineering trade-off between autonomy and centralization in multi-agent system design. FIPA protocols are specified using AUML (Agent Unified Modeling Language). Protocols include several technical devices represented in Figure 9.1, including *roles*, which agents occupy in the protocol; *lifelines*, which indicate the duration of time that an agent is active in its role in the protocol; *parallelism*, which allows communicative acts to occur simultaneously; and *guards*, which are conditions that must be met before a communicative act can be performed. Note that FIPA protocols are somewhat rigid; there is no mechanism, for example, for representing undelivered messages, and in many real-world applications protocols become unmanageably complex, as developers are forced to add exception after exception to handle unexpected communication developments (Foundation for Intelligent Physical Agents, 1999). Furthermore, protocols do not have independent ontological status, like Collins's (1981) interaction ritual chains; rather, direct copies of the protocols must be stored within each agent, sidestepping issues of intersubjectivity and thus making the system less interesting to sociologists. These practical and theoretical concerns have motivated the increasing focus on improvisational, collaborative agents (see the next section).

Cognitive agent ACLs support communication based on beliefs, goals, and plans. For example, agents must be able to request actions from other agents, to accept or deny such requests, or to partially accept a request. Because agents often reason based on knowledge of the beliefs and goals of other agents, agents must be capable of communicating about their own beliefs and goals and occasionally correcting incorrect impressions held by other agents. BDI formalisms follow directly from such conceptions of the agent, and the communications supported by cognitive agent ACLs are designed to support BDI logics.

Compared with reactive agent systems, very different emergence processes and outcomes are observed, and these could only emerge in a system with a speech act–based ACL. Yet, even speech acts are radically simple compared with human language use as described in most theories of such use (Sawyer 2003a). In the next section, I discuss several advanced artificial societies with even more sophisticated communication languages.

Collaborative agent societies: Improvisational dialogue and teamwork

The most sophisticated agent communication is found in the *distributed artificial intelligence (DAI)* tradition. Several of the researchers in this tradition are exploring virtual collaboration and teamwork in teams composed of multiple computational agents but also occasionally with the participation of human users. Owing to the active participation of humans, many of these researchers attempt to support natural language communication so that humans and computational agents can interact. As in all collaborative teamwork settings, the outcome is emergent from the communicative processes among the group members (Sawyer 2003c).

Most complexity researchers assume that systems must contain a large number of distinct components to display complex behavior. But complex behavior can be seen in small groups, owing to *collaborative emergence* (Sawyer 1999, 2003c). A system with a small number of agents can exhibit complex behavior when the agents are complex and the communication language is complex; these complexities make up for the lack of a large number of distinct agents. In fact, many collaborative systems focus on emergence with as few as two agents engaged in shared cooperative activity (e.g., Bratman 1992).

P. R. Cohen and Levesque (1991) made a seminal early attempt to formalize teamwork in terms of *joint intentions* (also see M. Gilbert 1989; Searle 1990). A joint intention exists when two or more agents mutually know that they each intend the collective action to occur and that they each intend to do their share, so long as the action has not yet occurred and is still believed to be attainable. In a team, the group acts "as a single agent with beliefs, goals, and intentions of its own, over and above the individual ones" (Levesque, Cohen, and Nunes 1990, 94). Levesque, Cohen, and Nunes (1990) contrasted ordinary traffic (interaction but no collaboration) with a convoy (collaboration), with the latter demonstrating the emergent properties of a team. Joint intentions are "shared commitments to perform an action" (p. 94) and as such are emergent from communicative interaction.

Many computer scientists have explored the kinds of communication that are necessary to sustain such group action (P. R. Cohen and Levesque 1991; Grosz and Sidner 1990; Jennings 1993, 1995; P. R. Cohen, Morgan, and Pollack 1990; Rich, Sidner, and Lesh 2001; Tambe 1997). Designers of such artificial societies are particularly interested in agents that do not necessarily have identical beliefs; this is a common case in complex real-world environments. Groups can collaboratively accomplish tasks even when members hold different information and have different understandings of the task (P. R. Cohen and Levesque 1991). One resulting research question is, What would hold a team together when individual members have distinct private beliefs about the shared activity? Collaborative systems thus touch on the key sociological issue of intersubjectivity; the need to continually manage intersubjectivity requires sophisticated communication (P. R. Cohen and Levesque 1991, 489). Agents in teams must be able to reason with and communicate about group goals and actions in addition to the individual representations and communications supported by the ACLs of cognitive agents.

Much of this theoretical work has explored the relations between individual intentions and joint intentions; for example, if a team jointly intends to do an action involving a sequence of steps, then the agent responsible for any step "will intend to do that part relative to the larger intention" (P. R. Cohen and Levesque 1991, 505). Philosophers who have influenced this simulation work (e.g., see the essays in P. R. Cohen, Morgan, and Pollack 1990) have debated issues related to social emergence: Is collective intentionality reducible to individual intentions or does it necessarily have a distinct ontological status? Some philosophers (M. Gilbert 1989; Searle 1990) argue that collective intentionality is not reducible. But most collaborative systems do not explicitly model collective intentions (see Tambe 1997, 113–14).

Bratman (1992) identified three features that define shared cooperative activity: mutual responsiveness, commitment to the joint activity, and commitment to mutual support (p. 328). Much of this discussion reduces cooperation to the intentions of individual participants "in favor of" a joint activity (Bratman 1992, 329; Levesque, Cohen, and Nunes 1990; Grosz 1996). As Bratman, Grosz, and others have argued, although intentions are typically thought to be related only to the possessing individual's actions, in fact intentions are often realized to be "elements of partial plans" (Bratman 1992, 330) that are understood to unfold over longer periods of time, and in cooperative activity these plans are understood by all involved to require the activities of multiple participants to be successfully carried out. Thus, in a sense, an intention to perform an action understood to be an element of such a collective plan is a collective intention. When a jazz drummer gets a nod from the soloing saxophonist indicating his solo is coming to an end, and the drummer plays a flourish designed to build up and end dramatically in unison with the soloist at the end of the 32-bar form, the drummer's intention only makes sense in the context of the group activity and also only makes sense if the soloist does indeed terminate his solo as the drummer is anticipating. The notion of collective improvisationality is implicit in all such discussions of collaborative agent systems and has been explicitly explored by a few researchers (Agre and Chapman 1987; Hayes-Roth, Brownston, and van Gent 1995; Sawyer 2001b).

Much of this work incorporates notions of complex hierarchical plans that are composed of many successive actions that must be executed over an extended period of time before the goal can be reached. Agents not only have goals and plans – perhaps partial and incomplete – but also have complex nested subplans and subgoals. Thus to coordinate joint activity, agents must be able to communicate about these complexly organized plans and to negotiate differences not only in goals and overall plans but also in subplans. Further, when actions have unexpected effects due to an uncertain environment, these complex plan-subplan hierarchies may need to be improvisationally modified (Agre and Chapman 1987; Hayes-Roth, Brownston, and van Gent 1995), and these modifications must also be mutually responsive (Bratman 1992, 339). Consequently, these improvised modifications are emergent from the group's communication processes. Without the capability for improvisational communication, joint plans are nothing more than what Bratman (1992) called "prepackaged cooperation" (p. 339), and such plans are "brittle" in engineering terms – not robust to the vagaries of real-world environments.

Grosz (1996) and Tambe (1997) have developed some of the most sophisticated collaborative systems. In Grosz's *SharedPlan* system, different participants have different knowledge about how to proceed to solve a problem, and they must work together as equals to solve the problem. Agents have different beliefs, intentions, and capabilities; collaboration requires that agents have the ability to reason about other agents' beliefs and intentions; and agents must be able to collaborate in both planning and acting. Planning and acting are not sequential but interleave, as the unexpected results of actions force rethinking of plans, and the plans and actions that result in such systems are emergent group phenomena, emerging not only from agent interaction but also from the unpredictability of interaction with the environment. Most importantly, Grosz and Sidner (1990) argue that these emergent group plans cannot be understood as the sum of individual plans (Grosz 1996, 73) and that agents must be designed to plan differently if they are to collaborate toward emergent planning (Grosz and Kraus 1996). For example, agents must have intentional states that are directed toward the collective group plan. Grosz and Kraus (1996) identify two such states, *intending to* (the intention of an agent to accomplish a subtask of the group's task) and *intending that* (the indirect intention of a requesting agent that is depending on another agent to accomplish a subtask). "Intending that" carries implications for the requesting agent: It should not expect other subtasks to be accomplished by the subtask agent at the same time, and it has a commitment to provide help when asked. Both states involve commitment and responsibility even though only one of the agents is directly responsible for the subtask.

In these collaborative systems, collective intentions and group plans are emergent. They emerge when agents have a mutual belief in the plan – on the overall outline of how they are going to execute the plan. There must be individual or group plans for each of the subactions; and unique to groups, there must be an "intention that" the group will do the action, and indirect commitments that other agents are able to do their actions, "intentions that" the collaborators succeed. But before this emergent state can be reached, the agents have to undergo a process of reaching at least a partial agreement on a group plan.

These forms of social emergence cannot occur unless the participating agents have explicit representations of mutual beliefs, team plans, and team goals and are capable of communicating to negotiate and coordinate their beliefs and plans (Tambe 1997, 85). Although each agent performs only a small part of the group activity, each agent must be able to represent and reason about it. These collective representations are not supported in cognitive agent architectures nor in the ACLs that they use.

Tambe (1997) noted that prior systems, particularly Grosz's Shared-Plans, typically have only two or three agents, and part of his motivation in developing his STEAM system was to support teams of more agents; systems have been developed with eight, eleven, and sixteen agents. A classic example is the RoboCup soccer tournament, in which different research groups each develop a multi-agent soccer team with eleven agents as team members (www.robocup.org, accessed 2 April 2005). STEAM systems start with joint intentions and then build up hierarchical structures that parallel Grosz's theory of partial SharedPlans.

Joint intentions theory prescribes that team members attain mutual beliefs, but it ignores the cost of attaining mutual beliefs, specifically the cost of communication itself. Pynadath and Tambe (2002) provided a series of proofs outlining how an agent can evaluate the cost of communicating to attain mutual beliefs; in some situations, an agent may rationally choose not to communicate, instead calculating that other agents are likely to observe the same phenomena and come to the same belief on their own. This represents one of the first attempts by agent researchers to represent what linguists call *metapragmatics* – thinking and talking about communication itself (see the next section).

Collaborative agent research is fundamentally interested in how teams improvisationally respond to unexpected developments as they operate in complex and changing environments, each agent possessing only partial information about the environment and about other agents. In such environments, plans cannot be developed in advance, with subtasks parceled out to team members; rather, the distribution of the subtasks must emerge dynamically as the team proceeds. Agents must be able to communicate when they realize they cannot complete a task that they have previously committed to; this also requires that agents be able to perceive the impact of this difficulty on the overall group plan and decide what information is necessary to communicate to its partners (also see Levesque, Cohen, and Nunes 1990). Team members must be jointly committed to such plan "repair," and this process requires sophisticated interagent communication. Collaborative systems represent the current leading edge of artificial society research – with the most complex agent models and the most complex communication languages. Emergence in these systems is found in the dynamically changing configurations of agents responding in distributed teamlike fashion to unexpected developments as the task proceeds. Very little of this technology has been used by social simulation researchers, who have generally preferred simulations with large numbers of simpler agents.

In some of these collaborative systems, disagreements are resolved by a team or subteam leader rather than by negotiation among team members. Yet researchers remain keenly interested in modeling "distributed leadership" in such systems so that agents can negotiate their plans without a leader (Tambe 1997, 115); this is thought to require as-yet untheorized enhancements to agent communication languages. In a situation in which people do not share a mental state of joint intention, they can still collaborate and improvisationally generate emergent properties. But this can only happen when *metapragmatics* are introduced to the communication language (Sawyer 2001b). In an empirical study of improvised dialogues (Sawyer 2003d), I demonstrated that the metapragmatic features of human communication lead to unintended emergent effects and that these emergent effects have causal consequences for the future flow of the encounter (see the next section). Yet metapragmatics have not yet been implemented in agent communication languages.

This body of research has found that collaborative emergence is deeply sensitive to the nature of the communication language used by the agents. Communication is necessary to resolve resource conflicts (shared objects that different agents each need to execute their portion of the group plan) and to negotiate to resolve unexpected failures in response to unexpected environmental behaviors. In other words, executing group plans necessarily requires collective improvisation (Hayes-Roth, Brownston, and van Gent 1995) because the group needs to be able to adapt in response to unexpected developments, interleaving planning and acting.

The accounts of artificial societies with collaborating agents outlined here are strikingly similar to microsociological accounts of mutually contingent behavior (such as Lawler, Ridgeway, and Markovsky 1993). In both treatments, agents engage in cooperative activity by being mutually responsive and negotiating distinct plans, such negotiation resulting in the emergence of the eventual collective action. In sociology, the emergent pattern of the group encounter is thought of as an *interaction ritual chain* (Collins 1981) or, in artificial societies, as a plan for collective action. A key difference is that sociologists like Collins and Giddens are typically concerned with structures that emerge and perdure across repeated encounters, thus resulting in something approximating macrosocial structure, whereas in collaborative systems, researchers are more focused on the success of problem solving in a single encounter (although Tambe 1997, 115, noted a recent interest in exploring how collaborating agents might learn to repeat successful emergent routines). For example, in expectation states theory (Fararo and Skvoretz 1986), status microstructures develop whenever agents engage in collective goal-oriented encounters (just as in collaborative systems). Agents form expectations about the usefulness of one another's contributions; these expectations are updated based on the competence demonstrated by an agent after an action. However, once formed, such expectations tend to be self-fulfilling and begin to shape future goal-related behaviors. Thus stable status microstructures form in which agents perceived to be more competent engage in more actions, engage in more important actions, and receive requests from other agents more frequently, whereas other agents play a more supportive, background role.

Metapragmatics and improvised dialogue

In the preceding section, I demonstrated that different communication languages result in different emergence processes and outcomes. Artificial societies suggest that symbolic communication is not epiphenomenal in social systems and that theories of social emergence must fundamentally incorporate a theory of symbolic communication. Such a theory must be explicitly specified to the level of detail found in artificial societies owing to the extreme sensitivity of emergence to subtle changes in the agent communication language.

However, this is only the beginning of the problem because the ACLs used even in collaborative agent societies are much simpler than human natural languages (Sawyer 2003a). In particular, recent microsociological studies of improvised discourse highlight the importance of *metapragmatics* in emergence (Sawyer 2001a, 2003d). Speakers use the metapragmatic function of language to reflexively communicate about the emergent process and flow of the encounter or about the ground rules and the communication language itself. In an improvisational theater performance, when no dialogue or plot is specified in advance, how do actors determine the variables of the interactional frame – the characters, motivations, relationships, and plot events and sequence? In my study of emergence in improvising theater groups (Sawyer 2003d), I found that the interactional frame emerged from the metapragmatic properties of the discourse.

These frames emerge from the collaborative efforts of the entire group. No single participant creates the frame; it emerges from the give and take of conversation. The interactional frame includes all of the pragmatic elements of a small-group encounter: the socially recognized roles and practices enacted by each participant, the publicly shared and perceived motives of those individuals, the relationships among them, and the collective definition of the joint activity they are engaged in. The frame is constructed turn by turn; one person proposes a new development for the frame, and others respond by modifying or embellishing that proposal.

Each new proposal for a development in the frame is the creative inspiration of one person, but that proposal does not become a part of the frame until it is evaluated by the others. In the subsequent flow of dialogue, the group collaborates to determine whether to accept the proposal, how to weave that proposal into the frame that has already been established, and then how to further elaborate on it.

Example 9.3 presents the first few seconds of dialogue from a scene that the actors knew would last about five minutes. The audience was asked to suggest a proverb, and the suggestion given was "Don't look a gift horse in the mouth."

Example 9.3. Lights up. Dave is at stage right, Ellen at stage left. Dave begins gesturing to his right, talking to himself

1	Dave	All the little glass figurines in my menagerie, The store of my dreams. Hundreds of thousands everywhere!	Turns around to admire.
2	Ellen		Slowly walks toward Dave.
3	Dave	Yes, can I help you?	Turns and notices Ellen.
4	Ellen	Um, I'm looking for uh, uh, a present?	Ellen is looking down like a child, with her fingers in her mouth.
5	Dave	A gift?	
6	Ellen	Yeah.	
7	Dave	I have a little donkey?	Dave mimes the action of handing Ellen a donkey from the shelf.
8	Ellen	Ah, that's – I was looking for something a little bit bigger . . .	
9	Dave	Oh.	Returns item to shelf.
10	Ellen	It's for my dad.	

By turn 10, elements of the frame are starting to emerge. We know that Dave is a storekeeper and Ellen a young girl. We know that Ellen is buying a present for her dad and, because she is so young, probably needs help from the storekeeper. These dramatic elements have emerged from the creative contributions of both actors. Although each turn's incremental contributions to the frame can be identified, none of these turns fully determines the subsequent dialogue, and the emergent dramatic frame is not chosen, intended, or imposed by either of the actors. (Also note that the dialogue is not obviously derived from the audience's suggestion, although the actors will later integrate it with the emerging frame.)

The emergence of the frame cannot be reduced to the actor's intentions in individual turns because in many cases an actor cannot know the meaning of his or her own turn until the other actors have responded. In turn 2, when Ellen walks toward Dave, her action has many potential meanings; for example, she could be a coworker arriving late to work. Her action does not carry the meaning "A customer entering the store" until after Dave's query in turn 3. In improvised dialogues, many actions do not receive their full meaning until after the act has occurred; the complete meaning of a turn is dependent on the flow of the subsequent dialogue. This sort of retrospective interpretation is quite common in improvised dialogue, and it is one reason that the emergent frame is analytically irreducible to the intentions or actions of participants in individual turns of dialogue. (Note in particular that such retrospective intentions are beyond the scope of recent work on collaborative agent systems.)

Emergent properties are usually associated with the *unintended effects* of action; effects that are intended are, by definition, not emergent because their origin can be traced to the individual motivations and advance plans of specific individuals. In improvised dialogues like the one in Example 9.3, the actors do not have beliefs, desires, and intentions as conceived of in artificial societies; rather, these are attributed to individual actions retrospectively as the dialogue evolves. In spite of their lack of plans and intentions, actors are able to coordinate their actions to generate a plausible, coherent dialogue, and stable macropatterns emerge.

In an extended study of metapragmatics and social emergence, I compared emergence processes in two different sixty-minute improvised plays, both performed by professional groups in Chicago in the early 1990s (Sawyer 2003d). The first group, called The Family, used a format that they called "The Movie"; in The Movie, actors are allowed to step out of character and to explicitly metacommunicate about the ongoing drama, using "director talk" as if they were the director or playwright. The second group, called Jazz Freddy, did not allow their actors to step out of character at all. As a result, all of their metapragmatic negotiation had to be accomplished while speaking in character. Both groups created their sixty-minute play from a combination of two- to four-minute scenes. The edits between these short scenes were not timed or planned in advance; these were emergent and collaboratively accomplished by the actors. I found that in The Movie all scene edits were done with director talk; of course, in Jazz Freddy all scene edits had to be done while the actors remained in character.

I pursued this comparison to determine whether the metapragmatic level of interaction had causal power over social emergence. Upon analyzing the two emergent frames, I found major differences. The Jazz Freddy frame that emerged over the course of the one-hour performance emphasized character and relationship development, but its plot was not very complex. In contrast, The Movie's emergent frame had multiple interwoven plot lines but had weak characters and relationships.

Could these differences in socially emergent outcomes be attributed to the differences in the metapragmatic communications used? To answer this question, I used conversation analytic methods to identify the step-by-step processes of this emergence. I found that the metapragmatic differences were indeed responsible for these different emergent outcomes, largely owing to the dramatic demands associated with scene edits. The actor initiating a scene edit has to metacommunicate which other actors should join him or her on stage to start the new scene. The Movie actors would simply state explicitly which actors were to participate in the next scene:

Example 9.4. "We now see John and Mary, sitting in a coffeehouse, talking about what just happened." (After which, the actors playing John and Mary would walk onstage, pull up chairs, and sit down and mime the act of drinking coffee, and the actor initiating the edit would leave the stage and allow the scene to begin.)

In contrast, the Jazz Freddy actors had to execute their scene edits while remaining in character. Unlike in The Movie, the actor initiating the scene edit had to be in the new scene; otherwise, there would be no dramatically plausible reason for him or her to be onstage in the first place. The most effective way for an actor to implicitly metacommunicate who should join him or her on stage was to address another character (the one meant to come on stage) by name. To execute the same edit as The Movie did in Example 9.4, the actor playing the character of Mary would have to walk on stage, pull up a chair and sit down, and say something like:

Example 9.5. "John, could you bring some creamer over with our coffees?"

My conversation analyses showed that because the actors in Jazz Freddy were required to accomplish scene edits in character, they tended to use metapragmatic strategies like these relationship-focused edits, and these had the unintended effect of causing a frame to emerge that was rich in relationship and character information. These data demonstrate that communication is not epiphenomenal; it has causal influence over micro-to-macro processes of social emergence.

I also found that once these frames emerged – about one-third of the way through each performance – they then began to exert downward causal influence over the communication strategies that actors used in scene edits. This causal influence became progressively stronger as the frames became increasingly elaborated and complex. For example, as The Movie's plots became progressively more complex, the actors used edits that drew on these plots, and as Jazz Freddy's characters and relationships become more developed, the actors used edits that invoked those characters and relationships. In other words, edits like Example 9.5 became easier and thus more common after a rich set of relationships had emerged. This social causation occurred even though none of the actors were aware it was happening. These data demonstrate that conversation scholars must take unintended emergent effects into consideration in their analyses.

There is rarely conscious awareness of such emergence processes in small groups, in part because dialogue exchanges happen so quickly. For example, the actors in The Movie and in Jazz Freddy were not aware of these contrasts between their performances. As Harvey Sacks was perhaps the first to point out (1992, 11), during conversation people respond so fast that they could not conceivably have consciously planned and decided their action. The psychological processes underlying conversational behavior are largely preconscious and are difficult to explain with the agency theories of contemporary sociology. For example, Giddens claimed that people know pretty much everything that is sociologically relevant about social life and that since people know what they're doing, we should just ask them (1984). Even sociologists that reject structuration theory nonetheless generally believe that the causal impact of macrosocial forces must be mediated through individual's perceptions of them (as in interpretivist and subjectivist theory; see Chapter 10). However, in improvised dialogue, people act without conscious awareness or reflection.

Furthermore, prior research has demonstrated that speakers have great difficulty becoming aware of the metapragmatic function of their own utterances, even when they consider an interaction in retrospect (Silverstein 1979, 1981). This is why so much of social emergence results from the implicit metapragmatics of dialogue. In improvised dialogues, most new dramatic ideas are introduced using implicit metapragmatics: An actor speaks as if the proposed state of affairs was already the case (as in turns 2 and 3 in Example 9.3 and as in the Jazz Freddy scene edit in Example 9.5). These dialogues can only be explained by reference to the metapragmatic strategies used in successive turns.

The metapragmatic properties of communication are not represented in current ACLs, and this may prevent them from being extended to collaboratively improvised distributed leadership. Collaborative agent systems improvisationally respond as a group when plans must be altered owing to a mismatch of goals or subplans or to unexpected environmental events. Yet developers are now facing unresolved coordination issues as they expand beyond systems of two or three agents and attempt to do so with true distributed leadership. As the cutting edge of intelligent collaborative system research implements increasingly complex agents, and as it increases the number of agents and the task complexity, truly distributed leadership will require more sophisticated ACLs. Of particular relevance will be studies of improvised dialogues and how different dialogues result in different emergence processes and outcomes.

Conclusion

In this chapter, I have explored the undertheorized role of symbolic communication in social emergence. In the artificial societies reviewed here, stable macrostructures emerge, and these differ depending on the communication language that agents use. Different communication languages result in different outcomes and processes of social emergence. And in improvised dialogues, the metapragmatic properties of interaction are largely responsible for social emergence. These examples demonstrate that a theory of communication must be a core component of a theory of social emergence. And they demonstrate the close relationship between group improvisation and social emergence.

A theory of social emergence requires an explicit theorization of symbolic communication and dynamic processes. Yet for the most part, sociological theorists who focus on the micro-macro link have not theorized communication, nor the role that communication plays in micro-macro relations. I propose an explanation for why this might be in Chapter 10.

The perspective provided by artificial societies problematizes three sociological forms of reductionism. First, it suggests that social explanation cannot be reduced to social structure. The extreme structuralist position cannot be maintained – the position that macrostructure is the only appropriate subject of analysis for sociology and that individuals and communications do not need to be theorized (e.g., Black 2000; Mayhew 1980). Second, it suggests that methodological individualism does not allow a complete explanation of social phenomena. The extreme individualist position cannot be maintained – that a theory of the individual as, for example, a maximizing rational actor is sufficient and that communication languages can be simplified into exchange values. Third, it suggests that social explanation cannot be reduced to symbolic interaction, as proposed by the interactional reductionisms associated with ethnomethodology and conversation analysis. All three of these prominent sociological paradigms fail to theorize the multileveled nature of society that is brought into focus by artificial societies: individual, communication, and emergent social properties. In Chapter 10, I further elaborate these three forms of reductionism, contextualizing them within a broader history of sociological theory and emergence.

Symbolic communication must be a central component of social emergence theory. In artificial societies, interaction among agents is a central and essential element of the paradigm. Emergence does not occur if there is no interaction among agents in a complex system, but, more significantly, different collective properties emerge and the processes of their emergence are different when the agent communication language is changed. All sociological theory – not only microsociology – must take into account the interactions and communications among agents.

Even though artificial societies have demonstrated the critical role of interagent communication, to date most of them use quite simple communication languages. Simulations that most explicitly focus on social emergence use primarily reactive agents, with radically simple interaction mechanisms. Emergence in systems of cognitive and collaborative agents has only recently been examined, and although emergence processes occur – particularly with the improvisational group dynamics of collaborative agents – developers of such systems have not developed systematic theories of the process. But even the advanced languages used by collaborative agents are more simplistic than human communication and omit the metapragmatic function, one of the most sociologically essential aspects of symbolic interaction. The metapragmatic function is critical to social emergence – because it is not reducible to individual intention, because its outcome is collaborative and unintended, and because individuals are rarely conscious of it.

In Chapter 10, I elaborate these points in some detail, and I propose a new vision for sociology, one that reconciles microsociology and macrosociology. Sociologists interested in the micro-macro link must broaden their focus to include the empirical study of symbolic communication, and microsociologists can contribute their expertise to micro-macro concerns. This chapter, by demonstrating that the theory of social emergence requires a sophisticated account of human symbolic communication, can be viewed as a prelude to Chapter 10.

10 The Emergence Paradigm

> The problems which [the social sciences] try to answer arise only in so far as the conscious action of many men produce undesigned results, in so far as regularities are observed which are not the result of anybody's design. If social phenomena showed no order except in so far as they were consciously designed, there would indeed be no room for theoretical sciences of society and there would be, as is often argued, only problems of psychology.
>
> F. A. von Hayek

Social emergence is the central phenomenon of the social sciences. The science of social emergence is the basic science underlying all of the social sciences, because social emergence is foundational to all of them. Political science, economics, education, history, and sociology study phenomena that socially emerge from complex systems of individuals in interaction. In this concluding chapter, I argue that sociology should become the basic science of social emergence, and I outline a theoretical framework to guide this study. This new sociology would be as Comte and Durkheim originally envisioned: By concerning itself with the foundational processes of social emergence, sociology would be at the core of the social sciences.

But this is not the sociology we see today; few sociologists study social emergence. In the second half of the twentieth century, economics has made the best case for being the foundational social science, by making social emergence central to its theory and practice. Perhaps the most important strength of the neoclassical economic approach is that it has rigorous formalisms for modeling the ways that individual action generates aggregate outcomes at the level of an entire population (Bowles 2001; Durlauf and Young 2001). Because social emergence is the central phenomenon of the social sciences, and economics has developed the most successful model of social emergence, this has naturally led to "economic imperialism," with neoclassical economists beginning to analyze noneconomic phenomena traditionally associated with sociology (Boulding 1969, 8; Hirshleifer 1985; Radnitzky and Bernholz 1987;

Tullock 1972).[1] These imperialists argue that economics is "the universal grammar of social science" (Hirshleifer 1985, 53) and that it simply represents "straight thinking" applied to social science (Radnitzky 1992, 15). And in fact microeconomics has been the only game in town for those interested in studying social emergence.

However, there are many problems with the models of social emergence dominant in microeconomics. Critics such as the "New Economic Sociologists" (see Krier 1999; Zafirovsky 1999) claim that the microeconomic account of social emergence is empirically unfounded, is methodologically individualist, neglects the social embeddedness of actors, neglects the importance of institutions and social networks, and neglects the unavoidable inefficiencies introduced by institutions, power, and path dependence. Joining these critics, I focus on the argument that microeconomics radically simplifies important elements of social emergence. My account of social emergence emphasizes the key role played by symbolic communication; as we learned in Chapter 9, different communication languages change the processes of social emergence. This leads to a new critique of rational choice models: Such models of social emergence have a radically simplified account of human interaction.[2] At the end of this chapter, I argue that as sociology reformulates itself as the science of social emergence, and as microeconomics begins to develop more empirically grounded and theoretically sophisticated models of social emergence, research into social emergence currently conducted by microeconomists should migrate into the discipline of sociology. Until this disciplinary reconfiguration occurs, microeconomics will continue to operate with inadequate models of social emergence, and the social sciences will continue without an adequate foundation.

Unfortunately, twentieth-century sociology did not focus on social emergence. Sociology as a discipline has failed to recognize the importance of social emergence to the foundational issues facing the discipline (Coleman 1987; Saam 1999; see Chapter 5). In some cases, an expressed interest in emergence is seen as synonymous with

---

[1] The term "economic imperialism" was coined by Souter (1933), although it is often attributed to Boulding (1969). Souter wrote that economic imperialism "invades the territories of its neighbors, not to enslave or to swallow them up, but to aid and enrich them and promote their autonomous growth" (p. 94n91).

[2] Some attempts have been made to include the strength of the interaction as a factor in the utility equation (Blume and Durlauf 2001; Brock and Durlauf 2001; Durlauf 2001), although this is a minority position and most economists believe that actors' social relations are nothing more than "a frictional drag that impedes competitive markets" (Granovetter 1985, 484). And in any case these formalisms do not attempt to represent the symbolic nature of communication.

Table 10.1. *The Recent History of Sociological Theory*

	Structure Paradigm 1950s–1960s	Interaction Paradigm 1960s–1990s	Emergence Paradigm 1990s-present
Sociological Theory	Structural-functionalism, structural sociology, micro-macro theory	Ethnomethodology, conversation analysis, interpretivism, structuration theory	Social emergence
Emphasis	Top down causation; Abstract, impersonal collective entities; people as "judgmental dopes"	Bottom-up causation or "emergence"; people as creative agents	Dialectic of emergence and social causation; mediation by ephemeral and stable emergents

methodological individualism because it is primarily methodological individualists who have emphasized the importance of emergence to sociology. For example, Coleman's emphasis on "foundations" was an attempt to address the failure of sociologists to develop models of social emergence (Coleman 1987, 171), and social mechanists have also proposed methodologically individualist versions of emergence (see Sawyer 2004a).

If sociology becomes the science of social emergence, it will be different from the sociology that we have today. The study of social emergence requires a simultaneous focus on three levels of analysis: individuals, their interactional dynamics, and the socially emergent macroproperties of the group. In this final chapter, I present a brief history that explains why sociology has not yet combined these levels into an integrated study of social emergence, I describe what the new sociology of social emergence would look like, I explain how this new sociology would relate to past sociological theory and practice, and I outline how this reformulated sociology could transform the disciplinary boundaries of the social sciences, with a particularly strong impact on economics.

I begin the chapter by presenting a narrative account of twentieth-century sociology from the perspective of social emergence (see Table 10.1). I describe this history using a simple dialectic: the thesis of the Structure Paradigm, followed by the antithesis of the Interaction Paradigm. I show how each is an inadequate theory of society because each fails to develop an adequate account of social emergence. Then in the bulk of the chapter, I describe a synthesis of these two paradigms that I call the Emergence Paradigm.

The Structure Paradigm focuses on the relations between individuals and societies. Parsonsian structural-functionalism is the canonical approach of the Structure Paradigm; this version of the Structure Paradigm was dominant in the 1950s and 1960s, and other forms of the

Social Structure
Roles, positions, networks, power, distribution, material resources and systems
Individual
Intention, agency, cognition, rationality

Figure 10.1. The Structure Paradigm.

Structure Paradigm continue today. The Structure Paradigm was followed by the Interaction Paradigm. The Interaction Paradigm rejected almost everything central to the Structure Paradigm and proposed a new alternative not considered within the Structure Paradigm: that communicative interaction, not the structure nor the individual, was central to sociological explanation.

The Emergence Paradigm is a classic synthesis: the inherent tensions of the Interaction Paradigm drive theory's movement toward it, and it combines the central elements of both the Structure Paradigm and the Interaction Paradigm. The Emergence Paradigm emphasizes both individual-society relations and communicative interaction, arguing that the individual-society relation cannot be explained without recourse to sophisticated theories of communication and of emergence from communication.

The Structure Paradigm

The Structure Paradigm focuses on the relations between two distinct levels of analysis: the *individual* and the *social* (see Figure 10.1). Structure Paradigm theories tend to fall into one of three types:

- *Structural determinism.* Social structure is foundational, and the individual is socioculturally determined. Structure is the driving causal force in social life, determining even properties of the individual such as consciousness, rationality, and cognitive capacities. In Figure 10.1, the critical causal arrow points downward from social structure to the individual. Structural determinism is characteristic of Marxism, French structuralism, structural sociology, and many forms of social constructivism.
- *Methodological individualism.* Methodological individualism posits that properties of the individual – actions, behaviors, mental states, beliefs, intentions – are primary and that properties of individuals determine social structure. In Figure 10.1, the critical causal arrow points upward from the individual to social structure. This is the notion of

emergence found in neoclassical microeconomics and in rational choice approaches more generally, in social mechanistic approaches, and in many theories of collective action.

- *Hybrid theories*. Both individual and structure have autonomous reality, and sociology must explain both upward and downward causal force. Hybrid theories include Parsonsian structural-functionalism, Archer's morphogenetic social realism, and Alexander's neo-functionalism.

There is some disagreement about whether individualism or structuralism is currently dominant in sociology. Mayhew (1980, 339) claimed that most U.S. sociologists were individualist, whether concerned with the subjective or objective aspects of human behavior. However, King (1999b) and Porpora (1987) disagreed. For example, Porpora claimed, "Structural Sociology has become a dominant perspective in the discipline; some people even label it 'Standard American Sociology'" (p. 12). I believe that this disagreement reflects a confusion about the definition of "structure" that originates in sociology's neglect of social emergence.

I examine each of these three variants of the Structure Paradigm and conclude that each fails because it cannot explain emergence processes and dynamics. Ultimately, the Structure Paradigm cannot explain social emergence because it has no theory of communicative interaction and its role in emergence processes.

Structural determinism

Sociological reductionism can be defined as the arbitrary reduction of all social phenomena to the level of structure. It assigns ontological preference to structure and maintains, by definition, that any nonstructural phenomenon is not social. (DiTomaso 1982, 15)

Structural determinists argue that the primary ontological phenomenon is society and that everything else about social life is caused by social properties. Of the classic sociological traditions, Marxism perhaps makes the strongest claim that human nature derives from social structures: "This sum of productive forces, capital funds and social forms of intercourse...is the real basis of what the philosophers have conceived as 'substance' and 'essence of man'" (Marx 1978, 165). In the 1930s, the Frankfurt School extended these notions by arguing that knowledge itself is socially constructed; in the 1960s, French structuralists such as Levi-Strauss, Barthes, and Foucault argued that even our concept of the "individual" had been a byproduct of a certain period in capitalism. Much of Marxist theory and debate has been devoted to identifying the exact mechanisms for these downward causal processes. For example, Althusser's structuralist Marxism explained determination from the structural level by introducing a theory of ideology and its relation to both material conditions and to consciousness.

Structural determinism is also a focus of the *structural sociologists* (Black 2000; Blau 1970b, 1977; Mayhew 1980, 1981; Porpora 1993). Structuralists argue that social phenomena can be studied objectively and scientifically without a concern for individual-level properties. As Blau wrote in a critique of Homans's psychological reductionism, "the behavior of organized aggregates follows its own principles, and the discovery of these explanatory principles does not require detailed knowledge of the principles that govern the behavior of sub-units" (1970a, 338). Blau rejected the methodologically individualist study of social emergence, arguing that "there is no reason to assume that empirical relationships between variables that characterize collectivities are more likely to be deducible from a limited number of general psychological propositions, which refer to connections between properties of individuals and their behavior, than from a set of general sociological propositions, which refer to connections between various aspects of the organization of collectivities and their consequences" (1970a, 339). And Mayhew (1980) rejected hybrid theories that examined the relation between individual and structure: "[Q]uestions about the relationship between 'the individual' and 'society' ... are not central to sociology" (p. 358).

Many structuralists emphasize the explanatory power of networks. The idea is that "a concrete social structure is a network of relations among social entities" (Fararo and Skvoretz 1986, 591) and that "social systems are bundles of interconnected social relations" (p. 592). The metaphor is that of a wiring diagram; social systems are sets of pairwise relationships between members of the population.

Network theory is often presented as reductionist. Ritzer (2000) grouped network theory with exchange theory and rational choice theory, both of which are explicitly reductionist. In fact, some scholars have advocated a hybrid known as "network exchange theory" (e.g., Cook 1987; Cook and Whitmeyer 1992). Granovetter (1990) noted that "network analysis often takes the individual as a fundamental unit of analysis [and] it is methodologically more individualist than some other sociological traditions" (p. 95).

Yet many network theorists affiliate with complexity theory and reject reductionist explanation. Granovetter (1990) continued, "But the underlying conception of network arguments lends itself to a fundamental critique of the atomized conception of action in neoclassical theory" (p. 95). For example, Wellman (1983) held that network theorists "dismiss as non-structural any explanation that treats social processes as the sum of individual actors' personal attributes and internalized norms" (p. 162).

For network theory to avoid being a sophisticated version of methodological individualism, it will have to develop a theory of social emergence. Social emergence is not a central part of contemporary network theory; networks may or may not manifest emergent properties, and whether they do has not been a central question in network theory. And networks themselves are generally not analyzed as emergent phenomena. As a result, studies of social networks rarely focus on dynamics and change (cf. Latané, Nowak, and Liu 1994, 18).

Structuralist theories are a part of the Structure Paradigm because they lack a sufficient level of sophistication in their theory of node-to-node communication. Structuralist theories have not incorporated a theory of communication, nor have they developed a theory of social emergence.

Methodological individualism

The methodological individualist holds that the primary ontological phenomenon is the individual and that all properties of social groups are derivative from properties of individuals in combination. This position is associated with social mechanist approaches and with rational choice theory.

The doctrine of methodological individualism is rooted in Smith, Hobbes, and Mill and was elaborated by the Austrian economists Mises and von Hayek. Watkins (1957) stated the canonical version of methodological individualism: "[T]he ultimate constituents of the social world are individual people.... Every complex social configuration or event is the result of a particular configuration of individuals, their dispositions, situations, beliefs" (p. 106). Methodological individualists invert the causal arrow of the structural determinists: Instead of top-down causation, they focus on bottom-up causation, which they often refer to as "emergence." Everything about society is determined by properties of individuals, whether human nature, the nature of consciousness or subjective experience, or the predetermined cognitive structures of the brain.

Coleman (1990) was an influential advocate of methodological individualism in sociology. Coleman argued that rational choice theory provided a microlevel base for the explanation of macrophenomena, and he considered emergence to be central to the project. Rational choice theorists are the prototypical methodological individualists. They model each individual's behavior and then run a model that aggregates many individuals acting in similar fashion. Coleman argued that the aggregation mechanisms proposed by neoclassical microeconomists were overly simplistic, and he attempted to introduce some sociological sophistication into rational choice models of social emergence.

Several sociological theorists have advocated *social mechanistic* approaches as a way to move beyond the deductive-nomological covering law model associated with logical empiricism (see Hedström and Swedberg 1998; Pickel 2004). Rather than explanation in terms of laws and regularities, mechanists provide explanations by postulating the processes constituted by the operation of mechanisms that generate the observed phenomena. Social mechanists are methodological individualists in that they do not consider the possibility that emergent social properties are real (Abbott 1996, 3; Sawyer 2004a).[3]

Hybrid theories

Hybrid theories hold that both the individual and structure have ontological autonomy and that their mutual causal relations must be explained. Toward the end of the twentieth century, there was renewed interest in hybrid theories of the micro-macro link (e.g., J. C. Alexander et al. 1987; Knorr-Cetina and Cicourel 1981) and of the structure-agency link (Archer 1995). Increasingly since the 1980s, sociologists working within the Structure Paradigm have developed hybrid theories that incorporate both the microlevel and the macrolevel; the development of these theories has been called a "third phase" of postwar sociology (Alexander and Colomy 1990, 43), and several theorists believe it is the central focus of contemporary sociology (J. C. Alexander and Giesen 1987; Archer 1995). The micro-macro debate tends to focus on relations between the microsociological study of interaction and the macrosociological study of structure, and the structure-agency debate tends to focus on the relation between subjectively conceived agents and the objectivity of social structure. These debates are sometimes construed as manifestations of the same theoretical divide, but I argue below that these two have very little in common; theories that incorporate microinteraction represent a shift to the Interaction Paradigm, whereas theories that relate structure and agency belong in the Structure Paradigm.

Some sociological theorists have realized that the Structure Paradigm is inadequate and have argued that the problem is the paradigm's objectivity and positivism. They attempt to fix sociological theory by introducing

---

[3] Some social theorists (Bhaskar [1975] 1997; Bunge 1997) focus on the generating mechanisms underlying social reality, but they reject methodological individualism. For a discussion of these issues, see Sawyer 2004a.

subjectivity and agency (Ritzer 2000). Yet this solution still falls within the Structure Paradigm, and most structure-agency theories fail because they have no theory of the mechanisms of social emergence that connect these two levels of analysis. Lacking a theory of social emergence, there is no theory of how individual agency could have causal effects on the structural level. This problem is evidenced by the fact that many agency theorists allow groups to possess agency but do not provide a theory of how individual agencies combine to result in the emergence of group agency (among others, this move is taken by Coleman 1990; Giddens 1984, 25; Ritzer 1996, 558). Groups could not have agency unless that property emerged from the agency of the constituent individuals, and structure-agency theorists rarely theorize this emergence. An account of emergence requires an account of the interactional mechanisms that give rise to processes of emergence; structure-agency theories are subject to the same criticism that the Interaction Paradigm makes against the Structure Paradigm (see "The Interaction Paradigm").

Problems with the Structure Paradigm

The Structure Paradigm cannot explain social emergence because it does not incorporate theories of process, mechanism, and interaction. Consequently, it cannot explain

- The emergence of structure. Either no mechanism is proposed for the emergence of structure from individual actions, or the proposed mechanism is overly simplistic.
- Emergent processes of maintenance, reproduction, change, and conflict.
- Symbolic interaction and the joint construction of social reality.
- Social causation. Of course, social causation is assumed in many variants of the Structure Paradigm; however, the causal vector operates directly on the individual, resulting in theories of socialization and internalization. Yet such theories are susceptible to methodologically individualist explanation as well (see Granovetter 1985). And such theories are susceptible to Giddens's critique that social constraint could not work unless agents were aware of it. When interaction is added to the mix, social causation is mediated by communication in ways that agents are not aware of (as in the improvisation examples in Chapter 9).

The Structure Paradigm fails because it is missing a critical mediating link: interactions between individuals (cf. Rawls 1987; Ritzer and Gindoff 1992; Wiley 1988). In the 1960s, an important alternative to the Structure Paradigm began to emerge: the Interaction Paradigm. The

Social Structure
Social structures; cultural meaning systems; norms
Interaction
Discourse patterns, symbolic interaction, collaboration, intersubjectivity
Individual
Intention, agency

Figure 10.2. The Interaction Paradigm.

Interaction Paradigm represented a fundamental break; it focused on the processes and mechanisms of interaction neglected by the Structure Paradigm. After summarizing the Interaction Paradigm, I ultimately conclude that it too results in inadequate theory because it also neglects emergence, although for a very different set of reasons.

The Interaction Paradigm

The level of interaction, then, is one of the thorniest problems in social theory, largely because so many theorists have omitted or misconceived this level. (Wiley 1988, 258)

Like the Structure Paradigm, the Interaction Paradigm directly addresses the fundamental problem of sociology: the relation between the social and the individual. Its defining feature is the addition of a third level of analysis in between the individual and the social: interaction (see Figure 10.2). The properties of interaction are not derivable from the individual actions or agency of the members of the group, nor can they be derived from social structure; interaction is an ontologically distinct level of analysis.

The Interaction Paradigm holds that there are fundamental properties and laws of interaction – based, for example, on semiotics, cybernetics, or communication theory – that are not reducible either to individual properties or structural characteristics. Because interaction is not reducible to individuals or structure, it is an autonomous level of analysis. Structure Paradigm theorists tend to conceive of "levels" in terms of the size of the group and the degree of complexity of its internal structure (e.g., Ritzer 2000, 499). That is partly why theorists working within the Structure Paradigm generally do not recognize interaction to be a level of analysis: because interaction is a level of reality but not a level of organization. The claim that interaction is a level of analysis with ontological status implies that it possesses properties that participate in causal relations, with causal effects on both structure and individuals.

Interaction is at the center of an old sociological tradition associated with Simmel, Cooley, Mead, and the Chicago School of symbolic interactionism. Simmel famously explained social life in terms of interaction: "The large systems and the super-individual organizations that customarily come to mind when we think of society, are nothing but immediate interactions that occur among men constantly every minute" (1950, 10). Beginning in the 1960s and 1970s, symbolic communication became central to a remarkably wide range of theories. Interaction Paradigm theorists have taken different positions on the relationship between interaction, individuals, and structure; what unifies them is that, in contrast to Structure Paradigm theorists (who believed that interaction was epiphenomenal), they give symbolic communication a prominent role. The prototype of the Interaction Paradigm is the microsociology associated with late twentieth century U.S. sociology, including symbolic interactionism, ethnomethodology, and conversation analysis. Interaction Paradigm theories in Europe include Bourdieu's notion of *habitus* ([1972] 1977), Foucault's discussions of *discourse* ([1969] 1972), and Habermas's theory of *communicative action* (1987). In both Europe and the United States, the Interaction Paradigm emerged at about the same time, in both cases as a response to the inherent tensions of the Structure Paradigm. It is an antithesis to the Structure Paradigm because it rejects exactly what the Structure Paradigm views as central: the autonomous causal power of structure in social life, or the reducibility of social life to individuals. Instead, the Interaction Paradigm argues that interaction is central and even that structure can be explained in terms of interaction.

The Interaction Paradigm represents the most significant theoretical attempt to address the most commonly noted problems with the Structure Paradigm: that it generates models that are too static and thus neglect history, models that are unable to deal effectively with processes of social change, and models that are unable to deal with conflict.[4] Interaction Paradigm theorists all agree that the Structure Paradigm is inadequate to fully capture social behavior in groups and to account for the relationship between the individual and the social.

---

[4] Few social theorists have formulated twentieth-century theoretical developments in this way (see Lawler, Ridgeway, and Markovsky 1993 for an exception). In many canonical accounts of twentieth-century sociology, 1960s era conflict theory is often considered to be the antithesis to structural-functionalism; but in my account, conflict theory also belongs to the Structure Paradigm.

Within the Interaction Paradigm, theories tend to take one of two forms:

- *Interactional reductionism.* All phenomena at the level of structure and the level of the individual are derivative from interaction; interaction is the foundational social reality (Mead, Blumer, Collins; symbolic interactionism, ethnomethodology, conversation analysis).
- *Hybrid theories.* As with the Structure Paradigm, hybrid theories are those that hold that each of the three levels has ontological autonomy and that sociology must theorize all three levels and their relations (Althusser, Foucault, Habermas, Pêcheux; critical discourse analysis).

The Interaction Paradigm denies that the social world has an objective, irreducible structure that constrains individuals in interaction. Macrolevel concepts such as social structure and culture are considered to be abstractions that "only describe what men do in generalized terms" but do not really exist nor have any causal force over individuals (Shibutani 1961, 175). Social reality can only be ascribed to concrete interactional processes, and it can only be studied in terms of the participating individuals' interpretations of it (Blumer 1962, 190). The symbolic interactionist Herbert Blumer was explicit in contrasting this stance with the Structure Paradigm (1962, 1966). Rather than structure, symbolic interactional processes are the fundamental units of social life: "[T]he essence of society lies in an ongoing process of action – not in a posited structure of relations" (Blumer 1966, 541). Macrostructural forces never operate directly on individuals but are mediated through their interpretation by those individuals.

Ethnomethodology was closely related to symbolic interactionism (see Fine 1990; Wallace 1969, 35n152). Like symbolic interactionism, ethnomethodology defined itself in opposition to the then dominant Structure Paradigm approach of structural-functionalism. It argued that social reality could only exist in participants' perceptions of it and observable orientations toward it. In developing this theoretical orientation, ethnomethodology was heavily influenced by the phenomenological sociology of Schutz (1967) and the interpretivism of Winch (1958), Berger and Luckmann (1966), and others. Ethnomethodology rejected social realism and countered that the analyst could only understand social phenomena by studying their meanings to the participants and the situated practices which individuals engaged in. The ethnomethodological approach of conversation analysis emphasized the study of individual creativity and situated social practice. Social life was seen to be collaboratively improvised, a joint accomplishment of shared meaning in interaction. Shared orientations to the situation emerge from meaningful interaction;

these orientations include mutual understandings of the roles participants enact and the rules according to which they interact.

Many sociocultural psychologists (see Chapter 7) fall into the Interaction Paradigm in their emphasis on the close microgenetic study of small-group interaction. Their rejection of "social influence" models of behavior constitutes a rejection of the Structure Paradigm (Rogoff 1998). Sociocultural psychology was foundationally influenced by several strands of Interaction Paradigm theory: American pragmatism, linguistic anthropology, and the interwar Soviet psychology of Vygotsky and Bakhtin.

The Interaction Paradigm was a necessary intellectual development because it enabled researchers to undertake the close empirical study of the interactional processes of social life – an advance over Structure Paradigm studies of interaction, as represented by Robert Bales, with their observational coding of interactional moves based on the structural functions they served (Bales 1950). These interactional processes had not been studied by the Structure Paradigm; a static synchronic focus led them to neglect the dynamic contingency of situated discourse. Thus, the rejection of structuralist approaches enabled the close empirical study of creativity in naturally occurring discourse.

However, in making this antithetical move, the Interaction Paradigm was left with a problematic orientation toward emergent frames and structures. The Interaction Paradigm is uncomfortable with the idea that social phenomena might be irreducibly emergent. For example, the interactional frame remains undertheorized because a theory of the frame is necessarily partially collectivist and partially structuralist, and consequently any theory of the frame seems to suffer from the same problems as the Structure Paradigm (Sawyer 2003d). This assumption has made it difficult for the Interaction Paradigm to study several aspects of social emergence, including how individual participants are constrained by macrosocial forces extending far beyond the encounter and how individual actions collectively result in the emergence of macrosocial phenomena (cf. Blommaert 2001; Duranti 1997, 267–70; Hanks 1996, 142).[5]

Interactional reductionism

The Structure Paradigm recognizes two forms of reduction: reduction to structure and reduction to individuals. The Interaction Paradigm introduces a third possible form: reduction to interaction.

---

[5] And of course those sociologists who focus on macrosociological concerns have long claimed that microanalytic approaches like conversation analysis are insufficient to explain large-scale institutional and enduring macrosocial patterns (e.g., J. C. Alexander and Giesen 1987, 27–8).

The early twentieth century Chicago School of sociology introduced the groundwork for interactional reductionism. The philosopher George Herbert Mead, for example, argued that interaction was primary and that the self and the mind derived from interaction: "The process out of which the self arises is a social process which implies interaction of individuals in the group" (1934, 164).

Robert Bales had been deeply influenced by the Chicago interactionist tradition before arriving at Harvard to study with Talcott Parsons. Like Mead, Bales was an interactional reductionist; he argued that the "interaction system" is the key theoretical starting point and that from it can be derived personality, social system, and culture. The social structure of a group is "a system of solutions to the functional problems of interaction which become institutionalized in order to reduce the tensions growing out of uncertainty and unpredictability in the actions of others" (1950, 65–6). Following Cooley, Mead, James, and Peirce (see Archer 2003), Bales held that properties of the individual reduce to interaction:

[W]hat we usually regard as individual problem-solving, or the process of individual thought, is essentially in form and in genesis a social process; thinking is a re-enactment by the individual of the problem-solving process as he originally went through it with other individuals. It can probably be maintained with considerable success that the best model we have for understanding what goes on *inside* the individual personality is the model of what goes on *between* individuals in the problem-solving process. The component parts – acts in a system of action – are identical. (1950, 62)

Today, this line of thought is common among socioculturalists and is sometimes called "Vygotskian," even though its foundations are American pragmatism as much as Vygotsky's Soviet psychology (also see Chapter 7).

Within contemporary sociology, interactional reductionism is found in the various strands of what Collins (1981) called "radical microsociology" – particularly in ethnomethodology and conversation analysis. Interactional reductionists are perhaps the prototypical theorists of the Interaction Paradigm because of the purity of their rejection of sociological realism: "[M]acrophenomena are made up of aggregations and repetitions of many similar microevents" (Collins 1981, 988); social patterns and institutions "do not *do* anything" (p. 989). Sociologists should explain social structures by reducing them to "interaction ritual chains" (p. 985).[6]

---

[6] Such ethnomethodologically inspired ideas were common through the 1970s; for an example, see Hawes's 1974 review of texts on organizational behavior, which argued that "a social collectivity *is* patterned communicative behavior; communicative behavior does not occur *within* a network of relationships but *is* that network" (p. 500).

Perhaps the best-known argument for reducing social structure to inter-action is the *demonstrable relevance* argument of the conversation analysts. Following ethnomethodology's rejection of the Structure Paradigm, con-versation analysts argue that the causal effects of macrosocial forces are not analytically distinct but can only be understood by analyzing partic-ipants' orientations toward them as revealed in the talk itself. Schegloff (1992, 195–6) referred to this distinction as that between "external context" and "discourse context" and made the standard conversation-analytic argument that the researcher can treat all context as discourse context because the external context is only important to the extent that it is "demonstrably relevant to participants" (1992, 215; also see Schegloff 1991). This was in part a rejection of positivism and in part a claim for the methodological efficiency of interactional study: The best way to study the influence of structural properties on individuals is to look for conversational evidence of that influence.

Interactional reductionists focus primarily on small-group encounters and do not directly address the micro-macro link. Many interactional reductionists are committed to a process ontology and are resistant to theorizing emergence processes because that seems to involve ontolog-ical commitments to both component individuals and emergent social structures (Chapter 7).

Hybrid theories

Interactional reductionists do not engage with the Structure Paradigm; instead they reject it entirely: Only interaction is real, and both structure and individuals derive from it. Hybrid theorists cannot avoid a more sub-stantial engagement with the Structure Paradigm because they accept the ontological independence of all three levels. They argue that the relation between individuals and structure cannot be properly theorized nor empirically studied without incorporating an intermediate level of symbolic communication. Communication has causal influences both on individuals (it mediates the downward causal effects of social struc-ture) and on social structure (it mediates the upward emergence of social structure from the collective actions of individuals).

Although interactional reductionism is the dominant form of the Inter-action Paradigm, there are a few hybrid theorists who have attempted to analyze both interaction and structure and their mutual relations. Hybrid theories within the Interaction Paradigm are important because they rec-ognize the theoretical tensions driving the dialectic toward the Emergence Paradigm. However, lacking a theory of social emergence, hybrid inter-action theories are unstable and tend to migrate toward interactional reductionism.

Various contemporary sociologists have argued that interaction mediates between individual action and macrosocial structure (Collins 1981; Ellis 1999; Lawler, Ridgeway, and Markovsky 1993; Rawls 1987, 1990; Ritzer and Gindoff 1992). Stryker (1980) advocated the incorporation of macrostructure into studies of symbolic interaction, emphasizing the causal and constraining role that structure exerts over interaction. Lawler, Ridgeway, and Markovsky (1993) argued that the micro-macro problem can only be solved by considering encounters between individuals. They argued that microsociology has always been fundamentally concerned with the emergence of social structure from individual action (p. 269), and their account of the emergence of microstructures within a macrostructural network is compatible with the local neighborhoods that emerge in many artificial societies (Chapter 8). However, in fact most microsociology along these lines – including symbolic interactionism and conversation analysis – has emphasized that social structures emerge from the joint actions of actors in symbolic encounters, while deemphasizing the causal constraint of such emergent structures over action (cf. Sawyer 2003d). Ritzer and Gindoff (1992) termed their own position *methodological relationism* because it approaches the micro-macro link by examining relations among individuals.

In Germany, Habermas (1987) developed a hybrid interaction theory, the theory of *communicative action*. Communicative action was a level of analysis distinct from individual agency: "[T]he acts of reaching understanding, which link the teleologically structured plans of action of different participants and thereby first combine individual acts into an interacting complex, cannot themselves be reduced to teleological actions" (vol. 1, 288). In introducing communicative action, Habermas partially resolved the tensions within the Structure Paradigm and the Interaction Paradigm. However, he did not provide an account of the processes of social emergence. Although such processes are implicit in his account – for example, he referred to "linking" and "combining" individual acts "into an interacting complex" (p. 288) – he never provided an emergence account of how these links and combinations occur, nor of how they result in macrostructural phenomena.

The concept of *discourse* has been central to many hybrid interaction theories. It originated in 1970s French discourse analysis, then was integrated into British cultural studies theory, and today is found primarily in critical discourse analysis (Sawyer 2002a). During the 1970s, French discourse analysts such as Paul Henry and Michel Pêcheux developed Althusser's concept of ideology into a theory of discourse. Pêcheux ([1975] 1982) explored the relations that discourses have with ideologies; discourses, like ideologies, develop out of clashes with one another, and there is always a political dimension to writing and speech. Pêcheux explored the relationship between discursive formations and *ideological formations*; for Pêcheux, the discursive formation was the key concept that provided the causal link between social structures and individual consciousness: "Individuals are 'interpellated' as speaking-subjects (as subjects of *their* discourse) by the discursive formations which represent 'in language' the ideological formations that correspond to them" (p. 112). Discourse is a level of analysis that intermediates structure and individual. However, Althusserian discourse theory did not explore how structures emerge from interaction; rather, it empha-sized that interaction is determined by structure.

Beginning in the 1990s, a type of analysis known as "critical discourse analysis" emerged from British cultural studies, building on these 1970s notions of discourse and ideology (Fairclough 1995). Critical discourse analysis shares with Althusserian discourse analysis the attempt to simul-taneously study both interaction and social structure, considering each to be an autonomous level of social reality. But by the 1990s, agency and individual creativity were more central concerns in social theory than in the 1970s, and compared with 1970s discourse analysis, critical dis-course analysis is more concerned with the agency and potential freedom of action of individual speakers.

However, in practice, critical discourse analysis has rarely documented or explained specific cases in which structural phenomena emerge from interaction. In most cases, the empirical studies of critical discourse anal-ysis demonstrate how social structures reproduce themselves through interaction. These studies often demonstrate the mechanisms of class reproduction – a traditional Marxian concern – in spite of (or with the unwitting participation of) the creative agency of individuals. Critical discourse analysis has not proposed a theory of social emergence.

Problems with the Interaction Paradigm

The Structure Paradigm failed because it did not theorize the processes and mechanisms of social emergence, and these are necessary compo-nents of any explanation of the relation between individuals and social structure. The Interaction Paradigm is a necessary first step toward a sci-ence of social emergence because it emphasizes interaction, process, and mechanism. But it is limited by internal theoretical contradictions that prevent it from fully explaining social emergence.

Problem 1: No mechanism proposed between social structure and interaction   The interactional reductionists deny that social structure has any autonomous reality, so they reject the possibility that interaction is constrained by social phenomena. In contrast, the hybrid theories of the critical discourse analysts and the cultural studies theorists examined how interaction itself might be causally constrained by social structure. But they have not explained the mechanisms by which macrosocial phenomena causally influence interaction. For example, this was where Pêcheux's discourse theory came up short; he never identified the mechanisms of the causal relations between ideological frameworks and discursive frameworks.

More important, the Interaction Paradigm does not explain how interaction could causally influence social structure; what is required is a theory of social emergence focused on explaining how interactional processes result in the emergence of social properties. Without a well-developed account of how interactional processes result in social emergence, Interaction Paradigm theorists have been unable to convince other sociologists that communication is central to sociological theory. Although a few hybrid interaction theorists have argued for the need to incorporate communication into micro-macro theories, none has sufficiently articulated the role of communication in social emergence.

Problem 2: No mechanism proposed between the individual and interaction   Interactional reductionists hold that the individual is constituted by and through interaction, and they deny that the individual has autonomous existence prior to and apart from interaction. Hybrid interactionists introduce the theoretical possibility of examining how interaction causally constrains individuals. Yet, in practice, hybrid interactionists rarely consider the individual; rather, they focus on relations between interaction and social structure. Sociocultural psychologists have made the most empirical progress in this area, with their close studies of cultural practices and socialization processes.

Problem 3: No theory of social emergence   The Structure Paradigm ultimately fails to explain social emergence because it has no theory of interaction. After the antithesis of the Interaction Paradigm, it is no longer possible to deny the importance of symbolic interaction. The unresolved tension in the Interaction Paradigm is how to bring social structure back into sociological theory.

• The Interaction Paradigm rejects the necessity of examining individuals (the realm of psychology) and macrosocial structures (the realm of macrosociology). Thus it seems that no concept of emergence is necessary.

- The Interaction Paradigm lacks ontological depth; its conception of reality has a narrow scope around the interaction level, and it neglects the causally autonomous properties of both structures and individuals.
- The Interaction Paradigm has not theorized social constraint; in fact, interactional reductionists reject the existence of such constraint.

In sum, the Interaction Paradigm has no theory of social emergence – no explanation of how stable structures emerge from the joint collective actions of individuals engaged in social interaction. Accounting for causal relations between structure, interaction, and individual is a central goal of the Emergence Paradigm.

An aside: Interpretivism and agency

Intent is too intimate a thing to be more than approximately interpreted by another. It even escapes self-observation. . . . An act cannot be defined by the end sought by the actor, for an identical system of behavior may be adjustable to too many different ends without altering its nature. (Durkheim [1897] 1951, 43)

Before describing the Emergence Paradigm, I here discuss the place of agency theory in the history of the two paradigms reviewed in the preceding sections. Agency theory requires an aside because it does not fit comfortably into either the Structure Paradigm or the Interaction Paradigm, and its uncomfortable position results from theoretical confusion within agency theory. Many sociologists consider microsociology to include both agency theories and interaction theories. The usual result has been that the autonomous properties of interaction are neglected because interaction is conflated with agency. For example, in Ritzer's (1996) scheme, "micro" sociology includes both patterns of interaction and subjective mental states: "Depending on who is offering the definition, the micro level can range from psychological phenomena to individuals to interaction patterns among individuals" (p. 493). And Wiley (1988) wrote, "I will use 'micro' to refer to the bottom two levels, self and interaction" (p. 255).

The conflation of agency and interaction is a serious error. When many agentive individuals begin interacting, socially emergent phenomena occur; but when a single agent acts in isolation, there is no social emergence. Interaction can be studied objectively within the positivist tradition, whereas agency is a subjectivist, interpretivist notion. In the Interaction Paradigm, interactional regularities are properties of interaction *qua* interaction, not reducible to participants' agency or intentions.

Some interaction theorists and agency theorists have unwittingly encouraged this confusion by themselves conflating agency and interaction.

These *interpretivists* include many scholars who reject positivism and objectivism, such as phenomenological and subjectivist social scientists. Conversation analysts, for example, believe that what emerges during an encounter can only be explained in terms of the strategic actions taken by individuals and the demonstrated interpretations held by individuals in successive turns of an encounter. Interpretivists believe that macrostructural forces never constrain individuals directly; rather, social causation is always mediated by the interpretations that individuals hold.

Giddens (1984) is one of the best-known contemporary advocates of interpretivism: "Structural constraints, in other words, always operate via agents' motives and reasons" (p. 310). Giddens's account of interpretivism is a variant of 1960s phenomenology and ethnomethodology, developed in the context of 1960s and 1970s British Marxist thought. Many Marxians at that time developed hybrid interpretations of Marx that combined the subjectivity of consciousness with the objectivity of economic and social relations. One of the first such interpretations of Marx was that of Peter Berger and colleagues (Berger and Luckmann 1966; Berger and Pullberg 1965), who noted that the world "must be constructed and re-constructed over and over again" (Berger and Pullberg 1965, 201). Berger and Pullberg (1965) called this process *structuration*: Social structure is "a medium for the production of a world, while at the same time it is itself a produced moment of that world. Clearly, the relationship just described is a dialectical one. That is, social structure is produced by man and in turn produces him" (p. 202).[7] Various combinations of Marxist theory and phenomenology focused on routines, habitualized action, temporality, the ontological dependence of social order on human activity, and the dialectic between the individual and the social world (Berger and Luckmann 1966; Bourdieu [1972] 1977; Garfinkel 1967; Giddens 1984).

Giddens attempted to retain the theoretical benefits of structure with his notion of the *social system*: "reproduced relations between actors or collectivities organized as regular social practices" (1984, 25). This concept of the social system requires a theory of interaction ("relations between actors") and a theory of how collectivities emerge (else they could not be entities capable of having relations); yet no theories of interaction or

---

[7] Many of Giddens' readers talk as if he is a theorist of social emergence, when they refer to the process of structuration as a process of individuals co-creating structures that then constrain and enable their further course of action. However, this is a misreading of Giddens; Giddens explicitly rejected any form of social emergence. He explicitly rejected that social emergents are real, and argued that they have no autonomous causal power (see Chapters 5 and 7).

emergence appear in Giddens's writings. In Giddens's theory, *situated social practice* is central. Although he never made clear whether "situated social practice" is a theory of agency or a theory of interaction, in practice he remained focused on individual agency and never outlined a theory of interaction.

Interpretivists are opposed to atomist reductionism and methodological individualism. The philosopher Charles Taylor (1985) presented a prototypical argument that meaning and interpretation cannot be reduced to physical-level explanations. However, like most interpretivists, Taylor did not base his argument against physicalism on emergence; rather, he made an argument based on the irreducibly subjective nature of consciousness. In the context of systems theory, interpretivists use a "special case" argument against reductionism of the individual level – they argue that human subjectivity is the one special natural phenomenon that will not submit to natural science analysis. And in making this move, interpretivism finesses social emergence, denying that objective social phenomena exist apart from subjective orientations toward them and interpretations of them.

Agency theorists like Taylor and Giddens are ultimately focused on individuals; they hold that subjective interpretation explains social life and that there is no need for an autonomous science of society. If interpretivists are correct, then the social level of analysis does not exist. Interpretivists have the same attitude about social phenomena as methodological individualists: Social phenomena do not exist, they are mere epiphenomena of human action (and humans in interaction). As Granovetter (1985) noted, in such an oversocialized conception of actors, "Social influences are all contained inside an individual's head" (p. 486), and the ultimate effect is that these individuals can be considered to be "as atomized as any *Homo economicus*" (p. 486).

Contemporary interpretivism is a strange and unstable combination of subjectivist agency theories (e.g., Giddens) and objectivist empirical studies of interaction (e.g., conversation analysis). Interpretivism is unstable because it overlaps both agency theory (part of the Structure Paradigm) and interactionism (part of the Interaction Paradigm). This has had unfortunate implications for sociological theory. It has allowed many sociologists to mistakenly conflate agency theories and interaction theories and to group theories of the individual and theories of communication into "micro" sociology, when in fact they have very little in common. It has obscured the need for symbolic communication in sociological theory. Its anti-objectivism has distracted sociology from its primary task: to be the science of social emergence.

The Emergence Paradigm

The Interaction Paradigm is a necessary antithesis to the Structure Paradigm. It emphasizes critical features of social emergence that have no place in the Structure Paradigm: process, interaction, symbolic communication, and social mechanism. However, the Interaction Paradigm is also incomplete because it either rejects the structural level of analysis (in the case of interactional reductionists) or fails to theorize emergence (in the case of hybrid theorists). Ultimately, both paradigms fail because neither provides an account of social emergence.

As a result of inverted neglects – the Structure Paradigm neglecting symbolic interaction, the Interaction Paradigm neglecting structural properties – there has not been any sustained study of the role that symbolic interaction plays in social emergence. This is unfortunate, because if structural properties can be said to emerge from collective microfoundations of action, then that emergence must be the result of interaction among individuals; without interaction among elements in a complex system of dynamic connections, there can be no emergence. It is time for sociology to reconcile the best features of these two paradigms, time to synthesize the thesis of the Structure Paradigm and the antithesis of the Interaction Paradigm. In the rest of this chapter, I propose a synthesis: the Emergence Paradigm.

The micro-macro issue in sociology is a theoretical issue regarding how to relate two paradigms in sociological research that have, for the most part, remained independent. One paradigm, *microsociology* – which studies interactions between individuals – includes ethnomethodology, symbolic interactionism, conversation analysis, and, to some extent, sociolinguistics. The other paradigm, *macrosociology*, studies large-scale social phenomena such as institutions (schools, governments, economies, corporations, markets) and roles and statuses (social class, gender, race). Recent attempts to bridge the micro-macro divide are driven by the dialectic that I described earlier, and the Emergence Paradigm continues this late twentieth century endeavor.

The Emergence Paradigm introduces two additional levels of social reality: *stable emergents* and *ephemeral emergents* (see Figure 10.3). In any social situation, there is a continuing dialectic: social emergence, where individuals are co-creating and co-maintaining ephemeral and stable emergents, and downward causation from those emergents. The new, modified versions of the emergents at Levels C and D continually constrain the flow of the interaction. During conversational encounters, interactional frames emerge, and these are collective social facts that can be characterized independently of individuals' interpretations of them. Once

Social Structure (Level E)
Written texts (procedures, laws, regulations); material systems and infrastructure (architecture, urban design, communication and transportation networks)
Stable emergents (Level D)
Group subcultures, group slang and catchphrases, conversational routines, shared social practices, collective memory
Ephemeral emergents (Level C)
Topic, context, interactional frame, participation structure; relative role and status assignments
Interaction (Level B)
Discourse patterns, symbolic interaction, collaboration, negotiation
Individual (Level A)
Intention, agency, memory, personality, cognitive processes

Figure 10.3. The Emergence Paradigm.

a frame has emerged, it constrains the possibilities for action. Although the frame is created by participating individuals through their collective action, it is analytically independent of those individuals, and it has causal power over them. I refer to this process as *collaborative emergence* (Sawyer 2003d) to distinguish it from models of emergence that fail to adequately theorize interactional processes and emergence mechanisms. The Emergence Paradigm emphasizes the identification of the mechanisms of collaborative emergence that lead to ephemeral and stable emergents. By introducing these intermediate levels and the corresponding notion of collaborative emergence, my goal is to move beyond various undeveloped conceptions of emergence in sociology, which try to make too large a jump from the individual to the structural level.

In hybrid variants of the Interaction Paradigm, the theorized relations between structure and interaction conflate three distinct processes of social emergence; Levels C, D, and E are all considered to be part of the structure level. Likewise in the Structure Paradigm, emergents at Levels C and D are considered to be part of social structure. For both sociological paradigms, collaboratively emergent phenomena are incorrectly associated with the structural level and are thus perceived as being overly static rather than dynamic and processually emergent.

In much of traditional sociological theory, lower levels represent smaller groups of people, and higher levels represent larger groups. The emergents at Levels C and D are not structures in the traditional sociological sense of organizations and networks. They are emergent properties of sociological events and have an existence independent of any particular configuration of individuals. Although Levels C and D are at lower levels than social structure, they do not necessarily correspond to smaller groups. Rather, they represent emergent properties of groups of any size.

The Interaction Paradigm and the Structure Paradigm have complementary strengths in their approaches to social emergence. Whereas the Interaction Paradigm is known for its empirically rigorous approaches, in general it has not demonstrated how these methods could be applied to broader theoretical concerns. In contrast, Structure Paradigm treatments of emergence have been almost exclusively theoretical (Ritzer 1990, 363). The synthesis of the Interaction Paradigm and the Structure Paradigm provides an empirical method to study the micro-macro link; after all, this link must be mediated by successive interactions among individuals. Thus the Emergence Paradigm takes from the Interaction Paradigm the close empirical focus on processes of symbolic interaction, and it takes from the Structure Paradigm the belief that emergent social phenomena are ontologically distinct and have autonomous causal influence on individuals.[8]

The Emergence Paradigm accepts an important role for methodological individualism in sociology; it can play an important role in identifying the mechanisms and processes of social emergence in specific token instances. But methodological individualism is incomplete because, unlike the Emergence Paradigm, it does not support a social realism in which emergents have autonomous causal powers (as argued in Chapter 5). Due to social emergence, social life cannot be fully explained by analyzing the actions or mental states of the participant individuals and

---

[8] Compare Layder (1981), who outlined a similar conflict between theories of structure and of interaction and who made a similar critique of Interaction Paradigm theories as "interactive determinism" (p. 75): They reduce the social world to "the notion of the 'accomplishments' of active subjects" (p. 116) and thus cannot account for structural constraints on interaction. Despite Giddens's and Bourdieu's attempts to incorporate some notion of structure, Layder argued that both ultimately are "on the same terrain as the ethnomethodologists and the phenomenologists" because social structure for them "is nothing other than the ephemeral constructions and reality negotiations of situated actors" (p. 75). Layder proposed to distinguish interaction structure (emergent anew in each encounter) from contextual structure (objective, preconstituted structure; see the figure on p. 108). Although his proposed relation is subtly different from the Emergence Paradigm, there is much overlap.

then analyzing the interactions of these individuals, working "upward" to an explanation of the emergents. This sort of analysis can partially explain the collaborative emergence of ephemeral interactional frames but cannot adequately represent the analytic independence of emergents and the ways that they causally constrain and enable participants.

The Emergence Paradigm is a positivist, objectivist, scientific approach, and consequently it rejects subjectivism and interpretivism. It argues that the causal power of emergents cannot be explained solely in terms of individuals' representations of them, their demonstrated orientations to them, or their subjective interpretations of them. Properties at higher levels have autonomous causal force. They are unintended emergent effects, and they are causal even when individuals have no knowledge of them. Of course, in many cases individuals do have some knowledge of these emergents, and individuals' perceptions can have socially relevant effects. But in the Emergence Paradigm, most of the explanatory power comes from emergent properties and their processes of emergence, and individuals' subjective interpretations of emergents are generally not necessary in social explanation.

The Emergence Paradigm attempts to explain the causal forces that originate in an emergent that was created by the participants. Emergence Paradigm research focuses on the micro-interactional mechanisms by which shared social phenomena emerge and on how those emergents constrain those mechanisms.

Level C: Ephemeral emergents

In order that there may be a social fact, several individuals, at the very least, must have contributed their action; and in this joint activity is the origin of a new fact. (Durkheim [1895] 1964, lvi)

Level C includes the interactional frames of conversation analysis. In conversation, an interactional frame emerges from collective action and then constrains and enables collective action. These two processes are always simultaneous and inseparable. They are not distinct stages of a sequential process – emergence at one moment and then constraint in the next; rather, each action contributes to a continuing process of collaborative emergence at the same time that it is constrained by the shared emergent frame that exists at that moment. The emergent frame is a dynamic structure that changes with each action. No one can stop the encounter at any one point and identify with certainty what the frame's structure is. It is always subject to continuing negotiation, and because of its irreducible ambiguity, there will always be intersubjectivity issues, with different participants having different interpretations of the frame's constraints and affordances.

The collaborative emergence of frames has been studied by several researchers in interactional sociolinguistics and conversation analysis, including Deborah Tannen, Alessandro Duranti, and Charles Goodwin (Duranti and Goodwin 1992; Tannen 1993). This tradition represents an Interaction Paradigm antithesis to the linguistic tradition of pragmatics, which presumes the prior existence of a context within which individuals engage in conversation – analogous to Structure Paradigm conceptions of social structure. In most of pragmatics, context is presumed to influence an individual's conversational behavior in a given turn, but individuals are not considered to be participating in the creation of that context.

The Interaction Paradigm shifted the focus to how participants collectively create their context. However, due to the interpretivist theoretical foundations of most Interaction Paradigm researchers, they have been resistant to arguments that the emergent frame is a real social phenomenon with autonomous social properties. Rather, the frame is considered to exist only to the extent that it is "demonstrably relevant" (Schegloff, 1992) to participants, a classic interpretivist stance. Due to these interpretivist assumptions, the Interaction Paradigm fails to explain social emergence.

Level D: Stable emergents

The second form of collaborative emergence is from Level B to Level D, with a complicated mediation through Level C. Level D represents the shared, collective history of a group. Stable emergents of small groups include group learning (Hertz-Lazarowitz and Miller 1992), group development (Frey 1994), peer culture (Corsaro 1985), and collective memory (Wertsch 2002). Stable emergents of an entire society include its culture and its language; their collaborative emergence has been studied by cultural and linguistic anthropology.

The line between stable and ephemeral emergents is a fine one; for purposes of definition, I consider an emergent to be stable if it lasts across more than one encounter. Stable emergents have different degrees of stability; some are stable over generations, and others are stable only for weeks or months. From most to least stable, examples of stable emergents include language, catchphrases, trends and tastes, cohort private jokes and stories, and the ensemble feel of a theater group during a month-long run of a play. The issue of how stable emergents are related to ephemeral emergents is still unresolved within social science. In different ways, the issue is central to folkloristics, ethnomusicology, popular culture studies, the study of peer cultures and subcultures, and collective behavior studies of rumors and fads.

Ephemeral emergence occurs within a single encounter. Most sociological discussions of emergence have focused on the broader macrostructures that emerge and how those emergent patterns constrain future interaction. Yet these studies have not had much success in tracing the exact details of the moment-to-moment emergence processes whereby macrostructures are collectively created. In contrast, the Interaction Paradigm has focused exactly on the moment-to-moment details of how ephemeral emergents result from interaction. However, in shifting their focus to interactional process, they have tended to neglect the nature of what emerges and of what perdures across repeated encounters.

The collaborative emergence of stable emergents is the concern of the field known as "collective behavior," the study of phenomena such as mob actions, riots, mass delusions, crazes, fads, and fashions. Park and Burgess (1921) first noted a special kind of behavior that they called "collective behavior." Lang and Lang (1961) called it "collective dynamics": "*Those patterns of social action that are spontaneous and unstructured inasmuch as they are not organized and are not reducible to social structure*" (p. 4, original italics). They were also concerned with how collective action transforms into stable emergents, and during the 1960s, this became the concern of social movements researchers (Evans 1969, 10).

But these classic theories of collective behavior went from the individual to the emergents directly, without an examination of the mechanisms of interaction. These theorists used extremely simplistic notions of interaction such as "social contagion" (Blumer 1939) or "milling" (Park and Burgess 1921); historically, this is because these writings on collective behavior predated the development of sophisticated methodologies for analyzing interaction. The sociology of collective behavior never made connections to the study of how stable emergents are created over time – oral culture, ritual change, and related subjects from linguistic anthropology. It is time to revisit these phenomena of collective behavior with the additional sophistication provided by the Emergence Paradigm.

I agree with Coleman's (1990) critique of this line of research: It assumes that people transform into unreflective, irrational beings when grouped into certain unstructured social forms. Collective behavior researchers essentially studied any behavior that was not institutionalized. This is a historical artifact of the fact that the Structure Paradigm was dominant at the time, and the Structure Paradigm had no way to study creative social emergence; the collective behavior researchers chose to avoid this limitation by claiming they were studying an altogether different sort of social behavior, behavior that did not occur within the constraints of institutions and norms. But in the Emergence Paradigm, social emergence is found in all social interaction, regardless of the degree of formalization or institutionalization.

Several social theorists have recognized the theoretical benefits of introducing stable emergents as a mediator between individuals and macrostructure. These include Collins's (1981) *repetitive patterns of behavior*, Giddens' (1984) *situated social practices*, and Lawler, Ridgeway, and Markovsky's (1993) *microstructures*. For Lawler, Ridgeway, and Markovsky, microstructures "emerge from and organize particular encounters" (1993, 272). Stable emergents are symbolic phenomena that have a degree of intersubjective sharing among some (more or less stable) group of individuals.

Some network analysts have argued that in many cases institutions are crystallizations of emergent activity patterns and personal networks. Granovetter (1990) cited two historical examples of such institutional emergence: the development of the electrical utility industry in the United States between 1880 and 1930 and the professionalization of psychiatric practice. In both cases, the original institutions were "accretions of activity patterns around personal networks" (p. 105). Empirical and historical study suggests that these economic institutions emerged from the same processes as other social institutions. This sort of historical analysis of institutional emergence demonstrates that institutions are contingent and are socially constructed; the processes of their emergence must be studied empirically, and they cannot be predicted from neoclassical economic theory. As Granovetter (1990) concluded, explanations of institutions that do not incorporate the contingencies of social emergence "fail to identify causal mechanisms; they do not make an adequate connection between micro and macro levels, and so explain poorly when historical circumstances vary from the ones under which they were formulated" (p. 106).

Downward causation and the bidirectional dialectic

The central theoretical problems [of sociology are] how the purposive actions of the actors combine to bring about system-level behavior, and how those purposive actions are in turn shaped by constraints that result from the behavior of the system. (Coleman 1986, 1312)

As [interactions] crystallize, they attain their own existence and their own laws, and may even confront or oppose spontaneous interaction itself. (Simmel 1950, 10)

As levels of reality, stable and ephemeral emergents have an independent ontological status, and they have causal powers. These causal powers result in constraining and enabling effects on individuals. For example, in a conversation, once an interactional frame has emerged, it then constrains the future interaction of the participants, constraining interaction (at Level B) by acting directly on the interactional semiotics of the interaction and also constraining individuals directly (at Level A). Numerous examples of both forms of causation are documented in my 2003 book *Improvised Dialogues*.

Influence of emergents on the individual   Participants are constrained by stable and ephemeral emergents. For example, the strategic options that the ephemeral emergent frame makes available are limited, and the limiting of the selection set is a form of constraint, although not a strictly deterministic one. Social encounters are often improvisational, and in improvisational encounters there is always contingency and actions are never fully constrained.

There are four distinct types of downward causation operating on individuals:

- Structures constraining individuals (E → A)
- Stable emergents constraining individuals (D → A)
- Ephemeral emergents constraining individuals (C → A)
- Properties of interaction constraining individuals (B → A)

Interpretivists are correct to note that complex social systems have a unique feature not held by any other complex system: Individuals are aware of the social products that emerge from their encounters. In no other complex system do the components internalize representations of the emergents that they participated in creating. When sociologists have considered social causation, they have largely limited their analysis to this form of "interpretivist" downward causation.

However, many complex systems manifest downward causation (Andersen et al. 2000); for example, philosophers of mind generally accept that mental states are emergent from the physical brain and yet have causal powers over the physical brain. Note that this downward causation does not require that neurons have awareness or agency; by analogy, there is no reason why individuals could not be constrained even when they are not aware of it.

The Structure Paradigm does not recognize interaction as an autonomous level of reality, and the first three forms of downward causation are conflated within the Structure Paradigm, which places Levels C and D at the structural level. Because the Structure Paradigm does not distinguish these types of emergents, it has difficulty accounting for the mechanisms whereby emergent properties constrain individuals.

Within the Interaction Paradigm, interactional reductionists do not recognize downward causation because they deny that levels C, D, and E have ontological status apart from interaction. Hybrid theorists within this paradigm have not theorized stable and ephemeral emergents, although critical discourse analysis has made contributions to our understanding of how structures and interaction constrain individuals (E → A and B → A).

Anthropologists – both French structuralist anthropologists of the 1960s and Chicago-style symbolic anthropologists of the 1970s – have argued that cultures provide *emblems* or *ready-mades* to individuals and that these combine to form a shared system of knowledge that individual actors can then use in interaction. This is a downward causal force from the stable emergents that make up culture. These emblems and ready-mades are stable emergents from prior interaction. Anthropologists have not adequately examined the historical processes of collaborative emergence, typically considering that the symbolic structures of the culture are relatively stable and preexist any given encounter.[9]

Influence of the emergents on interaction   Because interaction is an autonomous level of analysis, there is downward causation onto Level B that is not mediated through individual representations at Level A:

- Structures constrain interaction (E → B) (this was a focus of Althusserian discourse analysis).
- Stable emergents constrain interaction (D → B) (the focus of much of linguistic anthropology).
- Ephemeral emergents constrain interaction (C → B) (the focus of Sawyer 2003d).

Emergents constrain the kinds of discursive patterns that can occur, and this is a strictly semiotic, interactional phenomenon, independent of human agency. Linguistic anthropologists and sociolinguists have demonstrated a wide range of situations where interaction patterns are directly constrained by the situation, even in cases where that situation has been collaboratively negotiated by the participants. This causal arrow is analytically distinct from any participating individuals – their strategic intentions or agency – because it operates directly on interaction processes themselves. Examples include studies of politeness and formality (Brown and Levinson 1978), strategic register switches (Friedrich 1971), greeting rituals (Irvine 1974), and collaborative joke-telling (Brenneis 1984).

---

[9] There are some exceptions: The "invention of tradition" theories of Hobsbawm and Ranger (1983) and the creativity and anthropology approach represented by Lavie, Narayan, and Rosaldo (1993).

Accounting for the dialectic between emergence and downward causation requires a semiotic argument about the nature of interaction (e.g., Sawyer 2003c).

Within the Structure Paradigm, there is no recognition that interaction itself can be constrained because interaction is not theorized as a distinct level of analysis. The only notion of downward causation is the social force that operates on the individual. This is why agency, subjectivity, and interaction are so frequently conflated in the Structure Paradigm. Within the Interaction Paradigm, most theorists are interactional reductionists who reject the autonomous existence of Levels C, D, and E. Those hybrid theorists that accept the autonomous existence of social structures – such as the critical discourse analysts – have made some progress at understanding the ways that interaction is itself constrained by social structure, but they have conflated Levels D and E and have generally failed to theorize Level C.

The circle of emergence

The Emergence Paradigm is a vision of sociology as the foundational social science. The basic science of social emergence has the explanatory scope inscribed by the circle in Figure 10.4. The Emergence Paradigm cannot explain everything of interest to the social sciences – only the phenomena within the circle of emergence. Most of the phenomena outside of the circle should be studied by disciplines other than sociology, because they are not foundational.

Level E: Structure

Level E represents stable emergents that have become fixed in objective material form. These include the technological and material systems of a society – communication networks, systems of highways and rail lines, residential population distributions, urban architecture, physical locations of goods and services, distribution networks for goods and services, and many other such features (Collins 1981, 994–5). Level E also includes those stable emergents that have become codified externally through writing technology: schedules, project plans, organizational charts, procedural and operations manuals, audit procedures, legal codes, constitutions.[10]

---

[10] Some theorists would argue that all of these elements I choose to place at Level E, including both the material and the documentary, are not objective because they only take on meaning once interpreted and used in some concrete encounter between individuals. This position is part of the subjectivist interpretivism that I have already rejected.

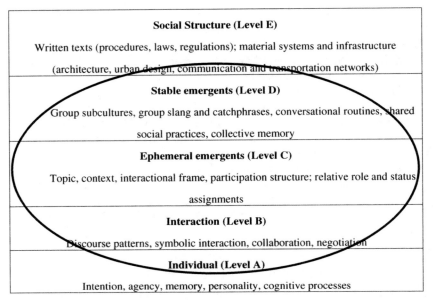

Figure 10.4. The circle of emergence.

Many Level E phenomena are already the purview of other social sciences:

- Political systems are fixed by the documents and records that support institutions. These systems are studied by political science.
- Economic systems are fixed by patterns and technologies of distribution of goods, the status of contemporary technology (the means of production), locations of factories, and financial communication technologies that make possible international interbank transfers and letters of credit, which in turn make international trade possible. These systems are studied by economics.
- Educational systems are fixed by the locations of schools, by their classroom architectures, by the documents and records that support the institutions of schooling, and by the textbooks that encode knowledge. These systems are studied by education researchers.

Durkheim recognized a distinction between stable emergents and fixed structures. He referred to emergents at the lower end of Level D as "currents" and used the term "crystallized currents" to refer to currents with a higher degree of stability: "All sorts of currents come, go, circulate everywhere, cross and mingle in a thousand different ways, and just because they are constantly mobile are never crystallized in an objective form" ([1897] 1951, 315). Durkheim's examples of social currents include joyous confidence, individualism, philanthropy, and cosmopolitanism. When a current takes on an objective material form, Durkheim called it a materialized social fact (see Chapter 6). In his time, there was no technology available to study the emergence of social currents – that would require videotape and audiotape records. His only empirical option was the study of materialized currents – and in this category Durkheim included databases, bureaucratic records, and demographic statistics. Perhaps owing to these methodological limitations, Durkheim claimed that materialized currents and crystallized currents were not significantly different from the (noncrystallized) currents they originated in: "There is thus a whole series of degrees without a break in continuity between the facts of the most articulated structure and those free currents of social life which are not yet definitely molded. The differences between them are, therefore, only differences in the degree of consolidation they present. Both are simply life, more or less crystallized" ([1895] 1964, 12).

In responding to the claim that society includes only individuals, Durkheim referred to these "materialized" aspects of society: "It is not true that society is made up only of individuals; it also includes material things, which play an essential role in the common life. The social fact is sometimes so far materialized as to become an element of the external world" ([1897] 1951, 313). His examples include types of architecture, networks of communication and transportation, technologies of production, and written language techniques.

The physical world is fixed in a way that stable emergents are not. Level E phenomena are not subject to normal social emergence, and they fall outside of the scope of the Emergence Paradigm as outlined here – with its emphasis on symbolic interaction – because their emergence from interaction is lost to history and their continued existence does not depend on interactional phenomena at Level B. For the most part, these material phenomena are resistant to explanation in terms of social emergence. Level E phenomena always socially emerge from historical processes, although their emergence is often too distant in the historical past to be of empirical interest to sociologists, and as a result they are usually studied by historians rather than sociologists.

Modern transportation infrastructures are examples of Level E phenomena. Before the industrial era in the United States, shipping and travel tended to follow inland waterways. In the nineteenth century, rail lines – materialized social emergents – increasingly influenced the development of the United States. They influenced the settlement patterns of the American West and determined the rise and fall of many midwestern cities. Once established, these transportation networks had causal power over individuals. In the second half of the twentieth century, another complex set of materialized social facts emerged: the automobile, interstate highways, and cheap fossil fuel. Generally it is historians, rather than sociologists, who explain these historical cases of emergence. The Emergence Paradigm could be combined with social history to help us explain the emergence of Level E structures through historical time. But questions within the circle of emergence are more central to sociology, and sociology proper should focus on the empirical study of social emergence.[11]

Sociologists often conflate Levels C, D, and E into the "macrostructure" and Levels A and B into the "microlevel." Introducing the distinction between Levels D and E results in a rethinking of the notion of social structure because many conceptions of structure include Level D phenomena. From the perspective of the Emergence Paradigm, it is critical to clarify the divide between levels D and E because Level D phenomena fall under the purview of the Emergence Paradigm whereas Level E phenomena do not.

Level A: Individuals

The lower limit of the circle of emergence occurs within Level A. To the extent that the individual can be studied outside of the circle of emergence, the individual will be the subject of the discipline of psychology. This psychology will be much more limited in scope than the current discipline because much of what we think of as "the individual" is subject to emergence processes, and these aspects of the individual must be studied via social emergence.

Individual brains have properties that are not subject to downward causation from the upper levels, and the task of psychology is to identify those properties of individual brains that are universal across sociocultural contexts and across individuals. These properties include such things as memory capacity, processing speed, abilities to multitask, factors of personality, and cognitive developmental pathways. All of these things may,

---

[11] Of course, many historians use great skill in reconstructing encounters that the historical record shows to have taken place, but in doing so they necessarily use historical methods rather than microsociological ones. When we do not have access to the many conversational encounters that were the foundations of historical emergence, microsociological methods cannot be applied.

at least in principle, be ultimately tied to the genotype of the organism and to its expression during development. To that extent, they are not subject to downward causal forces and consequently would fall outside the realm of social emergence.[12]

The Emergence Paradigm is of interest whenever properties of Levels B, C, or D begin to influence or constrain the way individuals think, solve problems, or behave. Social causation is significant during socialization; contemporary sociocultural research has found that a large part of the child's development depends on social and cultural context. Social causation also plays a significant role throughout adult life when situations influence individual behavior; many such cases have been documented by both social psychologists and sociologists.

To the extent that individuals are influenced and constituted by their social situation, the study of the individual will be a part of the Emergence Paradigm. For example, to the extent that developing individuals can change during development to reflect the society or culture that they are in, the study of individual development would fall within the Emergence Paradigm. This study is currently the purview of psychologists, but only of psychologists of a certain persuasion – sometimes known as "cultural psychologists" or "sociocultural psychologists"; the mainstream of psychology is still focused on those universal, biologically based behavioral phenomena that are constant across situations.

The Emergence Paradigm reveals that the discipline of psychology as it is currently configured is unstable: The circle of emergence slices directly through the center of contemporary psychology. If the Emergence Paradigm takes hold, then psychology will split into two distinct disciplines. The first, the study of biologically based universal properties of human brains, will increasingly merge with neuroscience. The second, which studies those phenomena that cannot be explained by reduction to neuroscience, will migrate to the new sociology of social emergence. Alternatively, as the universalist elements of psychology merge with neuroscience, the discipline of psychology may give itself new life by reformulating itself as emergence psychology, a psychology broken free from its reductionist theoretical assumptions.[13]

---

[12] I consider the existence of such properties to be well documented by decades of psychological and neuroscientific research. Although a few die-hard social constructivists may still wish to argue that everything about the individual is malleable and socially constructed, I believe this extreme stance is fading from serious consideration within the social sciences.

[13] Similar observations have led many social theorists to deny that psychology is a distinct discipline, beginning famously with Comte.

Toward a new social science

The Emergence Paradigm addresses the critical weaknesses of both the Structure Paradigm and the Interaction Paradigm, acting as a synthesis of the central features of both – a synthesis designed to reformulate sociology as the foundational science of social emergence. If sociology indeed becomes the science of social emergence, there are ramifications for many other social sciences as well, because the science of social emergence would provide the foundation for all of the social sciences.

First, the Emergence Paradigm addresses several of the inadequacies of the Structure Paradigm. The first weakness is that, within the Structure Paradigm, Levels C and D are assumed to be a part of social structure. Some theorists consider them to be distinct, but even those theorists generally consider them to be largely determined by Level E. Perhaps the one exception is cultural anthropology, which is particularly invested in a symbolic cultural sphere autonomous from material conditions and which consequently emphasizes stable emergents (Level D) and largely neglects Level E. The second weakness is that the Structure Paradigm does not recognize interaction as a mediator between individuals and structure. It does not account for how interaction itself can be constrained by structure, nor how interaction can have causal effects on social structure (via social emergence) and on individuals (via downward causation). The failure to account for interaction results in the fundamental weakness of the Structure Paradigm: There is no way to account for the mechanisms and processes of social emergence.

Second, the Emergence Paradigm shows that the Interaction Paradigm did not go far enough in addressing the failings of the Structure Paradigm. For example, even within hybrid variants of the Interaction Paradigm, levels C, D, and E are conflated, just as in the Structure Paradigm. The Interaction Paradigm tends toward one of two positions, neither of them capable of accounting for social emergence: either interactional reductionism (such as conversation analysis) or a social determinism that views interaction as a mediating but not a causally independent level (such as Althusserian discourse analysis and critical discourse analysis). The fundamental failing of the Interaction Paradigm is that, in its desire to reject the structural determinism of the Structure Paradigm, it went too far in denying the autonomous causal reality of emergent social phenomena.

Although sociology has failed to explain social emergence, its recent history – thesis followed by antithesis – has led us to an important point: As a result of the findings of the Interaction Paradigm, it is no longer possible to deny that the foundations of the social sciences must centrally incorporate symbolic communication. No social theory can be complete without a consideration of the intermediate levels of interaction and emergents because these levels mediate structure and agency, society and the individual.

The Emergence Paradigm suggests that the social sciences are currently misconfigured in three ways that result from the failure of sociology to define itself as the foundational study of social emergence. First, much of what is currently considered to be part of psychology should be located in the discipline of sociology. Second, sociology has an important role to play in explaining collective symbolic products, such as those studied by cultural anthropology, folkloristics, and popular culture studies. These disciplines study stable emergents, yet none has adequate theoretical foundations for explaining how its objects of study emerge, maintain themselves, and change over time. Sociology has always had an uncertain relationship with cultural phenomena; note the interesting theoretical discussions in the "sociology of culture" and "cultural sociology." A sociology centered on social emergence would provide these social sciences with theoretical foundations.

The relation between economics and sociology

And third, the microeconomic study of social emergence should be located in the discipline of sociology. My argument here is consistent with a long line of scholars who have argued that economics is a subdiscipline of sociology because the economic system is part of the social system (scholars making such an argument include Comte, Weber, Mises, and other Austrian School economists).

Since the 1980s, there has been increasing discussion about the relation between economics and sociology. Economic sociologists (e.g., Smelser and Swedberg 1994) and social economists (e.g., Durlauf and Young 2001) disagree about what the new division of labor between economics and sociology should be. I add to this debate my proposal that the sociology of social emergence is the foundational, basic science and that economics is one of the applied social sciences. Economics is the science of economic institutions, but the study of how they emerge is a question for sociology.

The Emergence Paradigm is consistent with the foundational assumptions of economic sociology: Economic action is a form of social action, economic action is socially situated, and economic institutions are social institutions (Granovetter and Swedberg 1992). Both economic sociology and the Emergence Paradigm are positivist and reject interpretivism (Krier 1999). I accept the criticisms of neoclassical microeconomics made by the economic sociologists: the rejection of neoclassical assumptions

regarding market efficiency and individual optimization or utility maximization (Etzioni 1991). The social emergence of economic institutions is no different from the social emergence of any other institution
(Granovetter and Swedberg 1992); all social phenomena emerge from
individual collective action, and there is no reason to believe that there
are different emergence processes for different social phenomena. Economic action is a form of social action, and economic institutions are
social institutions. Economists who import rational choice models into
sociological problems agree with this but assume that rational economic
action is the fundamental form of social action. However, empirical evidence has made this assumption increasingly difficult to maintain. Empirically grounded, theoretically rich sociological models of action simulated
using multi-agent systems will result in models of social emergence that
will then become foundational to economics, replacing the mathematical
formalisms of rational choice.

If the Emergence Paradigm takes hold, then academic departments are
currently configured in a theoretically unstable fashion, because microeconomics should be a part of sociology to the extent that it studies
emergence processes in general and how they give rise to stable emergents. This disciplinary reconfiguration leaves to economics the study of
emergent economic phenomena, just as it leaves to political science the
study of emergent political systems, to education the study of emergent
educational systems, and so on. However, it removes a chunk of microeconomics as currently practiced: the use of rational choice models of
individuals, combined with simple aggregation assumptions, to develop
microexplanations of macroeconomic phenomena. The study of social
emergence has taken place largely in microeconomics because sociology
has not been receptive to studies of social emergence; those scholars interested in it have had no choice but to affiliate with microeconomics. But its
models of social emergence are simplistic, are empirically ungrounded,
and have largely failed (see the critiques of Granovetter 1985 and Etzioni
1991). They persist in the face of such problems because social science
needs a foundation in social emergence, and at present microeconomics
has the only one.

It is frequently observed that microeconomics has a radically simplified theory of both the individual and of the social. The neoclassical
microeconomics model of the individual is a *homo economicus* who has
complete, certain information and rationally maximizes exchange value,
and only this simplified model of the individual has allowed the study
of social emergence to operate within economics. However, toward the
end of the twentieth century, experimental economists and behavioral
economists began to challenge the assumptions of rationality, certainty,

and complete information, drawing on experimental findings from psychology that show that individuals operate with bounded rationality, bounded willpower, and bounded self-interest.[14] Social economists (Durlauf and Young 2001) have introduced heterogeneity in individuals, direct interaction as well as interaction mediated by market prices (peer groups, social networks, and role models), individual preferences that are influenced by these interactions, and the use of dynamical systems theory and models. As these challenges continue and expand, it will become increasingly obvious that the study of social emergence belongs within sociology.

Sociologists have focused their critiques of microeconomics on its inadequate model of the individual rather than on its simplistic approach to interaction and aggregation – exchange of goods, price, and the interaction between demand and supply. Rather than focus my critique on its assumptions of rational action, I think economics has a more significant weakness vis-à-vis sociology: The forms of symbolic interaction that give rise to the emergence of social phenomena are not amenable to study using economic concepts. As Coleman (1986) observed, sociologists have not realized that "the major theoretical obstacle to social theory built on a theory of action is not the proper refinement of the action theory itself, but the means by which purposive actions of individuals *combine* to produce a social outcome" (p. 1321). Before the approaches to social emergence found in neoclassical microeconomics can expand to incorporate an empirically valid theory of interaction and emergence, they will have to merge into sociology's trajectory through the Interaction Paradigm into the Emergence Paradigm. Although communication has been neglected in micro-macro sociological theory – because such theory has remained within the Structure Paradigm – it is not even a part of the vocabulary in economics.[15]

Unlike economics, sociology has a long history of studying situated symbolic interaction. For economics to model social emergence as I have described it, economics would have to import whole subdisciplines of sociological theory and practice, subdisciplines whose object of study has no obvious relation to rational economic action – conversation analysis,

---

[14] The seminal reference is to Simon (1955). Particularly influential work has been done by Daniel Kahneman and Amos Tversky (resulting in a Nobel prize in 2002 for Kahneman) and Richard Thaler (for an overview of behavioral economics, see Mullainathan and Thaler 2001).

[15] Birner and Ege (1999) showed that Hayek's writings acknowledge the importance of "communication structure," but they noted that this is "very unusual" in economics (p. 761). Hayek argued that efficient markets require a perfect communication structure and that such a structure could not exist in reality.

symbolic interaction, and interactional sociolinguistics. Such a disciplinary redefinition would make no sense for economics. Yet for sociology, the redefinition required to incorporate the study of social emergence is a natural development, a synthesis of the two dominant twentieth-century sociological paradigms.

The microeconomic study of social emergence has held fast to the methodological individualism of rational choice theory; it has firmly rejected social realism. Of course, this is also true of individualist emergentists within sociology, but the discipline has collectively realized that social emergence is compatible with both social realism and methodological individualism (see Chapter 5). To the extent that the realist components of social emergence hold true, the study of social emergence cannot be reductively individualist but must also incorporate irreducibly causal, emergent macro-social properties. Even some economists have begun to realize that strict forms of methodological individualism cannot be maintained. Economist Kenneth Arrow (1994) argued that economics must use social categories, because they are "irreducible," not just "figures of speech" (p. 1), and that "social variables, not attached to particular individuals, are essential in studying the economy or any other social system and that, in particular, knowledge and technical information have an irremovable social component, of increasing importance over time" (p. 8). And several economists have noted that the market mechanism, required to coordinate and communicate prices, is not explained by neoclassical theory and yet is a macro-social institution that must exist before rational choice models can work.

If sociology begins to reformulate itself as the foundational study of social emergence, and if microeconomists who study social emergence increasingly modify their models to incorporate interaction and emergence mechanisms, the two strands of social emergence study will begin to converge. And as microeconomists increasingly address the flaws in their models of social emergence, they will find it increasingly inappropriate to be housed in departments of economics – because economic institutions emerge from the same human actions and through the same emergence processes as all other social institutions. Sophisticated models of emergence from communicative interaction are not likely to rest comfortably in a department of economics.

It is a historical accident that many studies of social emergence are now conducted by economists. Eventually, such studies will be grouped in a single discipline, and that discipline will be sociology. The emergence of macrophenomena cannot be explained with a narrow focus on maximizing utility – not even the emergence of macro-economic phenomena can be explained this way.

This reconfiguration will happen only after many years, perhaps decades: after sociology reconfigures itself as the basic science of social emergence, and after microeconomics revamps its models to incorporate socially embedded individuals interacting using complex communication systems. This new unified discipline will study ephemeral and stable emergents as symbolic emergents of interaction, combining empirical rigor and theoretical foundations.

One claim microeconomics makes vis-à-vis sociology is the rigor of its mathematical method. The claim is that without mathematics sociology is not a science because it can only provide discursive accounts of phenomena one by one: That is, it is historicism or storytelling rather than a lawful science of regularities. But the sociology of social emergence now has an equally powerful and equally rigorous methodology: multi-agent–based simulation. The power and rigor of sociology's new methodology will replace the mathematics of utility maximization because those formalisms cannot be expanded to model symbolic communication and emergence mechanisms.

Conclusion

Social emergence is a return to the big questions that helped to found sociology over a hundred years ago. Yet the Emergence Paradigm is not a grand theory in the Parsonsian sense because it does not theorize any specific, concrete social phenomena. Instead, the Emergence Paradigm is a metatheory of middle-range theories, combined with a proposed methodology for studying middle-range phenomena.[16] This methodology combines the close focus on interaction associated with conversation analysis with the independent analysis of the ephemeral and stable emergents that result. A case study of such a methodology can be found in my 2003 book *Improvised Dialogues*. The Emergence Paradigm does not propose any definite answers to long-standing sociological questions, but it has significant implications for how sociological theory and methodology should proceed.

The Emergence Paradigm shows that we cannot answer the fundamental question of the Structure Paradigm – How do individuals and collectivities mutually make each other up? – without close analysis of the bidirectional mechanisms interacting between these three intermediate

---

[16] Thus following Merton's (1968) recommendation that sociologists should pursue middle-range theories of social mechanism to unify micro- and macrotheories, and Swedberg's (1987) recommendation that the best way to respond to economic imperialism is to develop a middle-range economic sociology.

levels. The micro-macro debate largely neglects the most important components of the mechanism – the phenomena at the center of the circle of emergence.

The Emergence Paradigm shows that we cannot answer the key question raised by the Interaction Paradigm – What is the relation between interaction and both social structure and the individual? – without a theory of social emergence. Social emergence is the process linking interaction with stable and ephemeral emergents. The link between interaction and the structures of Level E is just at the limits of the Emergence Paradigm, but most of what sociologists consider to be structure falls at Level D and participates in emergence processes.

In his 1937 book, Parsons documented the phenomenon of *theoretical convergence* – his claim that four different theorists working in different disciplines and in different countries, without significant influence on one another, developed essentially the same "voluntaristic theory of action" and rejected utilitarian and positivistic theories of action. He claimed that this convergence itself provided an argument for the validity of the theory ([1937] 1949, 722–6). The review that I have presented in this book can be viewed in a similar light: Because social emergence has been advocated by theorists in many disciplines, it represents a form of theoretical convergence. Social emergence is compatible with individualism and yet holds that reductionist methodology does not necessarily work for social phenomena. We do not know whether reductionism will ultimately be successful at explaining all complex natural systems, including the human mind and complex societies. Yet social emergence provides a scientifically plausible account of why reductionist explanation may not be possible for certain classes of complex social systems. The best way to determine which social properties are real, to determine the proper relation between individual action and social structure, to determine the role of symbolic interaction in the micro-macro link, and to identify the full complexity of the mechanisms of social emergence is to combine the empirical study of socially embedded communication with richly constructed artificial society models.

References

Abbott, Andrew. 1995. "Things of boundaries." *Social Research* 62:857–82.

Abbott, Andrew. 1996. "Mechanisms and relations." In: *Conference on Social Mechanisms*. Stockholm, Sweden.

Ablowitz, Reuben. 1939. "The theory of emergence." *Philosophy of Science* 6:1–16.

Adami, Christoph, Richard K. Belew, Hiroaki Kitano, and Charles Taylor, eds. 1998. *Artificial life VI: Proceedings of the Sixth International Conference on Artificial Life*. Cambridge, MA: MIT Press.

Agre, Philip E. 1995. "Computational research on interaction and agency." In: *Computational theories of interaction and agency*, edited by Philip E. Agre and Stanley J. Rosenschein (pp. 1–52). Cambridge, MA: MIT Press.

Agre, Philip E., and David Chapman. 1987. "Pengi: An implementation of a theory of activity." In: *Proceedings of the 6th National Conference on Artificial Intelligence (AAAI-97)* (pp. 268–72). San Mateo, CA: Morgan Kaufmann.

Agre, Philip E., and Stanley J. Rosenschein, eds. 1995. *Computational theories of interaction and agency*. Cambridge, MA: MIT Press.

Alexander, Samuel. 1920. *Space, time, and deity*. London: MacMillan. (Originally presented as the Gifford Lectures at Glasgow, 1916–18.)

Alexander, Jeffrey C. 1982. *Theoretical logic in sociology*. Vol. 2, *The antinomies of classical thought: Marx and Durkheim*. Berkeley: University of California Press.

Alexander, Jeffrey C., and Bernhard Giesen. 1987. "From reduction to linkage: The long view of the micro-macro link." In: *The micro-macro link*, edited by Jeffrey C. Alexander, Bernhard Giesen, Richard Münch, and Neil J. Smelser (pp. 1–42). Berkeley: University of California Press.

Alexander, Jeffrey C., and Paul Colomy. 1990. "Neofunctionalism today: Reconstructing a theoretical tradition." Pp. 33–67 in *Frontiers of social theory: The new syntheses*, edited by George Ritzer. New York: Columbia University Press.

Alexander, Jeffrey C., Bernhard Giesen, Richard Münch, and Neil J. Smelser, eds. 1987. *The micro-macro link*. Berkeley: University of California Press.

Allen, P. M., M. Sanglier, G. Engelen, and F. Boon. 1985. "Towards a new synthesis in the modeling of evolving complex systems." *Environment and Planning B* 12:65–84.

Andersen, Peter Bøgh, Claus Emmeche, Niels Ole Finnemann, and Peder Voetmann Christiansen, eds. 2000. *Downward causation: Minds, bodies and matter*. Aarhus, Denmark: Aarhus University Press.

Antona, M., F. Bousquet, C. LePage, J. Weber, A. Karsenty, and P. Guizol. 1998. "Economic theory of renewable resource management: A multi-agent system approach." In: *Multi-agent systems and agent-based simulation*, edited by Jaime S. Sichman, Rosaria Conte, and Nigel Gilbert (pp. 61–78). Berlin: Springer.

Archer, Margaret S. 1979. *Social origins of educational systems*. Beverly Hills, CA: Sage.

Archer, Margaret S. 1982. "Morphogenesis versus structuration: On combining structure and action." *British Journal of Sociology* 33:455–83.

Archer, Margaret S. 1988. *Culture and agency: The place of culture in social theory*. New York: Cambridge University Press.

Archer, Margaret S. 1995. *Realist social theory: The morphogenetic approach*. New York: Cambridge University Press.

Archer, Margaret S. 2000. "For structure: Its reality, properties and powers: A reply to Anthony King." *Sociological Review* 48:464–72.

Archer, Margaret S. 2003. *Structure, agency and the internal conversation*. New York: Cambridge University Press.

Arrow, Kenneth. 1951. *Social choice and individual values*. New York: Wiley.

Arrow, Kenneth J. 1994. "Methodological individualism and social knowledge." *American Economic Review* 84:1–9. Originally presented as the Richard T. Ely Lecture at the American Economics Association, Boston, January 3–5, 1994.

Arthur, W. Brian. 1999. "Complexity and the economy." *Science* 284:107–9.

Axelrod, Robert. 1984. *The evolution of cooperation*. New York: Basic Books.

Axelrod, Robert. 1995. "A model of the emergence of new political actors." In: *Artificial societies: The computer simulation of social life*, edited by Nigel Gilbert and Rosaria Conte (pp. 19–39). London: University College London Press.

Axelrod, Robert. 1997. *The complexity of cooperation: Agent-based models of competition and collaboration*. Princeton, NJ: Princeton University Press.

Axtell, Robert L. 2001. "Effects of interaction topology and activation regime in several multi-agent systems." Pp. 33–48 in *Multi-agent-based simulation*, edited by S. Moss and P. Davidsson. Berlin: Springer.

Axtell, Robert L. 2002. "A positive theory of emergence for multi-agent systems." Paper presented at the First Lake Arrowhead Conference on Computational Social Science and Social Complexity, May 9–12, Lake Arrowhead, CA.

Axtell, Robert L., and Joshua M. Epstein. 1999. "Coordination in transient social networks: An agent-based computational model of the timing of retirement." In: *Behavioral dimensions of retirement economics*, edited by Henry J. Aaron (pp. 161–83). New York: Russell Sage Foundation.

Ayala, Francisco J. 1974. "Introduction." In *Studies in the philosophy of biology: Reduction and related problems*, edited by Francisco Jose Ayala and Theodosius Dobzhansky (pp. vii–xvi). Berkeley: University of California Press.

Baas, Nils A. 1994. "Emergence, hierarchies, and hyperstructures." In: *Artificial life III* (SFI Studies in the Sciences of Complexity no. 17), edited by Christopher G. Langton (pp. 515–37). Reading, MA: Addison-Wesley.

Bailey, Kenneth D. 1994. *Sociology and the new systems theory: Toward a theoretical synthesis*. Albany, NY: SUNY Press.

Baker, Patrick L. 1993. "Chaos, order, and sociological theory." *Sociological Inquiry* 63:123–49.

Bales, Robert F. 1950. *Interaction process analysis: A method for the study of small groups*. Cambridge, MA: Addison-Wesley Press.

Batterman, Robert W. 2000. "Multiple realizability and universality." *British Journal of the Philosophy of Science* 51:115–45.

Bauman, Zygmunt. 1973. *Culture as praxis*. London: Routledge and Kegan Paul.

Bechtel, William, and Adele Abrahamson. 1991. *Connectionism and the mind: An introduction to parallel processing in networks*. Cambridge, MA: Blackwell.

Bechtel, William, and Robert C. Richardson. 1993. *Discovering complexity: Decomposition and localization as strategies in scientific research*. Princeton, NJ: Princeton University Press.

Beckermann, Ansgar, Hans Flohr, and Jaegwon Kim, eds. 1992. *Emergence or reduction? Essays on the prospects of nonreductive physicalism*. Berlin: de Gruyter.

Bedau, Mark. 2002. "Downward causation and the autonomy of weak emergence." *Principia* 6:5–50.

Bell, Daniel. 1973. *The coming of the post-industrial society: A venture in social forecasting*. New York: Basic Books.

Berger, Peter L., and Thomas Luckmann. 1966. *The social construction of reality: A treatise in the sociology of knowledge*. New York: Doubleday.

Berger, Peter, and Stanley Pullberg. 1965. "Reification and the sociological critique of consciousness." *History and Theory* 4:196–211.

Bergson, Henri. [1907] 1911. *Creative evolution*. New York: Henry Holt. Originally published as *L'évolution créatrice* (Paris: F. Alcan, 1907).

Bertalanffy, Ludwig von. 1968. *General systems theory: Foundations, development, applications*. New York: G. Braziller.

Berthelot, Jean-Michel. 1995. *1895 Durkheim: L'Avénement de la sociologie scientifique*. Toulouse, France: Presses Universitaires du Mirail.

Bhargava, Rajeev. 1992. *Individualism in social science*. New York: Oxford University Press.

Bhaskar, Roy. [1975] 1997. *A realist theory of science*. New York: Verso Classics.

Bhaskar, Roy. 1979. *The possibility of naturalism*. New York: Routledge.

Bhaskar, Roy. 1982. "Emergence, explanation, and emancipation." In: *Explaining human behavior: Consciousness, human action and social structure*, edited by Paul F. Secord (pp. 275–310). Beverly Hills, CA: Sage.

Birner, Jack, and Ragip Ege. 1999. "Two views on social stability: An unsettled question." *American Journal of Economics and Sociology* 58:749–80.

Black, Donald. 2000. "Dreams of pure sociology." *Sociological Theory* 18:343–67.

Blain, Robert R. 1971. "On Homan's psychological reductionism." *Sociological Inquiry* 41:3–25.

Blau, Peter M. 1955. *The dynamics of bureaucracy: A study of interpersonal relations in two government agencies*. Chicago: University of Chicago.

Blau, Peter M. 1964. *Exchange and power in social life*. New York: Wiley.

Blau, Peter M. 1970a. "Comment." In: *Explanation in the behavioural sciences*, edited by Robert Borger and Frank Cioffi (pp. 329–43). New York: Cambridge University Press.

Blau, Peter M. 1970b. "A formal theory of differentiation in organizations." *American Sociological Review* 35:201–18.

Blau, Peter M. 1977. "A macrosociological theory of social structure." *American Journal of Sociology* 83:26–54.

Blau, Peter M. 1981. "Introduction: Diverse views of social structure and their common denominator." In *Continuity in structural inquiry*, edited by Peter M. Blau and Robert K. Merton (pp. 1–23). Beverly Hills: Sage.

Blau, Peter M. 1987. "Microprocess and macrostructure." In *Social exchange theory*, edited by Karen S. Cook (pp. 83–100). Newbury Park, CA: Sage.

Blitz, David. 1992. *Emergent evolution: Qualitative novelty and the levels of reality*. Dordrecht, Netherlands: Kluwer Academic.

Blommaert, Jan. 2001. "Context is/as critique." *Critique of Anthropology* 21:13–32.

Blume, Lawrence E., and Steven N. Durlauf. 2001. "The interactions-based approach to socioeconomic behavior." In: *Social dynamics*, edited by Steven N. Durlauf and H. Peyton Young (pp. 15–44). Cambridge, MA: MIT Press.

Blumer, Herbert. 1939. "Collective behavior." In: *An outline of the principles of sociology*, edited by Robert E. Park (pp. 219–80). New York: Barnes and Noble.

Blumer, Herbert. 1962. "Society as symbolic interaction." In *Human behavior and social processes: An interactionist approach*, edited by Arnold M. Rose (pp. 179–192). Boston: Houghton Mifflin.

Blumer, Herbert. 1966. "Sociological implications of the thought of George Herbert Mead." *American Journal of Sociology* 71:535–44.

Blumer, Herbert. 1969. *Symbolic interactionism: Perspective and method*. Englewood Cliffs, NJ: Prentice-Hall.

Boring, E. G. 1929. *A history of experimental psychology*. 2nd ed. Englewood Cliffs, NJ: Prentice Hall.

Boulding, Kenneth E. 1969. "Economics as a moral science." *American Economic Review* 59:1–12.

Bourdieu, Pierre. [1972] 1977. *Outline of a theory of practice*. New York: Press Syndicate of the University of Cambridge. Originally published as *Esquisse d'une théorie de la pratique* (Geneva: Droz, 1972).

Boutroux, Émile. [1874] 1916. *The contingency of the laws of nature*. Chicago: Open Court. Originally published as a dissertation at the Sorbonne in 1874, titled *De la Contingence des Lois de la Nature*.

Boutroux, Émile. [1893] 1914. *Natural law in science and philosophy*. New York: Macmillan. From lectures presented at the Sorbonne 1892–1893.

Bowles, Samuel. 2001. "Comment: Individual behavior and social interactions." *Sociological Methodology* 31:89–96.

Brassel, Kai-H., Michael Möhring, Elke Schumacher, and Klaus G. Troitzsch. 1997. "Can agents cover all the world?" In: *Simulating social phenomena*, edited by Rosaria Conte, Rainer Hegselmann, and Pietro Terna (pp. 55–72). Berlin: Springer.

Bratman, Michael E. 1992. "Shared cooperative activity." *Philosophical Review* 101:327–41.

Brenneis, D. 1984. "Grog and gossip in Bhatgaon: Style and substance in Fiji Indian conversation." *American Ethnologist* 11:487–506.

Breton, Laurent, Jean-Daniel Zucker, and Eric Cl'ement. 2001. "A multi-agent based simulation of sand piles in a static equilibrium." Pp. 108–118. In *Multi-agent-based simulation*, edited by S. Moss and P. Davidsson. Berlin: Springer.

Broad, C. D. 1925. *The mind and its place in nature*. New York: Harcourt, Brace.

Brock, William A., and Steven N. Durlauf. 2001. "Discrete choice with social interactions." *Review of Economic Studies* 68:235–60.

Brodbeck, May. [1958] 1968. "Methodological individualisms: Definition and reduction." In: *Readings in the philosophy of the social sciences*, edited by May Brodbeck (pp. 280–303). New York: Macmillan. Originally published in *Philosophy of Science* 25 (1958):1–22.

Brooks, Rodney A., and Pattie Maes, eds. 1994. *Artificial life IV: Proceedings of the Fourth International Workshop on the Synthesis and Simulation of Living Systems*. Cambridge, MA: MIT Press.

Brown, Penelope, and Stephen Levinson. 1978. "Universals in language usage: Politeness phenomena." In: *Questions and politeness: Strategies in social interaction*, edited by Esther N. Goody (pp. 56–289). New York: Cambridge University Press.

Bruner, Jerome. 1990. *Acts of meaning*. Cambridge, MA: Harvard University Press.

Buckley, Walter. 1967. *Sociology and modern systems theory*. Englewood Cliffs, NJ: Prentice-Hall.

Bunge, Mario. 1977. "Commentary: Emergence and the mind." *Neuroscience* 2:501–9.

Bunge, Mario. 1996. *Finding philosophy in social science*. New Haven, CT: Yale University Press.

Bunge, Mario. 1997. "Mechanism and explanation." *Philosophy of the Social Sciences* 27:410–65.

Bunge, Mario. 2004. "How does it work? The search for explanatory mechanisms." *Philosophy of the Social Sciences* 34:182–210.

Burke, Peter J. 1997. "An identity model for network exchange." *American Sociological Review* 62:134–50.

Burt, Ronald S. 1982. *Toward a structural theory of action: Network models of social structure, perception, and action*. New York: Academic Press.

Byrne, David. 1998. *Complexity theory and the social sciences: An introduction*. London: Routledge.

Campbell, Donald T. 1974. "'Downward causation' in hierarchically organised biological systems." In: *Studies in the philosophy of biology: Reduction and related problems*, edited by Francisco Jose Ayala and Theodosius Dobzhansky (pp. 179–86). Berkeley: University of California Press.

Carelli, Maria Grazia. 1998. "Internalization, participation, and ethnocentrism." *Human Development* 41:355–9.

Cariani, Peter. 1991. "Emergence and artificial life." In: *Artificial life II* (SFI Studies in the Sciences of Complexity no. 10), edited by C. G. Langton, C. Taylor, J. D. Farmer, and S. Rasmussen (pp. 775–97). Reading, MA: Addison-Wesley.

Carley, Kathleen M., and Les Gasser. 1999. "Computational organization theory." In: *Multiagent systems: A modern approach to distributed artificial intelligence*, edited by Gerhard Weiss (pp. 299–330). Cambridge, MA: MIT Press.

Carley, Kathleen M., and Michael J. Prietula, eds. 1994. *Computational organization theory*. Hillsdale, NJ: Erlbaum.

Castelfranchi, Cristiano. 1998. "Simulating with cognitive agents: The importance of *cognitive emergence*." In: *Multi-agent systems and agent-based simulation*, edited by Jaime S. Sichman, Rosaria Conte, and Nigel Gilbert (pp. 26–44). Berlin: Springer.

Castelfranchi, Cristiano. 2001. "The theory of social functions: Challenges for computational social science and multi-agent learning." *Cognitive Systems Research* 2:5–38.

Castelfranchi, Cristiano, and Rosaria Conte. 1996. "Distributed artificial intelligence and social science: Critical issues." In: *Foundations of distributed artificial intelligence*, edited by G. M. P. O'Hare and N. R. Jennings (pp. 527–42). New York: Wiley.

Casti, John L. 1994. *Complexification: Explaining a paradoxical world through the science of surprise*. New York: HarperCollins.

Cederman, Lars Erik. 1997. *Emergent actors in world politics: How states and nations develop*. Princeton, NJ: Princeton University Press.

Cederman, Lars Erik. 2002. "Computational models of social forms: Advancing generative macro theory." Paper presented at Agent 2002: Social Agents: Ecology, Exchange, and Evolution, Chicago.

Chapman, David. 1987. "Planning for conjunctive goals." *Artificial Intelligence* 32:333–78.

Chwe, Michael Suk-Young. 1999. "Structure and strategy in collective action." *American Journal of Sociology* 105:128–56.

Cilliers, Paul. 1998. *Complexity and postmodernism: Understanding complex systems*. New York: Routledge.

Clark, Andy. 1997. *Being there: Putting brain, body, and world together again*. Cambridge, MA: MIT Press.

Clark, Terry N. 1969. "Introduction." In: *On communication and social influence*, edited by Terry N. Clark (pp. 1–69). Chicago: University of Chicago Press.

Clarke, R. 1999. "Nonreductive physicalism and the causal powers of the mental." *Erkenntnis* 51:295–322.

Cohen, Ira J. 1989. *Structuration theory: Anthony Giddens and the constitution of social life*. New York: St. Martin's Press.

Cohen, Philip R., and Hector J. Levesque. 1991. "Teamwork." *Noûs* 35:487–512.

Cohen, Philip R., Jerry Morgan, and Martha E. Pollack, eds. 1990. *Intentions in communication*. Cambridge, MA: MIT Press.

Cole, Michael. 1995a. "Socio-cultural-historical psychology: Some general remarks and a proposal for a new kind of cultural-genetic methodology." In: *Sociocultural studies of mind*, edited by James V. Wertsch, Pablo del Rio, and Amelia Alvarez (pp. 187–214). New York: Cambridge University Press.

Cole, Michael. 1995b. "The supra-individual envelope of development: Activity and practice, situation and context." In: *Cultural practices as contexts for development*, edited by Jacqueline J. Goodnow, Peggy J. Miller, and Frank Kessel (pp. 105–18). San Francisco: Jossey-Bass.

Cole, Michael. 1996. *Cultural psychology: A once and future discipline.* Cambridge, MA: Harvard University Press.

Cole, Michael, and Sylvia Scribner. 1978. "Introduction." In: *Mind in society: The development of higher psychological processes,* edited by Michael Cole, Vera John-Steiner, Sylvia Scribner, and Ellen Souberman (pp. 1–14). Cambridge, MA: Harvard University Press.

Coleman, James S. 1986. "Social theory, social research, and a theory of action." *American Journal of Sociology* 91:1309–35.

Coleman, James S. 1987. "Microfoundations and macrosocial behavior." In: *The micro-macro link,* edited by Jeffrey C. Alexander, Bernhard Giesen, Richard Münch, and Neil J. Smelser (pp. 153–73). Berkeley: University of California Press.

Coleman, James S. 1990. *Foundations of social theory.* Cambridge, MA: Harvard University Press.

Collier, Andrew. 1989. *Scientific realism and socialist thought.* Boulder, CO: Lynne Rienner Publishers.

Collins, Randall. 1981. "On the microfoundations of macrosociology." *American Journal of Sociology* 86:984–1014.

Comte, Auguste. [1842] 1854. *The positive philosophy of Auguste Comte.* New York: D. Appleton. Originally published in French in six volumes, from 1830 to 1842.

Comte, Auguste. [1854] 1966. *System of positive polity.* New York: B. Franklin. Originally published in French in four volumes, from 1851 to 1854.

Connah, David, and Peter Wavish. 1990. "An experiment in cooperation." In: *Decentralized A. I.: Proceedings of the First European Workshop on Modelling Autonomous Agents in a Multi-Agent World,* edited by Yves Demazeau and Jean-Pierre Müller (pp. 197–212). New York: Elsevier.

Conte, Rosaria, and Cristiano Castelfranchi. 1995. "Understanding the functions of norms in social groups through simulation." In: *Artificial societies: The computer simulation of social life,* edited by Nigel Gilbert and Rosaria Conte (pp. 252–67). London: University College London Press.

Conte, Rosaria, and Cristiano Castelfranchi. 1996. "Simulating multi-agent interdependencies: A two-way approach to the micro-macro link." In: *Social science microsimulation,* edited by Klaus G. Troitzsch, Ulrich Mueller, G. Nigel Gilbert, and Jim E. Doran (pp. 394–415). Berlin: Springer.

Conte, Rosaria, Bruce Edmonds, Scott Moss, and R. Keith Sawyer. 2001. "Sociology and social theory in agent based social simulation: A symposium." *Computational and Mathematical Organization Theory* 7:183–205.

Conte, Rosaria, Nigel Gilbert, and Jaime Samoa Sichman. 1998. "MAS and social simulation: A suitable commitment." In: *Multi-agent systems and agent-based simulation,* edited by Jaime S. Sichman, Rosaria Conte, and Nigel Gilbert (pp. 1–9). Berlin: Springer.

Conte, Rosaria, Rainer Hegselmann, and Pietro Terna, eds. 1997. *Simulating social phenomena.* New York: Springer.

Contractor, Noshir, Robert Whitbred, Fabio Fonti, Andrew Hyatt, Barbara O'Keefe, and Patricia Jones. 2005. "Structuration theory and the evolution of networks." Unpublished manuscript.

Cook, Karen S., ed. 1987. *Social exchange theory.* Newbury Park, CA: Sage.

Cook, K. S., and J. M. Whitmeyer. 1992. "Two approaches to social structure: Exchange theory and network analysis." *Annual Review of Sociology* 18:109–27.

Cooley, Charles Horton. 1902. *Human nature and the social order*. New York: Charles Scribner's Sons.

Corsaro, William A. 1985. *Friendship and peer culture in the early years*. Norwood, NJ: Ablex.

Cottrell, Alan. 1978. "Emergent properties of complex systems." In: *The encyclopaedia of ignorance: Everything you ever wanted to know about the unknown*, edited by Ronald Duncan and Miranda Weston-Smith (pp. 129–35). New York: Pocket Books.

Cox, S. J., T. J. Sluckin, and J. Steele. 1999. "Group size, memory, and interaction rate in the evolution of cooperation." *Current Anthropology* 40:369–76.

Craib, Ian. 1992. *Anthony Giddens*. New York: Routledge.

Crutchfield, James P. 1994. "The calculi of emergence: Computation, dynamics, and induction." *Physica D* 75:11–54.

Cunningham, Bryon. 2001. "The reemergence of "emergence"." *Philosophy of Science* 68 (Proceedings):S62–75.

Currie, Gregory. 1984. "Individualism and Global Supervenience." *British Journal for the Philosophy of Science* 35:345–58.

Cyert, Richard M., and James G. March. 1963. *A behavioral theory of the firm*. Englewood Cliffs, NJ: Prentice-Hall.

Darley, Vince. 1994. "Emergent phenomena and complexity." In: *Artificial life IV: Proceedings of the Fourth International Workshop on the Synthesis and Simulation of Living Systems*, edited by Rodney A. Brooks and Pattie Maes (pp. 411–16). Cambridge, MA: MIT Press.

Davidson, Donald. 1970. "Mental events." In: *Experience and theory*, edited by Lawrence Foster and J. W. Swanson (pp. 79–101). Amherst, MA: University of Massachusetts Press.

Davidson, Donald. 1993. "Thinking causes." In: *Mental causation*, edited by John Heil and Alfred Mele (pp. 3–17). Oxford: Oxford University Press.

Deutsch, Morton. 1954. "Field theory in social psychology." In: *Handbook of social psychology*, edited by Gardner Lindzey (pp. 181–222). Cambridge, MA: Addison-Wesley.

Dewey, John. 1934. *Art as experience*. New York: Perigree Books.

Dignum, Frank, Barbara Dunin-Keplicz, and Rineke Verbrugge. 2001. "Creating collective intention through dialogue." *Logic Journal of the IGPL* 9:289–303.

Dignum, F., D. Morley, E. A. Sonenberg, and L. Cavedon. 2000. "Towards socially sophisticated BDI agents." In: *Proceedings of the Fourth International Conference on Multiagent Systems* (ICMAS 2000; pp. 111–18). Boston: IEEE Computer Society.

DiPrete, Thomas A., and Jerry D. Forristal. 1994. "Multilevel models: Methods and substance." *Annual Review of Sociology* 20:331–57.

DiTomaso, Nancy. 1982. "'Sociological reductionism' from Parsons to Althusser: Linking action and structure in social theory." *American Sociological Review* 47:14–28.

Domingues, José Maurício. 1995. *Sociological theory and collective subjectivity*. New York: St. Martin's Press.

Doran, Jim, and Mike Palmer. 1995. "The EOS project: Integrating two models of Palaeolithic social change." In: *Artificial societies: The computer simulation of social life*, edited by Nigel Gilbert and Rosaria Conte (pp. 103–25). London: University College London Press.

Drogoul, Alexis, Bruno Corbara, and Steffen Lalande. 1995. "MANTA: New experimental results on the emergence of (artificial) ant societies." In: *Artificial societies: The computer simulation of social life*, edited by Nigel Gilbert and Rosaria Conte (pp. 190–211). London: University College London Press.

Duranti, Alessandro. 1997. *Linguistic anthropology*. New York: Cambridge University Press.

Duranti, Alessandro, and Charles Goodwin, eds. 1992. *Rethinking context: Language as an interactive phenomenon*. New York: Cambridge University Press.

Durkheim, Émile. [1893] 1984. *The division of labor in society*. New York: The Free Press. Originally published as *De la division du travail social: étude sur l'organisation des sociétés supérieures* (Paris: Alcan, 1893).

Durkheim, Émile. [1895] 1964. *The rules of sociological method*. New York: The Free Press. Originally published as *Les règles de la méthode sociologique* (Paris: Alcan, 1895).

Durkheim, Émile. [1897] 1951. *Suicide*. Glencoe, IL: The Free Press. Originally published as *Le Suicide: Etude de sociologie* (Paris: Alcan, 1897).

Durkheim, Émile. [1898–1899] 1960. "Prefaces to *L'Année Sociologique*." In: *Emile Durkheim, 1858–1917*, edited by Kurt H. Wolff (pp. 341–53). Columbus: Ohio State University Press.

Durkheim, Émile. [1898] 1953. "Individual and collective representations." In: *Sociology and philosophy* (pp. 1–34). Glencoe, IL: The Free Press. Originally published in *Revue de Metaphysique et de Morale 6* (1898).

Durkheim, Émile. [1900] 1960. "Sociology and its scientific field." In: *Emile Durkheim, 1858–1917*, edited by Kurt H. Wolff (pp. 354–75). Columbus, OH: Ohio State University Press.

Durkheim, Émile. [1901] 1964. "Author's preface to the second edition." In: *The rules of sociological method* (pp. xli–lx). New York: The Free Press. Originally published as "De la mèthode objective en sociologie," *Revue de synthese historique*, 2, 1901, 3–17.

Durkheim, Émile. [1903] 1982. "Sociology and the social sciences." In: *The rules of sociological method*, edited by Steven Lukes (pp. 175–208). New York: The Free Press Originally published, with Paul Fauconnet, as "Sociologie et sciences sociales," *Revue philosophique* 55 (1903):465–97.

Durkheim, Émile. [1907] 1982. "Letter to the director." In: *The rules of sociological method*, edited by Steven Lukes (pp. 258–60). New York: The Free Press. Originally published in *Revue neo-scolastique* (Louvain), 14 (1907): 612–14.

Durkheim, Émile. 1909–1912. "Review of Simon Deploige, *Le conflit de la morale et de la sociologie*." *L'Année Sociologique* 12:326–8.

Durkheim, Émile. [1912] 1915. *The elementary forms of the religious life*. New York: The Free Press. Originally published as *Les Formes élèmentaires de la vie religieuse: le système totèmique en Australie* (Paris: Alcan, 1912).

Durkheim, Émile. [1914] 1960. "The dualism of human nature and its social conditions." In: *Emile Durkheim, 1858–1917*, edited by Kurt H. Wolff (pp. 325–40). Columbus: Ohio State University Press.

Durlauf, Steven N. 2001. "A framework for the study of individual behavior and social interactions." *Sociological Methodology* 31:47–87.

Durlauf, Steven N., and H. Peyton Young. 2001. "The new social economics." In: *Social dynamics*, edited by Steven N. Durlauf and H. Peyton Young (pp. 1–14). Cambridge, MA: MIT Press.

Edel, Abraham. 1959. "The concept of levels in social theory." In: *Symposium on social theory*, edited by Lllewellyn Gross (pp. 167–95). Evanston, IL: Row, Peterson and Co.

Ellis, Donald G. 1999. "Research on social interaction and the micro-macro issue." *Research on Language and Social Interaction* 32:31–40.

Elman, Jeffrey L., Elizabeth A. Bates, Mark H. Johnson, Annette Karmiloff-Smith, Domenico Parisi, and Kim Plunkett. 1996. *Rethinking innateness: A connectionist perspective on development*. Cambridge, MA: MIT Press.

Elster, Jon. 1985. *Making sense of Marx*. New York: Cambridge University Press.

Elster, Jon. 1989. *Nuts and bolts for the social sciences*. New York: Cambridge University Press.

Elster, Jon. 1998. "A plea for mechanism." In: *Social mechanisms: An analytical approach to social theory*, edited by Peter Hedström and Richard Swedberg (pp. 45–73). New York: Cambridge University Press.

Emerson, Richard M. 1972. "Exchange theory." In: *Sociological theories in progress*, vol. 2, edited by J. Berger Jr., M. Zelditch, and B. Anderson (pp. 38–87). Boston: Houghton Mifflin.

Epstein, Joshua M., and Robert Axtell. 1996. *Growing artificial societies: Social science from the bottom up*. Cambridge, MA: MIT Press.

Etzioni, Amitai. 1991. "Socio-economics: A budding challenge." In: *Socio-economics: Toward a new synthesis*, edited by Amitai Etzioni and Paul R. Lawrence (pp. 3–7). Armonk, NY: M. E. Sharpe, Inc.

Evans, Robert R., ed. 1969. *Readings in collective behavior*. Chicago: Rand McNally and Co.

Fairclough, Norman. 1995. *Critical discourse analysis: The critical study of language*. New York: Longman.

Fararo, Thomas J., and John Skvoretz. 1986. "E-state structuralism: A theoretical method." *American Sociological Review* 51:591–602.

Fenton, Steve. 1984. *Durkheim and modern sociology*. New York: Cambridge University Press.

Fine, Gary Alan. 1990. "Symbolic interactionism in the post-Blumerian age." In: *Frontiers of social theory: The new syntheses*, edited by George Ritzer (pp. 117–57). New York: Columbia University Press.

Fitoussi, David, and Moshe Tennenholtz. 2000. "Choosing social laws for multi-agent systems: Minimality and simplicity." *Artificial Intelligence* 119:61–101.

Fodor, Jerry A. 1974. "Special sciences (Or: The disunity of science as a working hypothesis)." *Synthese* 28:97–115.

Fodor, Jerry A. 1989. "Making mind matter more." *Philosophical Topics* 17:59–79.

Fodor, Jerry A. 1997. "Special sciences: Still autonomous after all these years." *Philosophical Perspectives* 11:149–63.

Forman, Ellice A., Norris Minick, and C. Addison Stone, eds. 1993. *Contexts for learning: Sociocultural dynamics in children's development*. New York: Oxford University Press.

Forrester, Jay W. 1968. *Principles of systems*. Cambridge, MA: MIT Press.

Forrester, Jay W. 1971. *World dynamics*. Cambridge, MA: Wright-Allen.

Foucault, Michel. [1969] 1972. *The archeology of knowledge and the discourse on language*. New York: Pantheon Books. Originally published as *L'Archéologie du Savoir* (Paris: Editions Gallimard, 1969).

Foundation for Intelligent Physical Agents. 1999. "FIPA communicative act library specification." Available on-line at http://www.fipa.org/specs/fipa00037/SC00037J.pdf.

Frey, Lawrence R., ed. 1994. *Group communication in context: Studies of natural groups*. Hillsdale, NJ: Erlbaum.

Friedrich, P. 1971. "Structural implications of Russian pronominal usage." In: *Proceedings of the UCLA Sociolinguistics Conference, 1964*, edited by W. Bright (pp. 214–59). Los Angeles: Center for Research in Languages and Linguistics.

Gallagher, Richard, and Tim Appenzeller. 1999. "Beyond reductionism." *Science* 284:79.

Gane, Mike. 1988. *On Durkheim's rules of sociological method*. New York: Routledge.

Garfinkel, Harold. 1967. *Studies in ethnomethodology*. Englewood Cliffs, NJ: Prentice-Hall.

Gell-Mann, Murray. 1994. *The quark and the jaguar: Adventures in the simple and the complex*. New York: W. H. Freeman.

Gellner, Ernest. [1956] 1968. "Holism versus Individualism." In: *Readings in the philosophy of the social sciences*, edited by May Brodbeck (pp. 254–68). New York: Macmillan. Originally published as "Explanations in History," in *Proceedings of the Aristotelian Society*, suppl vol. 30 (1956):157–76.

Giddens, Anthony. 1970. "Durkheim as a review critic." *Sociological Review* 18:171–96.

Giddens, Anthony. 1977. *Studies in social and political theory*. New York: Basic Books.

Giddens, Anthony. 1979a. *Central problems in social theory: Action, structure, and contradiction in social analysis*. Berkeley: University of California Press.

Giddens, Anthony. 1979b. *Emile Durkheim*. New York: Viking Press.

Giddens, Anthony. 1984. *The constitution of society: Outline of the theory of structuration*. Berkeley: University of California Press.

Giddens, Anthony. 1989. "A reply to my critics." In: *Social theory of modern societies: Anthony Giddens and his critics*, edited by David Held and John B. Thompson (pp. 249–301). New York: Cambridge University Press.

Gilbert, Margaret. 1989. *On social facts*. Princeton, NJ: Princeton University Press.

Gilbert, Nigel. 1995. "Emergence in social simulations." In: *Artificial societies: The computer simulation of social life*, edited by Nigel Gilbert and Rosaria Conte (pp. 144–56). London: University College London Press.

Gilbert, Nigel. 1997. "A simulation of the structure of academic science." *Sociological Research Online*, 2:http://www.socresonline.org.uk//2/2/3.html.

Gilbert, Nigel. 1999a. "Multi-level simulation in Lisp-Stat." *Journal of Artificial Societies and Social Simulation* 2 [online], http://www.soc.surrey.ac.uk/JASSS/2/1/3.html.

Gilbert, Nigel. 1999b. "Simulation: A new way of doing social science." *American Behavioral Scientist* 42:1485–7.

Gilbert, Nigel. 2002. "Varieties of emergence in social simulation." Pp. 41–50 in *Social agents: Ecology, exchange, and evolution*, edited by C. Macal and D. Sallach. Chicago, IL: Argonne National Laboratory.

Gilbert, Nigel, and Jim Doran, eds. 1994. *Simulating societies: The computer simulation of social phenomena*. London: UCL Press.

Gilbert, Nigel, and Rosaria Conte, eds. 1995. *Artificial societies: The computer simulation of social life*. London: UCL Press.

Goldstein, Jeffrey. 1999. "Emergence as a construct: History and issues." *Emergence* 1:49–72.

Goldstein, Leon J. [1958] 1973. "Two theses of methodological individualism." In: *Modes of individualism and collectivism*, edited by John O'Neill (pp. 277–86). Hampshire, England: Gregg Revivals. Originally published in the *British Journal for the Philosophy of Science* 9 (1958):1–11.

Granovetter, Mark. 1985. "Economic action and social structure: The problem of embeddedness." *American Journal of Sociology* 91:481–510.

Granovetter, Mark. 1990. "The old and the new economic sociology: A history and an agenda." In: *Beyond the marketplace: Rethinking economy and society*, edited by Roger Friedland and A. F. Robertson (pp. 89–112). New York: Aldine de Gruyter.

Granovetter, Mark, and Richard Swedberg, eds. 1992. *The sociology of economic life*. Boulder, CO: Westview Press.

Gregson, Nicky. 1989. "On the (ir)relevance of structuration theory to empirical research." In: *Social theory of modern societies: Anthony Giddens and his critics*, edited by David Held and John B. Thompson (pp. 235–48). New York: Cambridge University Press.

Griffiths, P. E., and R. D. Gray. 1994. "Developmental systems and evolutionary explanation." *Journal of Philosophy* 91:277–304.

Grosz, Barbara J. 1996. "Collaborative systems." *AI Magazine* 17:67–85.

Grosz, Barbara, and Sarit Kraus. 1996. "Collaborative plans for complex group actions." *Artificial Intelligence* 86:269–357.

Grosz, Barbara J., and Candace Sidner. 1990. "Plans for discourse." In: *Intentions in communication*, edited by Philip R. Cohen, Jerry Morgan, and Martha E. Pollack (pp. 417–44). Cambridge, MA: MIT Press.

Habermas, J. 1987. *Theory of communicative action*. Boston: Beacon Press.

Hales, David. 1998. "Stereotyping, groups and cultural evolution: A case of 'second order emergence'?" In: *Multi-agent systems and agent-based simulation*, edited by Jaime S. Sichman, Rosaria Conte, and Nigel Gilbert (pp. 140–55). Berlin: Springer.

Halpin, Brendan. 1999. "Simulation in sociology." *American Behavioral Scientist* 42:1488–1508.

Hanks, William F. 1996. *Language and communicative practices*. Boulder, CO: Westview Press.

Hanneman, Robert A. 1988. *Computer-assisted theory building: Modeling dynamic social systems*. Newbury Park, CA: Sage.

Hannoun, Mahdi, Jaime Samoa Sichman, Olivier Boissier, and Claudette Sayettat. 1998. "Dependence relations between roles in a multi-agent system:

Towards the detection of inconsistencies in organization." In: *Multi-agent systems and agent-based simulation*, edited by Jaime S. Sichman, Rosaria Conte, and Nigel Gilbert (pp. 169–82). Berlin: Springer.

Harvey, David L., and Michael Reed. 1996. "Social science as the study of complex systems." In: *Chaos theory in the social sciences: Foundations and applications*, edited by L. Douglas Kiel and Euel Elliott (pp. 295–323). Ann Arbor: University of Michigan Press.

Hatano, Giyoo, and James V. Wertsch. 2001. "Sociocultural approaches to cognitive development: The constitutions of culture in mind." *Human Development* 44:77–83.

Hawes, Leonard C. 1974. "Social collectivities as communication: Perspective on organizational behavior." *Quarterly Journal of Speech* 60:497–502.

Hayek, F. A. von. 1942. "Scientism and the study of society," part 1. *Economica* 9:267–91.

Hayek, F. A. von. 1943. "Scientism and the study of society," part 2. *Economica* 10:34–63.

Hayek, F. A. von. 1944. "Scientism and the study of society," part 3. *Economica* 11:27–37.

Hayes-Roth, Barbara. 1992. "Opportunistic control of action in intelligent agents." *IEEE Transactions on Systems, Man, and Cybernetics* 23:1575–87.

Hayes-Roth, Barbara, Lee Brownston, and Robert van Gent. 1995. "Multiagent collaboration in directed improvisation." Pp. 148–154 in *ICMAS-95*, edited by Victor Lesser. Cambridge: MIT Press.

Hayes-Roth, Barbara, Erik Sincoff, Lee Brownston, Ruth Huard, and Brian Lent. 1995. "Directed improvisation with animated puppets." in *Conference on Human Factors in Computing Systems (CHI'95)* (pp. 79–80). New York, NY: ACM Press.

Healy, Kieran. 1998. "Conceptualising constraint: Mouzelis, Archer and the concept of social structure." *Sociology* 32:509–22.

Hedström, Peter, and Richard Swedberg, eds. 1998. *Social mechanisms: An analytical approach to social theory*. New York: Cambridge University Press.

Heil, John. 1998. "Supervenience deconstructed." *European Journal of Philosophy* 6:146–55.

Heil, John. 1999. "Multiple realizability." *American Philosophical Quarterly* 36:189–208.

Heil, John, and Alfred Mele, eds. 1993. *Mental causation*. Oxford: Clarendon Press.

Hempel, Carl G. 1965. *Aspects of scientific explanation and other essays in the philosophy of science*. New York: The Free Press.

Hertz-Lazarowitz, Rachel, and Norman Miller, eds. 1992. *Interaction in cooperative groups: The theoretical anatomy of group learning*. New York: Cambridge University Press.

Hinkle, Roscoe C. 1960. "Durkheim in American sociology." In: *Essays on sociology and philosophy*, edited by Kurt H. Wolff (pp. 267–95). New York: Harper and Row.

Hirshleifer, Jack. 1985. "The expanding domain of economics." *American Economic Review* 75:53–68.

Hobsbawm, Eric, and T. Ranger. 1983. *The invention of tradition*. New York: Cambridge University Press.

Holland, John H. 1995. *Hidden order: How adaptation builds complexity*. Reading, MA: Addison-Wesley.

Homans, George C. 1941. *English villagers of the thirteenth century*. Cambridge, MA: Harvard University Press.

Homans, George C. 1950. *The human group*. New York: Harcourt, Brace and World.

Homans, George C. 1958. "Social behavior as exchange." *American Journal of Sociology* 65:597–606.

Homans, George C. 1961. *Social behavior: Its elementary forms*. New York: Harcourt, Brace, and World.

Homans, George C. 1964a. "Commentary." *Sociological Inquiry* 34:221–31.

Homans, George C. 1964b. "Contemporary theory in sociology." In: *Handbook of modern sociology*, edited by Robert E. L. Harris (pp. 951–77). Chicago: Rand McNally.

Horgan, Terence. 1989. "Mental quasation." *Philosophical Perspectives* 3:47–76.

Horgan, Terence. 1993. "From supervenience to superdupervenience: Meeting the demands of a material world." *Mind* 102:555–86.

Horgan, Terence. 1994. "Nonreductive materialism." In: *The mind-body problem: A guide to the current debate*, edited by Richard Warner and Tadeusz Szubka (pp. 236–41). Cambridge, MA: Blackwell.

Horgan, Terence. 1997. "Kim on mental causation and causal exclusion." *Philosophical Perspectives* 11:165–84.

Hoyningen-Huene, Paul, and Franz M. Wuketits, eds. 1989. *Reductionism and systems theory in the life sciences*. Dordrecht, Netherlands: Kluwer Academic Publishers.

Huber, Joan. 1991. *Macro-micro linkages in sociology*. Newbury Park, CA: Sage.

Humphreys, Paul. 1997. "How Properties Emerge." *Philosophy of Science* 64:1–17.

Humphreys, Paul, Fritz Rohrlich, Alex Rosenberg, and William C. Wimsatt. 1997. "Symposium: Emergence and supervenience: Alternatives to unity by reduction." *Philosophy of Science* 64:S337–84.

Hutchins, Edwin. 1995. *Cognition in the wild*. Cambridge, MA: MIT Press.

Irvine, Judith T. 1974. "Strategies of status manipulation in the Wolof greeting." In: *Explorations in the ethnography of speaking*, edited by R. Bauman and J. Sherzer (pp. 167–91). New York: Cambridge University Press.

International Foundation for MultiAgent Systems. 2000. *Proceedings of the Fourth International Conference on MultiAgent Systems*. Los Alamitos, CA: IEEE Computer Society.

Jackson, Frank, and Philip Pettit. 1992. "Structural explanation in social theory." In: *Reduction, explanation, and realism*, edited by Kathleen Lennon and David Charles (pp. 97–131). Oxford: Clarendon Press.

James, William. 1890. *The principles of psychology*. New York: Henry Holt.

Jennings, Nick R. 1993. "Commitments and conventions: The foundation of coordination in multi-agent systems." *Knowledge Engineering Review* 8:223–50.

Jennings, Nick R. 1995. "Controlling cooperative problem solving in industrial multi-agent systems using joint intentions." *Artificial Intelligence* 75:195–240.

Johnson, Steven. 2001. *Emergence: The connected lives of ants, brains, cities, and software.* New York: Scribner's.

Jones, S. G. Stedman. 1995. "Charles Renouvier and Emile Durkheim: 'Les Règles de La Méthode Sociologique.'" *Sociological Perspectives* 38:27–40.

Kauffman, Stuart A. 1993a. *The origins of order: Self-organization and selection in evolution.* New York: Oxford University Press.

Kauffman, Stuart A. 1993b. "The sciences of complexity and 'origins of order.'" In: *Creativity: The reality club 4*, edited by John Brockman (pp. 75–107). New York: Simon and Schuster.

Kauffman, Stuart A. 1995. *At home in the universe: The search for laws of self-organization and complexity.* New York: Oxford University Press.

Keat, Russell, and John Urry. 1975. *Social theory as science.* London: Routledge.

Kennedy, James. 1997. "Minds and cultures: Particle swarm implications." In: *Socially intelligent agents: Papers from the 1997 AAAI fall symposium* (pp. 67–72). Menlo Park, CA: AAAI Press.

Kennedy, James, and Russell C. Eberhart. 2001. *Swarm intelligence.* San Francisco: Morgan Kaufmann Publishers.

Kiel, L. Douglas. 1991. "Lessons from the nonlinear paradigm: Applications of the theory of dissipative structures in the social sciences." *Social Science Quarterly* 72:431–42.

Kiel, L. Douglas, and Euel Elliott, eds. 1996. *Chaos theory in the social sciences.* Ann Arbor: University of Michigan Press.

Kim, Jaegwon. 1984. "Epiphenomenal and supervenient causation." *Midwest Studies in Philosophy* 9:257–70.

Kim, Jaegwon. 1992. "'Downward causation' in emergentism and nonreductive physicalism." In: *Emergence or reduction? Essays on the prospects of nonreductive physicalism*, edited by Ansgar Beckermann, Hans Flohr, and Jaegwon Kim (pp. 119–38). New York: Walter de Gruyter.

Kim, Jaegwon. 1993a. "The non-reductivist's troubles with mental causation." In: *Mental causation*, edited by John Heil and Alfred Mele (pp. 189–210). Oxford: Clarendon Press.

Kim, Jaegwon. 1993b. *Supervenience and mind.* New York: Cambridge University Press.

Kim, Jaegwon. 1999. "Making sense of emergence." *Philosophical Studies* 95:3–36.

Kincaid, Harold. 1990. "Defending laws in the social sciences." *Philosophy of the Social Sciences* 20:56–83.

Kincaid, Harold. 1997. *Individualism and the unity of science.* New York: Rowman and Littlefield.

King, Anthony. 1999a. "Against structure: A critique of morphogenetic social theory." *Sociological Review* 47:199–227.

King, Anthony. 1999b. "The impossibility of naturalism: The antinomies of Bhaskar's realism." *Journal for the Theory of Social Behavior* 29:267–88.

Knorr-Cetina, Karin D., and Aaron V. Cicourel, eds. 1981. *Advances in social theory and methodology: Toward an integration of micro- and macro-sociologies.* Boston: Routledge and Kegan Paul.

246   References

Köhler, Wolfgang. 1929. *Gestalt psychology*. New York: Horace Liveright.
Kontopoulos, Kyriakos M. 1993. *The logics of social structure*. New York: Cambridge University Press.
Krier, Dan. 1999. "Assessing the new synthesis of economics and sociology: Promising themes for contemporary analysts of economic life." *American Journal of Economics and Sociology* 58:669–96.
Krippendorff, Klaus. 1971. "Communication and the genesis of structure." *General Systems* 16:171–85.
Labrou, Yannis, and Tim Finin. 1997. "Towards a standard for an agent communication language." In: *Working notes of the AAAI fall symposium on communicative actions in humans and machines*. Cambridge, MA.
La Mettrie, Julien Offray de. [1748] 1912. *Man a machine*. Chicago: Open Court.
Lang, Kurt, and Gladys Engel Lang. 1961. *Collective dynamics*. New York: Thomas Y. Crowell Co.
Langton, Christopher G., ed. 1994. *Artificial life III* (Santa Fe Institute Studies in the Sciences of Complexity, proceedings vol. 17). Reading, MA: Addison-Wesley.
Latané, Bibb, Andrzej Nowak, and James H. Liu. 1994. "Measuring emergent social phenomena: Dynamism, polarization, and clustering as order parameters of social systems." *Behavioral Science* 39:1–24.
Lave, Jean. 1993. "The practice of learning." In: *Understanding practice: Perspectives on activity and context*, edited by Seth Chaiklin and Jean Lave (pp. 3–32). New York: Cambridge University Press.
Lave, Jean, and Etienne Wenger. 1991. *Situated learning: Legitimate peripheral participation*. New York: Cambridge University Press.
Lavie, Smadar, Kirin Narayan, and Renato Rosaldo, eds. 1993. *Creativity/anthropology*. Ithaca, NY: Cornell University Press.
Lawler, Edward J., Cecilia Ridgeway, and Barry Markovsky. 1993. "Structural social psychology and the micro-macro problem." *Sociological Theory* 11:268–90.
Lawrence, Jeanette A., and Jaan Valsiner. 1993. "Conceptual roots of internalization: From transmission to transformation." *Human Development* 36:150–67.
Lawson, Tony. 1997. *Economics and reality*. London: Routledge.
Layder, Derek. 1981. *Structure, interaction and social theory*. London: Routledge and Kegan Paul.
Layder, D. (1985). Power, structure and agency. *Journal for the Theory of Social Behaviour*, 15(2), 131–149.
Layder, Derek. 1987. "Key issues in structuration theory: Some critical remarks." *Current Perspectives in Social Theory* 8:25–46.
Lazarsfeld, Paul F., and Herbert Menzel. 1969. "On the relation between individual and collective properties." In: *A sociological reader on complex organizations*, edited by Amitai Etzoni (pp. 499–516). New York: Holt, Rinehart and Winston.
Le Bon, Gustave. [1895] 1896. *The crowd: A study of the popular mind*. London: T. Fisher Unwin Ltd. Originally published as *Psychologie des foules* (Paris: Alcan, 1895).

Le Boutillier, Shaun. 2001. "Theorising social constraint: The concept of super-venience." *Sociology* 35:159–75.

Lesser, Victor, ed. 1995. *ICMAS-95: First International Conference on Multi-Agent Systems*. Cambridge, MA: MIT Press.

Levesque, Hector J., Philip R. Cohen, and José H. T. Nunes. 1990. "On acting together." In: *Eighth National Conference on Artificial Intelligence* (AAAI-90; pp. 94–9). Boston: MIT Press.

Lévy-Bruhl, Lucien. [1910] 1925. *How natives think*. New York: Knopf. Originally published as *Les fonctions mentales dans les sociétés inférieures* (Paris: Alcan, 1910).

Lewes, George Henry. 1853. *Comte's philosophy of the sciences: Being an exposition of the principles of the Cours de philosophie positive of Auguste Comte*. London: H. G. Bohn.

Lewes, George Henry. 1875. *Problems of life and mind*. Ser. 1, vol. 2. London: Trubner and Co.

Lewis, Marc D. 2000. "The promise of dynamic systems approaches for an integrated account of human development." *Child Development* 71:36–43.

Liska, Allen E. 1990. "The significance of aggregate dependent variables and contextual independent variables for linking macro and micro theories." *Social Psychology Quarterly* 53:292–301.

Loar, Brian. 1992. "Elimination versus non-reductive physicalism." In: *Reduction, explanation, and realism*, edited by David Charles and Kathleen Lennon (pp. 239–63). Oxford: Oxford University Press.

Lomborg, Bjorn. 1992. "Game theory versus multiple agents: The iterated prisoner's dilemma." In: *Artificial social systems*, edited by Cristiano Castelfranchi and Eric Werner (pp. 69–93). Berlin: Springer-Verlag.

Lomborg, Bjorn. 1996. "Nucleus and shield: The evolution of social structure in the iterated prisoner's dilemma." *American Sociological Review* 61:278–307.

Lovejoy, Arthur O. 1927. "The meaning of 'emergence' and its modes." *Journal of Philosophical Studies* 2:167–89.

Lowe, E. J. 1993. "The causal autonomy of the mental." *Mind* 102:629–44.

Loye, David, and Riane Eisler. 1987. "Chaos and transformation: Implications of nonequilibrium theory for social science and society." *Behavioral Science* 32:53–65.

Luhmann, Niklas. [1984] 1995. *Social systems: Outline of a general theory*. Stanford, CA: Stanford University Press. Originally published as *Soziale Systeme. Grundreiner allgemeinen Theorie* (Frankfurt am Main: Suhrkamp, 1984).

Lukes, Steven. 1973. *Emile Durkheim: His life and work*. London: Penguin.

Lukes, Steven. 1982. "Introduction." In: *The rules of sociological method* (pp. 1–27). New York: The Free Press.

Macdonald, Graham, and Philip Pettit. 1981. *Semantics and social science*. London: Routledge.

Machlup, Fritz. 1951. "Schumpeter's economic methodology." *Review of Economics and Statistics* 33:145–51.

Macy, Michael W., and John Skvoretz. 1998. "The evolution of trust and cooperation between strangers: A computational model." *American Sociological Review* 63:638–60.

Macy, Michael W., and Robert Willer. 2002. "From factors to actors: Computational sociology and agent-based modeling." *Annual Review of Sociology* 28:143–66.

Mandelbaum, Maurice. 1951. "A note on emergence." In: *Freedom and reason: Studies in philosophy and Jewish culture, in memory of Morris Ralph Cohen,* edited by Salo W. Baron, Ernest Nagel, and Koppel S. Pinson (pp. 175–83). Glencoe, IL: The Free Press.

Mandelbaum, Maurice. 1957. "Societal laws." *British Journal of the Philosophy of Science* 8:211–24.

Margolis, Joseph. 1986. "Emergence." *Philosophical Forum* 17:271–95.

Marion, Russ. 1999. *The edge of organization: Chaos and complexity theories of formal social systems.* Thousand Oaks, CA: Sage.

Markovsky, Barry. 1987. "Toward multilevel sociological theories: Simulations of actor and network effects." *Sociological Theory* 5:101–17.

Marx, K. 1978. "The German ideology." In: *The Marx-Engels reader,* edited by R. C. Tucker (pp. 146–200). New York: Norton.

Maturana, Humberto R., and Francisco J. Varela. 1980. *Autopoeisis and cognition: The realization of the living.* Boston Studies in the Philosophy of Science no. 42. Dordrecht, Netherlands: D. Reidel.

Matusov, Eugene. 1998. "When solo activity is not privileged: Participation and internalization models of development." *Human Development* 41:326–49.

Mayhew, Bruce H. 1980. "Structuralism versus individualism." Part 1, "Shadowboxing in the dark." *Social Forces* 59:335–75.

Mayhew, Bruce H. 1981. "Structuralism versus individualism." Part 2, Ideological and other obfuscations." *Social Forces* 59:627–48.

Mayhew, Bruce H., Louis N. Gray, and Mary L. Mayhew. 1971. "The behavior of interaction systems: Mathematical models of structure in interaction sequences." *General Systems* 16:13–29.

McCulloch, W., and W. Pitts. 1943. "A logical calculus of the ideas immanent in nervous activity." *Bulletin of Mathematical Biophysics* 5:115–33.

McLaughlin, Brian P. 1992. "The rise and fall of British emergentism." In: *Emergence or reduction? Essays on the prospects of nonreductive physicalism,* edited by Ansgar Beckermann, Hans Flohr, and Jaegwon Kim (pp. 49–93). Berlin: Walter de Gruyter.

Mead, George Herbert. 1932. *The philosophy of the present.* Chicago: University of Chicago Press.

Mead, George Herbert. 1934. *Mind, self, and society.* Chicago: University of Chicago Press.

Meehl, P. E., and Wilfrid Sellars. 1957. "The concept of emergence." In: *Minnesota studies in the philosophy of science.* Vol. 1, *The foundations of science and the concepts of psychology and psychoanalysis,* edited by Herbert Feigl and Michael Scriven (pp. 239–52). Minneapolis: University of Minnesota Press.

Mellars, Paul A. 1985. "The ecological basis of social complexity in the Upper Paleolithic of southwestern France." In: *Prehistoric hunter-gatherers: The emergence of cultural complexity,* edited by T. D. Price and J. A. Brown (pp. 271–97). New York: Academic Press.

Mellor, D. H. 1982. "The reduction of society." *Philosophy* 57:51–75.

Mendonça, Wilson. 2002. "Mental causation and the causal completeness of physics." *Principia* 6:121–32.

Menger, Carl. [1883] 1963. *Problems of economics and sociology*. Urbana, IL: University of Illinois Press. Originally published in 1883 as *Untersuchungen über die Methode der Socialwissenschaften und der Politischen Oekonomie insbesondere*.

Merton, Robert K. 1968. "On sociological theories of the middle range." In: *Social theory and social structure*, edited by Robert K. Merton (pp. 39–72). New York: The Free Press.

Meyer, D. A., and T. A. Brown. 1998. "Statistical mechanics of voting." *Physical Review Letters* 81:1718–21.

Mihata, Kevin. 1997. "The persistence of 'emergence.'" In: *Chaos, complexity, and sociology: Myths, models, and theories*, edited by Raymond A. Eve, Sara Horsfall, and Mary E. Lee (pp. 30–8). Thousand Oaks, CA: Sage.

Mill, John Stuart. 1843. *A system of logic, ratiocinative and inductive: Being a connected view of the principles of evidence, and the methods of scientific investigation*. London: J. W. Parker.

Mill, John Stuart, and Auguste Comte. 1994. *The correspondence of John Stuart Mill and Auguste Comte*. New Brunswick, NJ: Transaction Publishers.

Miller, James G. 1978. *Living systems*. New York: McGraw-Hill.

Miller, Barbara D. 1995. "Precepts and practices: Researching identity formation among Indian Hindu adolescents in the United States." In: *Cultural practices as contexts for development*, edited by Jacqueline J. Goodnow, Peggy J. Miller, and Frank Kessel (pp. 71–85). San Francisco: Jossey-Bass.

Minsky, Marvin. 1985. *The society of mind*. New York: Simon and Schuster.

Möhring, Michael. 1996. "Social science multilevel simulation with MIMOSE." In: *Social science microsimulation*, edited by Klaus G. Troitzsch, Ulrich Mueller, G. Nigel Gilbert, and Jim E. Doran (pp. 123–37). Berlin: Springer.

Morgan, C. Lloyd. 1923. *Emergent evolution*. London: Williams and Norgate. Originally presented as the 1922 Gifford Lectures at the University of St. Andrews.

Moss, Scott. 1998. "Social simulation models and reality: Three approaches." In: *Multi-agent systems and agent-based simulation*, edited by Jaime S. Sichman, Rosaria Conte, and Nigel Gilbert (pp. 45–78). Berlin: Springer.

Moss, Scott. 2001. "Messy systems: The target for multi agent based simulation." In: *Multi-agent-based simulation*, edited by Scott Moss and Paul Davidsson (pp. 1–14). Berlin: Springer.

Moss, Scott, and Paul Davidsson, eds. 2001. *Multi-agent-based simulation*. Berlin: Springer.

Moulin, Bernard, and Brahim Chaib-Draa. 1996. "An overview of distributed artificial intelligence." In: *Foundations of distributed artificial intelligence*, edited by G. M. P. O'Hare and N. R. Jennings (pp. 3–55). New York: Wiley.

Mullainathan, Sendhil, and Richard H. Thaler. 2001. "Behavioral economics." In: *International encyclopedia of the social and behavioral sciences*, vol. 2, edited by Neil J. Smelser and Paul B. Baltes (pp. 1094–1100). New York: Elsevier.

Münch, Richard, and Neil J. Smelser. 1987. "Relating the micro and macro." In: *The micro-macro link*, edited by Jeffrey C. Alexander, Bernhard Giesen,

Richard Münch, and Neil J. Smelser (pp. 356–87). Berkeley: University of California Press.

Murray, David J. 1995. *Gestalt psychology and the cognitive revolution.* New York: Harvester Wheatsheaf.

Nagel, Ernest. 1961. *The structure of science: Problems in the logic of scientific explanation.* New York: Harcourt, Brace and World.

Némedi, Dénes. 1995. "Collective consciousness, morphology, and collective representations: Durkheim's sociology of knowledge, 1894–1900." *Sociological Perspectives* 38:41–56.

Newell, Allen, Herbert A. Simon, and J. C. Shaw. 1963. "GPS, a program that simulates human thought." In: *Computers and thought*, edited by E. A. Feigenbaum and J. Feldman (pp. 279–93). New York: McGraw-Hill.

Nicolis, G., and I. Prigogine. 1977. *Self-organization in nonequilibrium systems.* New York: Wiley.

Nicolopoulou, Ageliki, and Michael Cole. 1993. "Generation and transmission of shared knowledge in the culture of collaborative learning: The Fifth Dimension, its play-world, and its institutional contexts." In: *Contexts for learning: Sociocultural dynamics in children's development*, edited by Ellice A. Forman, Norris Minick, and C. Addison Stone (pp. 283–314). New York: Oxford University Press.

Nowak, Andrzej, and Bibb Latané. 1994. "Simulating the emergence of social order from individual behavior." In: *Simulating societies: The computer simulation of social phenomena*, edited by Nigel Gilbert and Jim Doran (pp. 63–84). London: UCL Press.

Nowostawski, Mariusz, Martin Purvis, and Stephen Cranefield. 2001. "Modelling and visualizing agent conversations." In: *Proceedings of the International Conference on Autonomous Agents (Agents '01)*, edited by Jörg P. Müller, Elisabeth Andre, Sandip Sen, and Claude Frasson (pp. 234–35). Montreal: ACM Press.

O'Hare, G. M. P., and N. R. Jennings, eds. 1996. *Foundations of distributed artificial intelligence.* New York: Wiley.

O'Neill, John, ed. 1973. *Modes of individualism and collectivism.* New York: St. Martin's Press.

Oyama, Susan. 1985. *The ontogeny of information: Developmental systems and evolution.* New York: Cambridge University Press.

Paolucci, Mario. 2002. "Review of *The edge of organization: Chaos and complexity theories of formal social systems*." *Journal of Artificial Societies and Social Simulation* 5, http://jasss.soc.surrey.ac.uk/5/4/reviews/paolucci.html.

Papineau, David. 1993. *Philosophical naturalism.* Oxford: Blackwell.

Park, Robert E., and Ernest W. Burgess. 1921. *Introduction to the science of sociology.* Chicago: University of Chicago Press.

Parsons, Talcott. [1937] 1949. *The structure of social action.* New York: The Free Press.

Parsons, Talcott. 1951. *The social system.* Glencoe, IL: The Free Press.

Parsons, Talcott. 1970. "On building social system theory: A personal history." *Daedalus* 99:826–81.

Parsons, Talcott, and Edward A. Shils. 1951. "Values, motives, and systems of action." In: *Toward a general theory of action*, edited by Talcott Parsons and Edward A. Shils (pp. 47–275). Cambridge, MA: Harvard University Press.

Parunak, H. Van Dyke, Robert Savit, and Rick L. Riolo. 1998. "Agent-based modeling vs. equation-based modeling: A case study and user's guide." In: *Multi-agent systems and agent-based simulation*, edited by Jaime S. Sichman, Rosaria Conte, and Nigel Gilbert (pp. 10–25). Berlin: Springer.

Pêcheux, Michel. [1975] 1982. *Language, semantics, and ideology*. New York: St. Martin's Press. Originally published as *Les vérités de La Palice: linguistique, sémantique, philosophie* (Paris: François Maspero, 1975).

Pepper, Stephen C. 1926. "Emergence." *Journal of Philosophy* 23:241–45.

Pettit, Philip. 1993. *The common mind: An essay on psychology, society, and politics*. Oxford: Oxford University Press.

Phillips, D.C. 1976. *Holistic thought in social science*. Palo Alto, CA: Stanford University Press.

Piaget, Jean. [1950] 1995. "Explanation in sociology." In: *Sociological studies*, edited by Leslie Smith (pp. 30–96). New York: Routledge. Originally published as *Introduction a' l'épistémologie génétique*, vol. 3 (Paris: Presses Universitaires de France, 1950).

Piaget, Jean. 1952. "Jean Piaget." In: *A history of psychology in autobiography*, edited by Edwin G. Boring, Herbert S. Langfeld, Heinz Werner, and Robert M. Yerkes (pp. 237–56). Worcester, MA: Clark University Press.

Piaget, Jean. 1995. *Sociological studies*. New York: Routledge.

Pickel, Andreas, ed. 2004. *Systems and mechanisms: A symposium on Mario Bunge's philosophy of social science*. Special issue, *Philosophy of the Social Sciences* 34, no. 2.

Pickering, W. S. F. 1984. *Durkheim's sociology of religion*. Boston: Routledge and Kegan Paul.

Pihlström, Sami. 2002. "The re-emergence of the emergence debate." *Principia* 6:133–81.

Pitt, Jeremy, Lloyd Kamara, and Alexander Artikis. 2001. "Interaction patterns and observable commitments in a multi-agent trading scenario." In: *Proceedings of the International Conference on Autonomous Agents* (Agents '01), edited by Jörg P. Müller, Elisabeth Andre, Sandip Sen, and Claude Frasson (pp. 481–8). Montreal: ACM Press.

Popper, Karl R. [1944–1945] 1957. *The poverty of historicism*. London: Routledge and Kegan Paul. Originally published in *Economica*, 1944–1945.

Popper, Karl R. 1962. *Conjectures and Refutations*. New York: Basic Books.

Porpora, Douglas V. 1983. "On the prospects for a nomothetic theory of social structure." *Journal for the Theory of Social Behaviour* 13:243–64.

Porpora, Douglas V. 1987. *The concept of social structure*. New York: Greenwood Press.

Porpora, Douglas V. 1993. "Cultural rules and material relations." *Sociological Theory* 11:212–29.

Porter, Theodore M. 1995. "Statistical and social facts from Quetelet to Durkheim." *Sociological Perspectives* 38:15–26.

Prietula, Michael J., Kathleen M. Carley, and Les Gasser, eds. 1998. *Simulating organizations: Computational models of institutions and groups*. Cambridge, MA: MIT Press.

Prigogine, Ilya, and Peter M. Allen. 1982. "The challenge of complexity." In: *Self-organization and dissipative structures: Applications in the physical and social sciences*, edited by William C. Schieve and Peter M. Allen (pp. 3–39). Austin: University of Texas Press.

Prigogine, Ilya, and Isabelle Stengers. 1984. *Order out of chaos: Man's new dialogue with nature*. New York: Bantam Books.

Pynadath, David V., and Milind Tambe. 2002. "Multiagent teamwork: Analyzing the optimality and complexity of key theories and models." In: *AAMAS'02* (pp. 873–80). Bologna, Italy: ACM.

Radnitzky, Gerard. 1992. "The economic approach." In: *Universal economics: Assessing the achievements of the economic approach*, edited by Gerard Radnitzky and Alvin M. Weinberg (pp. 1–68). New York: Paragon House.

Radnitzky, Gerard, and Peter Bernholz, eds. 1987. *Economic imperialism: The economic approach applied outside the field of economics*. New York: Paragon House.

Rao, Anand S., and Michael P. Georgeff. 1995. "BDI agents: From theory to practice." In: *ICMAS-95*, edited by Victor Lesser (pp. 312–19). Cambridge, MA: MIT Press.

Rawls, Anne Warfield. 1987. "The interaction order sui generis: Goffman's contribution to social theory." *Sociological Theory* 5:136–49.

Rawls, Anne Warfield. 1990. "Emergent sociality: A dialectic of commitment and order." *Symbolic Interaction* 13:63–82.

Rawls, Anne Warfield. 1996. "Durkheim's epistemology: The neglected argument." *American Journal of Sociology* 102:430–82.

Ray, Thomas S., and Joseph Hart. 1998. "Evolution of differentiated multithreaded digital organisms." In: *Artificial life VI*, edited by Christoph Adami, Richard K. Belew, Hiroaki Kitano, and Charles Taylor (pp. 295–304). Cambridge, MA: MIT Press.

Reed, Michael, and David L. Harvey. 1992. "The new science and the old: Complexity and realism in the social sciences." *Journal for the Theory of Social Behaviour* 22:353–80.

Reynolds, Craig W. 1987. "Flocks, herds, and schools: A distributed behavioral model." *Computer Graphics* 21:25–34.

Rich, Charles, Candace L. Sidner, and Neal B. Lesh. 2001. "COLLAGEN: Applying collaborative discourse theory to human-computer interaction." *Artificial Intelligence Magazine* 22:15–25.

Ritzer, George. 1990. "Micro-macro linkage in sociological theory: Applying a metatheoretical tool." In: *Frontiers of social theory: The new syntheses*, edited by George Ritzer (pp. 347–70). New York: Columbia University Press.

Ritzer, George. 1996. *Modern sociological theory*. 4th ed. Boston: McGraw-Hill.

Ritzer, George. 2000. *Modern sociological theory*. 5th ed. Boston: McGraw-Hill.

Ritzer, George, and Pamela Gindoff. 1992. "Methodological relationism: Lessons for and from social psychology." *Social Psychology Quarterly* 55:128–40.

Rogoff, B. 1982. "Integrating context and cognitive development." In: *Advances in developmental psychology*, edited by M. E. Lamb and A. L. Brown (pp. 125–70). Hillsdale, NJ: Erlbaum.

Rogoff, B. 1990. *Apprenticeship in thinking: Cognitive development in social context*. New York: Oxford University Press.

Rogoff, Barbara. 1992. "Three ways to relate person and culture: Thoughts sparked by Valsiner's review of *Apprenticeship in Thinking.*" *Human Development* 35:316–20.

Rogoff, Barbara. 1995. "Observing sociocultural activity on three planes: Participatory appropriation, guided participation, and apprenticeship." In: *Sociocultural studies of mind*, edited by J. V. Wertsch, P. del Rio, and A. Alvarez (pp. 139–64). New York: Cambridge University Press.

Rogoff, B. (1997). Evaluating development in the process of participation: Theory, methods, and practice building on each other. In E. Amsel & A. Renninger (Eds.), *Change and development* (pp. 265–285). Hillsdale, NJ: Lawrence Erlbaum.

Rogoff, Barbara. 1998. "Cognition as a collaborative process." In: *Handbook of child psychology*, 5th ed., vol. 2, *Cognition, perception, and language*, edited by Deanna Kuhn and Robert S. Siegler (pp. 679–744). New York: Wiley.

Rogoff, Barbara, Barbara Radziszewska, and Tracy Masiello. 1995. "Analysis of developmental processes in sociocultural activity." In: *Sociocultural psychology: Theory and practice of doing and knowing*, edited by Laura M. W. Martin, Katherine Nelson, and Ethel Tobach (pp. 125–49). New York: Cambridge University Press.

Rosenberg, Alex. 1997. "Reductionism redux: Computing the embryo." *Biology and Philosophy* 12:445–70.

Rueger, Alexander. 2000. "Physical emergence, diachronic and synchronic." *Synthese* 124:297–322.

Rumelhart, David E., and James L. McClelland. 1986. *Parallel distributed processing: Explorations in the microstructure of cognition.* Cambridge, MA: MIT Press.

Russell, E. S., C. R. Morris, and W. Leslie Mackenzie. 1926. "Symposium: The notion of emergence." *Aristotelian Society* 6:39–68.

Saam, Nicole J. 1999. "Simulating the micro-macro link: New approaches to an old problem and an application to military coups." *Sociological Methodology* 29:43–79.

Sacks, Harvey. 1992. *Lectures on conversation*, vol. 1. Cambridge, MA: Blackwell.

Sallach, David L., and Charles N. Macal, eds. 2001. *The simulation of social agents.* Special issue, *Social Science Computer Review.*

Sawyer, R. Keith. 1999. "The emergence of creativity." *Philosophical Psychology* 12:447–69.

Sawyer, R. Keith. 2001a. *Creating conversations: Improvisation in everyday discourse.* Cresskill, NJ: Hampton Press.

Sawyer, R. Keith. 2001b. "Simulating emergence and downward causation in small groups." In: *Multi-agent-based simulation*, edited by Scott Moss and Paul Davidsson (pp. 49–67). Berlin: Springer.

Sawyer, R. Keith. 2002a. "A discourse on discourse: An archeological history of an intellectual concept." *Cultural Studies* 16:433–56.

Sawyer, R. Keith. 2002b. "Nonreductive Individualism." Part 1, "Supervenience and wild disjunction." *Philosophy of the Social Sciences* 32:537–59.

Sawyer, R. Keith. 2003. "Assessing agent communication languages." Pp. 273–296 in *Challenges in social simulation.* Chicago, IL: Argonne National Laboratory.

Sawyer, R. Keith. 2003b. "Emergence in creativity and development." In: *Creativity and development*, edited by R. Keith Sawyer, Vera John-Steiner, Seana Moran, Robert Sternberg, David Henry Feldman, Mihaly Csikszentmihalyi, and Jeanne Nakamura (pp. 12–60). New York: Oxford University Press.

Sawyer, R. Keith. 2003c. *Group creativity: Music, theater, collaboration*. Mahwah, NJ: Erlbaum.

Sawyer, R. Keith. 2003d. *Improvised dialogues: Emergence and creativity in conversation*. Westport, CT: Greenwood.

Sawyer, R. Keith. 2003e. "Nonreductive individualism." Part 2, "Social causation." *Philosophy of the Social Sciences* 33:203–24.

Sawyer, R. Keith. 2004a. "The mechanisms of emergence." *Philosophy of the Social Sciences* 34:260–82.

Sawyer, R. Keith. 2004b. "Social explanation and computational simulation." *Philosophical Explorations* 7:219–31.

Schegloff, Emanuel A. 1991. "Reflections on talk and social structure." In: *Talk and social structure: Studies in ethnomethodology and conversation analysis*, edited by Deirdre Boden and Don H. Zimmerman (pp. 44–70). Berkeley: University of California Press.

Schegloff, Emanuel A. 1992. "In another context." In: *Rethinking context: Language as an interactive phenomenon*, edited by Alessandro Duranti and Charles Goodwin (pp. 191–227). New York: Cambridge University Press.

Schelling, Thomas C. 1971. "Dynamic models of segregation." *Journal of Mathematical Sociology* 1:143–86.

Schmaus, Warren. 1994. *Durkheim's philosophy of science and the sociology of knowledge*. Chicago: University of Chicago Press.

Schmaus, Warren. 1999. "Functionalism and the meaning of social facts." *Philosophy of Science* 66 (proceedings):S314–23.

Schutz, Alfred. 1967. *The phenomenology of the social world*. Evanston, IL: Northwestern University Press. Original work published 1932.

Searle, John R. 1990. "Collective intentionality." In: *Intentions in communication*, edited by P. R. Cohen, J. Morgan, and M. E. Pollack (pp. 401–15). Cambridge, MA: MIT Press.

Serrano, Juan Manual, and Sascha Ossowski. 2000. "Domain extensions to the FIPA-ACL: An application to decision support systems." In: *Simposio Español de Informática Distribuida* (SEID-2000; pp. 1–14). Ourense, Spain: University of Vigo.

Serrano, Juan Manuel, and Sascha Ossowski. 2002. "An organizational meta-model for the design of catalogues of communicative actions." In: *Intelligent agents and multi-agent systems*, edited by Kazuhiro Kuwabara and Jaeho Lee (pp. 92–108). Berlin: Springer-Verlag.

Servat, David, Edith Perrier, Jean-Pierre Treuil, and Alexis Drogoul. 1998. "When agents emerge from agents: Introducing multi-scale viewpoints in multi-agent simulations." In: *Multi-agent systems and agent-based simulation*, edited by Jaime S. Sichman, Rosaria Conte, and Nigel Gilbert (pp. 183–98). Berlin, Germany: Springer-Verlag.

Shibutani, Tamotsu. 1961. *Society and personality: An interactionist approach to social psychology*. Engelwood Cliffs, NJ: Prentice-Hall.

Shweder, Richard A. 1990. "Cultural psychology – What is it?" In: *Cultural psychology: Essays on comparative human development*, edited by James W. Stigler, Richard A. Shweder, and Gilbert Herdt (pp. 1–43). New York: Cambridge University Press.

Shweder, Richard A. 1995. "The confessions of a methodological individualist." *Culture and Psychology* 1:115–22.

Sichman, Jaime S., and Rosaria Conte. 1995. "DEPNET: How to benefit from social dependence." *Journal of Mathematical Sociology* 20:161–77.

Sichman, Jaime S., Rosaria Conte, and Nigel Gilbert, eds. 1998. *Multi-agent systems and agent-based simulation*. Berlin: Springer.

Sierra, Carles, Nicholas R. Jennings, Pablo Noriega, and Simon Parsons. 1998. "A framework for argumentation-based negotiation." In: *Intelligent agents IV: Agent theories, architectures, and languages*, edited by Munindar P. Singh, Anand S. Rao, and Michael Wooldridge (pp. 177–92). Berlin: Springer-Verlag. Proceedings of the Fourth International Workshop, ATAL'97, Providence, RI, July 24–26, 1997.

Silverstein, M. 1979. "Language structure and linguistic ideology." In: *The elements: A parasession on linguistic units and levels*, edited by P. R. Clyne (pp. 193–247). Chicago: Chicago Linguistic Society.

Silverstein, Michael. 1981. "The limits of awareness." Austin, TX: Southwest Educational Development Laboratory.

Simmel, Georg. 1950. *The sociology of Georg Simmel*. New York: The Free Press.

Simon, Herbert A. 1955. "A behavioral model of rational choice." *Quarterly Journal of Economics* 69:99–118.

Simon, Herbert A. 1969. *The sciences of the artificial*. Cambridge, MA: MIT Press.

Simon, Herbert A. 1999. "Karl Duncker and cognitive science." *From Past to Future: Clark Papers on the History of Psychology* 1:1–11.

Smart, J. J. C. 1981. "Physicalism and emergence." *Neuroscience* 6:109–13.

Smelser, Neil J., and Richard Swedberg, eds. 1994. *The handbook of economic sociology*. Princeton, NJ: Princeton University Press.

Smith, Joseph W., and Bryan S. Turner. 1986. "Constructing social theory and constituting society." *Theory, Culture and Society* 3:125–32.

Smith, Thomas S. 1997. "Nonlinear dynamics and the micro-macro bridge." In: *Chaos, complexity, and sociology: Myths, models, and theories*, edited by Raymond A. Eve, Sara Horsfall, and Mary E. Lee (pp. 52–63). Thousand Oaks, CA: Sage.

Smith, Thomas S., and Gregory T. Stevens. 1999. "The architecture of small networks: Strong interaction and dynamic organization in small social systems." *American Sociological Review* 64:403–20.

Sober, Elliott. 1999. "The multiple realizability argument against reductionism." *Philosophy of Science* 66:542–64.

Souter, Ralph William. 1933. *Prolegomena to relativity economics: An elementary study in the mechanics and organics of an expanding economic universe*. New York: Columbia University Press.

Spaulding, Edward Gleason. 1918. *The new rationalism: The development of a constructive realism upon the basis of modern logic and science, and through the criticism of opposed philosophical systems*. New York: Henry Holt.

Sperry, R. W. 1980. "Mind-brain interaction: Mentalism, yes; dualism, no." *Neuroscience* 5:195–206.

Steels, Luc. 1996. "Self-organizing vocabularies." In: *Proceedings of Alife V: Proceedings of the Fifth International Workshop on the Synthesis and Simulation of Living Systems*, edited by Christopher G. Langton and Katsunori Shimohara (pp. 179–84). Cambridge, MA: MIT Press.

Steels, Luc, and Frederic Kaplan. 1998. "Stochasticity as a source of innovation in language games." In: *Artificial life VI*, edited by Christoph Adami, Richard K. Belew, Hiroaki Kitano, and Charles Taylor (pp. 368–76). Cambridge, MA: MIT Press.

Stephan, Achim. 1997. "Armchair arguments against emergentism." *Erkenntnis* 46:305–14.

Stephan, Achim. 1998. "Varieties of emergence in artificial and natural systems." *Zeitschrift für Naturforschung C: A Journal of Biosciences* 53:639–56.

Stigler, James W., Richard A. Shweder, and Gilbert Herdt, eds. 1990. *Cultural psychology: Essays on comparative human development*. New York: Cambridge University Press.

Stone, Gregory P., and Harvey A. Farberman. 1967. "On the edge of rapprochement: Was Durkheim moving toward the perspective of symbolic interaction?" *Sociological Quarterly* 8:149–64.

Stryker, Sheldon. 1980. *Symbolic interactionism: A social structural version*. Menlo Park, CA: Benjamin/Cummings Publishing Co.

Suchman, Lucy A. 1987. *Plans and situated actions: The problem of human-machine communication*. New York: Cambridge University Press.

Suchting, Wal. 1992. "Reflections upon Roy Bhaskar's 'critical realism.'" *Radical Philosophy* 61:23–31.

Sullivan, David G., Barbara J. Grosz, and Sarit Kraus. 2000. "Intention reconciliation by collaborative agents." In: *Proceedings of the Fourth International Conference on Multiagent Systems* (ICMAS 2000; pp. 293–300). Boston: IEEE Computer Society.

Sumpter, David J. T., and D. S. Broomhead. 1998. "Formalising the link between worker and society in honey bee colonies." In: *Multi-agent systems and agent-based simulation*, edited by Jaime S. Sichman, Rosaria Conte, and Nigel Gilbert (pp. 95–110). Berlin: Springer.

Swedberg, Richard. 1987. "Economic sociology: Past and present." *Current Sociology* 35.

Symons, John. 2002. "Emergence and reflexive downward causation." *Principia* 6:183–202.

Sztompka, Piotr. 1991. *Society in action: The theory of social becoming*. Chicago: University of Chicago.

Sztompka, Piotr. 1994. "Society as social becoming: Beyond individualism and collectivism." Pp. 251–282 in *Agency and structure: Reorienting social theory*, edited by Piotr Sztompka. Yverdon, Switzerland: Gordon and Breach.

Tambe, Milind. 1997. "Towards flexible teamwork." *Journal of Artificial Intelligence Research* 7:83–124.

Tannen, Deborah, ed. 1993. *Framing in discourse*. New York: Oxford University Press.

Tarde, Gabriel de. 1969. *On communication and social influence: Selected papers.* Chicago: University of Chicago Press.

Taylor, Charles. 1985. *Human agency and language.* New York: Cambridge University Press.

Teller, Paul. 1992. "A contemporary look at emergence." In: *Emergence or reduction? Essays on the prospects of nonreductive physicalism,* edited by Ansgar Beckermann, Hans Flohr, and Jaegwon Kim (pp. 139–53). Berlin: Walter de Gruyter.

Thelen, E., and L. B. Smith. 1994. *A dynamic systems approach to the development of cognition and action.* Cambridge, MA: MIT Press.

Thompson, John B. 1989. "The theory of structuration." In: *Social theory in modern societies: Anthony Giddens and his critics,* edited by David Held and John B. Thompson (pp. 56–76). New York: Cambridge University Press.

Thrift, Nigel. 1999. "The place of complexity." *Theory, Culture and Society* 16:31–69.

Tullock, Gordon. 1972. "Economic imperialism." In: *Theory of public choice: Political applications of economics,* edited by James M. Buchanan and Robert D. Tollison (pp. 317–29). Ann Arbor: The University of Michigan Press.

Turner, Stephen P. 1986. *The search for a methodology of social science: Durkheim, Weber, and the nineteenth-century problem of cause, probability, and action.* Dordrecht, Netherlands: D. Reidel.

Turner, Stephen P. 1995. "Durkheim's *The Rules of Sociological Method*: Is it a classic?" *Sociological Perspectives* 38:1–13.

Turner, Stephen. 1996. "Durkheim among the statisticians." *Journal of the History of the Behavioral Sciences* 32:354–78.

Valsiner, J. (1989). *Human development and culture: The social nature of personality and its study.* Lexington, MA: Lexington Books.

Valsiner, Jaan. 1991. "Building theoretical bridges over a lagoon of everyday events." *Human Development* 34:307–15.

Valsiner, Jaan. 1998a. "Dualisms displaced: From crusades to analytic distinctions." *Human Development* 41:350–4.

Valsiner, Jaan. 1998b. *The guided mind: A sociogenetic approach to personality.* Cambridge, MA: Harvard University Press.

Varela, Charles R., and Rom Harré. 1996. "Conflicting varieties of realism: Causal powers and the problems of social structure." *Journal for the Theory of Social Behavior* 26:313–25.

Vygotsky, Lev S. 1971. *The psychology of art.* Cambridge, MA: MIT Press.

Vygotsky, Lev S. 1978. *Mind in society.* Cambridge: Harvard University Press.

Vygotsky, Lev S. 1981. "The genesis of higher mental functions." In: *The concept of activity in Soviet psychology,* edited by James V. Wertsch (pp. 144–88). Armonk, NY: M. E. Sharpe.

Wagner, Helmut R. 1964. "Displacement of scope: A problem of the relationship between small-scale and large-scale sociological theories." *American Journal of Sociology* 64:571–84.

Waldrop, M. Mitchell. 1992. *Complexity: The emerging science at the edge of order and chaos.* New York: Simon and Schuster.

Walker, Adam, and Michael Wooldridge. 1995. "Understanding the emergence of conventions in multi-agent systems." In: *ICMAS-95*, edited by Victor Lesser (pp. 384–9). Cambridge, MA: MIT Press.

Wallace, Walter L. 1969. *Sociological theory: An introduction*. Chicago: Aldine.

Wartofsky, M. W. (1979). *Models: Representation and the scientific understanding*. Dordrecht, Holland: D. Reidel.

Watkins, J. W. N. 1955. "Methodological individualism: A reply." *Philosophy of Science* 22:58–62.

Watkins, J. W. N. 1957. "Historical explanation in the social sciences." *British Journal for the Philosophy of Science* 8:104–17.

Watson, John B. 1913. "Psychology as the behaviorist views it." *Psychological Review* 20:158–77.

Weber, Max. 1968. *Economy and society*. New York: Bedminster Press.

Weick, Karl E. 2001. *Making sense of the organization*. London: Blackwell.

Wellman, Barry. 1983. "Network analysis: Some basic principles." In: *Sociological theory, 1983*, edited by Randall Collins (pp. 155–200). San Francisco: Jossey-Bass.

Wellman, Barry, and S. D. Berkowitz, eds. 1988. *Social structures: A network approach*. New York: Cambridge University Press.

Wertsch, James V. 1985. "Introduction." In: *Culture, communication, and cognition: Vygotskian perspectives*, edited by James V. Wertsch (pp. 1–18). New York: Cambridge University Press.

Wertsch, James V. 1993. "Commentary." *Human Development* 36:168–71.

Wertsch, J. V. (1994). The primacy of mediated action in sociocultural studies. *Mind, Culture, and Activity*, 1(4), 202–208.

Wertsch, J. V. (1995). The need for action in sociocultural research. In J. V. Wertsch, P.d. Rio, & A. Alvarez (Eds.), *Sociocultural studies of mind* (pp. 56–74). New York: Cambridge.

Wertsch, James V. 1998. *Mind as action*. New York: Oxford University Press.

Wertsch, James V. 2002. *Voices of collective remembering*. New York: Cambridge University Press.

Wheeler, William Morton. 1911. "The ant-colony as an organism." *Journal of Morphology* 22:307–25. A lecture prepared for delivery at the Marine Biological Laboratory, Woods Hole, MA, 2 August 1910.

Wheeler, William Morton. 1928. *Emergent evolution and the development of societies*. New York: Norton. Portions originally presented at the symposium on emergence held in Cambridge, MA, 14 September 1926.

Whitehead, Alfred North. 1926. *Science and the modern world*. New York: Macmillan.

Whitmeyer, Joseph M. 1994. "Why actor models are integral to structural analysis." *Sociological Theory* 12:153–65.

Wiley, Norbert. 1988. "The micro-macro problem in social theory." *Sociological Theory* 6:254–61.

Wimsatt, William C. 1986. "Forms of aggregativity." In: *Human nature and natural knowledge*, edited by Alan Donagan, Anthony N. Perovich Jr., and Michael V. Wedin (pp. 259–291). Dordrecht, Netherlands: D. Riedel.

Wimsatt, William C. 1997. "Aggregativity: Reductive heuristics for finding emergence." *Philosophy of Science* 64 (proceedings):S372–84.

Winch, Peter. 1958. *The idea of a social science*. Atlantic Highlands, NJ: Humanities Press International.

Wisdom, J. O. 1970. "Situational individualism and the emergent group-properties." In: *Explanation in the behavioural sciences*, edited by Robert Borger and Frank Cioffi (pp. 271–311). New York: Cambridge University Press.

Wooldridge, Michael. 1999. "Intelligent agents." In: *Multiagent systems: A modern approach to distributed artificial intelligence*, edited by Gerhard Weiss (pp. 27–77). Cambridge, MA: MIT Press.

Wooldridge, Michael. 2000. *Reasoning about rational agents*. Cambridge, MA: MIT Press.

Wundt, W. [1902] 1904. *Principles of physiological psychology*. London: Sonnenschein. Abridged translation of original work published as *Grundzüge der physiologischen Psychologie*, 5th ed. (Leipzig: W. Englemann, 1902–1903).

Wundt, Wilhelm. 1912. *An introduction to psychology*. New York: Macmillan.

Yablo, Stephen. 1992. "Mental causation." *Philosophical Review* 101:245–79.

Ye, Mei, and Kathleen M. Carley. 1995. "Radar-Soar: Towards an artificial organization composed of intelligent agents." *Journal of Mathematical Sociology* 20:219–46.

Zafirovsky, Milan. 1999. "Economic sociology in retrospect and prospect: In search of its identity within economics and sociology." *American Journal of Economics and Sociology* 58:583–627.

Index